CHRIST

< CHRONOLOGICAL >

CHRIST

< CHRONOLOGICAL >

CHRISTIAN STANDARD BIBLE®

HOLMAN® BIBLES

NASHVILLE, TENNESSEE

CSB Christ Chronological

Copyright © 2017 by 2K/DENMARK
Stenvej 25b, DK-8720 Højbjerg, Denmark
All rights reserved

Design and typesetting by 2K/DENMARK
Edited by Johs Krejberg Haahr, 2K/DENMARK
Introductory comments by Jake Pratt

The interior of the *CSB Christ Chronological* was designed and typeset by 2K/DENMARK, Højbjerg, Denmark. Proofreading was provided by Peachtree Editorial Services, Peachtree City, Georgia.

ISBN 978-1-4336-4603-4
Printed in China
1 2 3 4 — 19 18 17
RRD

INTRODUCTION

There are slightly over one hundred places in the four canonical Gospels—Matthew, Mark, Luke, and John—where the authors appear to be reporting on the same event or saying in the life of Jesus. In particular, the Synoptic Gospels—Matthew, Mark, and Luke—include considerable overlap in content. Yet, there are also noticeable differences among them, as each author presents the material from his own perspective and with his own emphases. To the modern reader, the relative unity and diversity between these narratives can prove to be quite perplexing. There are at least two reasons why such anxiety persists. First, it is difficult for the modern mind to grasp the relationship between history, literature, and theology within the compositional techniques of a first-century writer. Second, it is easy to impose a modern conception of historical and literary integrity upon an ancient text instead of deferring to the expectations of a first-century reader.

Regarding the relationship between history, literature, and theology, what exactly does one encounter in a canonical Gospel: early first-century history, pious literature, or a theological treatise? The answer is, "Yes." The Gospels are the history of the mission and vocation of Jesus Christ as remembered by his closest associates. Yet they are carefully crafted literary masterpieces as well. They continue the storytelling impulse in the Jewish Scriptures blended with aspects of Greco-Roman biography common in contemporary Hellenistic culture. Above all, however, they are unapologetically theological. It is this characteristic that makes the fourfold Gospel neither mere history nor mere literature.

Regarding the expectations of a first-century reader, I suggest that the ability of the earliest readers to retain a high view of the Gospels turns on their willingness to allow the Gospel writers to move freely among historical, literary, and theological concerns. Uppermost in their concern was the communication of the theological impact of this epic event in redemptive history. Yet as in OT Scriptures, that theology rests upon the framework of history, a series of events the core of which can be found in all four Gospels. Yet the authors' unique literary design of each Gospel allows for some flexibility on secondary events. Rather than scrutinizing every secondary historical fact, perhaps a better way forward is to ask how fitting a given account is in light of an author's literary style and theological purposes. This, I believe, better reflects the expectations of a first-century reader.[1]

[1] The present study will limit its focus only to variations between the four Gospels. Space precludes any treatment of apparent historical discrepancies unique to a given Gospel.

THE PREHISTORY AND BIRTH OF CHRIST

[1] In the beginning was the Word, and the Word was with God, and the Word was God. [2] He was with God in the beginning. [3] All things were created through him, and apart from him not one thing was created that has been created. [4] In him was life, and that life was the light of men. [5] That light shines in the darkness, and yet the darkness did not overcome it.

[6] There was a man sent from God whose name was John. [7] He came as a witness to testify about the light, so that all might believe through him. [8] He was not the light, but he came to testify about the light. [9] The true light that gives light to everyone, was coming into the world.

[10] He was in the world, and the world was created through him, and yet the world did not recognize him. [11] He came to his own, and his own people did not receive him. [12] But to all who did receive him, he gave them the right to be children of God, to those who believe in his name, [13] who were born, not of natural descent, or of the will of the flesh, or of the will of man, but of God.

[14] The Word became flesh and dwelt among us. We observed his glory, the glory as the one and only Son from the Father, full of grace and truth. [15] (John testified concerning him and exclaimed, "This was the one of whom I said, 'The one coming after me ranks ahead of me, because he existed before me.'") [16] Indeed, we have all received grace upon grace from his fullness, [17] for the law was given through Moses; grace and truth came through Jesus Christ. [18] No one has ever seen God. The one and only Son, who is himself God and is at the Father's side —he has revealed him.

Morna Hooker has observed the importance of a story's beginning and ending. In addition to creating intrigue at the beginning and "rounding things off" at the end, "each provides important clues about the meaning of the material that lies in between."[2] The Gospels are no exception. Matthew's genealogy (1:1-17) draws attention to the story behind the story of Jesus, namely God's covenant relationship with Israel. John's poetic prologue (1:1-18) captures the cosmic implications of Jesus's identity as the divine Word of God. The beginning of Mark has a more compressed style and is laden with OT overtones. Mark is signaling that what will follow in his account of "the gospel of Jesus Christ, the Son of God," is no less than the good news of God's salvation foretold by the OT prophets. Luke explains that he has compiled a narrative based on eyewitness testimony, hoping that his reader Theophilus might "know the certainty of the things" concerning Jesus.

[1] The beginning of the gospel of Jesus Christ, the Son of God.

[1] Many have undertaken to compile a narrative about the events that have been fulfilled among us, [2] just as the original eyewitnesses and servants of the word handed them down to us. [3] It also seemed good to me, since I have carefully investigated everything from the very first, to write to you in an orderly sequence, most honorable Theophilus, [4] so that you may know the certainty of the things about which you have been instructed.

[2] Morna D. Hooker, "Beginnings and Endings," in *The Written Gospel* (eds. Markus Bockmuehl and Donald A. Hagner; Cambridge: Cambridge University Press, 2005), 184.

In short, every name on Matthew's genealogy opens up a story that stands behind his story of Jesus. On the broadest level, that storyline is marked by the high points of Israel's history starting with Abraham and climaxing with David's reign, before ending on the tragic note of exile. Israel's exile casts its shadow over the ensuing account of Jesus. Situated between his account of Jesus's baptism and temptation, Luke's genealogy functions as a transition in the narrative. It is the author's emphasis on Jesus as the "beloved" (2:33), hereditary (3:38), and ultimately proven (4:3) Son of God that ties these narratives together. The latter is manifest in Satan's "If you are the Son of God."

[1] An account of the genealogy of Jesus Christ, the Son of David, the Son of Abraham:

2   Abraham fathered Isaac,
    Isaac fathered Jacob,
    Jacob fathered Judah and his brothers,
3   Judah fathered Perez and Zerah by Tamar,
    Perez fathered Hezron,
    Hezron fathered Aram,
4   Aram fathered Amminadab,
    Amminadab fathered Nahshon,
    Nahshon fathered Salmon,
5   Salmon fathered Boaz by Rahab,
    Boaz fathered Obed by Ruth,
    Obed fathered Jesse,
6   and Jesse fathered King David.
    David fathered Solomon by Uriah's wife,
7   Solomon fathered Rehoboam,
    Rehoboam fathered Abijah,
    Abijah fathered Asa,
8   Asa fathered Jehoshaphat,
    Jehoshaphat fathered Joram,
    Joram fathered Uzziah,
9   Uzziah fathered Jotham,
    Jotham fathered Ahaz,
    Ahaz fathered Hezekiah,
10 Hezekiah fathered Manasseh,
    Manasseh fathered Amon,
    Amon fathered Josiah,
11 and Josiah fathered Jeconiah and his brothers
    at the time of the exile to Babylon.
12 After the exile to Babylon
    Jeconiah fathered Shealtiel,
    Shealtiel fathered Zerubbabel,
13 Zerubbabel fathered Abiud,
    Abiud fathered Eliakim,
    Eliakim fathered Azor,
14 Azor fathered Zadok,
    Zadok fathered Achim,

23 As he began his ministry, Jesus was about thirty years old and was thought to be the
        son of Joseph, son of Heli,
24   son of Matthat, son of Levi,
        son of Melchi, son of Jannai,
        son of Joseph, 25 son of Mattathias,
        son of Amos, son of Nahum,
        son of Esli, son of Naggai,
26   son of Maath, son of Mattathias,
        son of Semein, son of Josech,
        son of Joda, 27 son of Joanan,
        son of Rhesa, son of Zerubbabel,
        son of Shealtiel, son of Neri,
28   son of Melchi, son of Addi,
        son of Cosam, son of Elmadam,
        son of Er, 29 son of Joshua,
        son of Eliezer, son of Jorim,
        son of Matthat, son of Levi,
30   son of Simeon, son of Judah,
        son of Joseph, son of Jonam,
        son of Eliakim, 31 son of Melea,
        son of Menna, son of Mattatha,
        son of Nathan, son of David,
32   son of Jesse, son of Obed,
        son of Boaz, son of Salmon,
        son of Nahshon, 33 son of Amminadab,
        son of Ram, son of Hezron,
        son of Perez, son of Judah,
34   son of Jacob, son of Isaac,
        son of Abraham, son of Terah,
        son of Nahor, 35 son of Serug,
        son of Reu, son of Peleg,
        son of Eber, son of Shelah,
36   son of Cainan, son of Arphaxad,
        son of Shem, son of Noah,
        son of Lamech, 37 son of Methuselah,
        son of Enoch, son of Jared,
        son of Mahalalel, son of Cainan,

Achim fathered Eliud,
15 Eliud fathered Eleazar,
Eleazar fathered Matthan,
Matthan fathered Jacob,
16 and Jacob fathered Joseph the husband of Mary,
who gave birth to Jesus who is called the Christ.

38 son of Enos, son of Seth,
son of Adam, son of God.

17 So all the generations from Abraham to David were fourteen generations; and from David until the exile to Babylon, fourteen generations; and from the exile to Babylon until the Christ, fourteen generations.

GABRIEL PREDICTS JOHN'S BIRTH

LK 1:5-25

5 In the days of King Herod of Judea, there was a priest of Abijah's division named Zechariah. His wife was from the daughters of Aaron, and her name was Elizabeth. 6 Both were righteous in God's sight, living without blame according to all the commands and requirements of the Lord. 7 But they had no children because Elizabeth could not conceive, and both of them were well along in years.

8 When his division was on duty and he was serving as priest before God, 9 it happened that he was chosen by lot, according to the custom of the priesthood, to enter the sanctuary of the Lord and burn incense. 10 At the hour of incense the whole assembly of the people was praying outside. 11 An angel of the Lord appeared to him, standing to the right of the altar of incense. 12 When Zechariah saw him, he was terrified and overcome with fear. 13 But the angel said to him: "Do not be afraid, Zechariah, because your prayer has been heard. Your wife Elizabeth will bear you a son, and you will name him John. 14 There will be joy and delight for you, and many will rejoice at his birth. 15 For he will be great in the sight of the Lord and will never drink wine or beer. He will be filled with the Holy Spirit while still in his mother's womb. 16 He will turn many of the children of Israel to the Lord their God. 17 And he will go before him in the spirit and power of Elijah, to turn the hearts of fathers to their children, and the disobedient to the understanding of the righteous, to make ready for the Lord a prepared people."

18 "How can I know this?" Zechariah asked the angel. "For I am an old man, and my wife is well along in years."

19 The angel answered him, "I am Gabriel, who stands in the presence of God, and I was sent to speak to you and tell you this good news. 20 Now listen. You will become silent and unable to speak until the day these things take place, because you did not believe my words, which will be fulfilled in their proper time."

21 Meanwhile, the people were waiting for Zechariah, amazed that he stayed so long in the sanctuary. 22 When he did come out, he could not speak to them. Then they realized that he had seen a vision in the sanctuary. He was making signs to them and remained speechless. 23 When the days of his ministry were completed, he went back home.

24 After these days his wife Elizabeth conceived and kept herself in seclusion for five months. She said, 25 "The Lord has done this for me. He has looked with favor in these days to take away my disgrace among the people."

[26] In the sixth month, the angel Gabriel was sent by God to a town in Galilee called Nazareth, [27] to a virgin engaged to a man named Joseph, of the house of David. The virgin's name was Mary. [28] And the angel came to her and said, "Greetings, favored woman! The Lord is with you." [29] But she was deeply troubled by this statement, wondering what kind of greeting this could be. [30] Then the angel told her: "Do not be afraid, Mary, for you have found favor with God. [31] Now listen: You will conceive and give birth to a son, and you will name him Jesus. [32] He will be great and will be called the Son of the Most High, and the Lord God will give him the throne of his father David. [33] He will reign over the house of Jacob forever, and his kingdom will have no end."

[34] Mary asked the angel, "How can this be, since I have not had sexual relations with a man?"

[35] The angel replied to her: "The Holy Spirit will come upon you, and the power of the Most High will overshadow you. Therefore, the holy one to be born will be called the Son of God. [36] "And consider your relative Elizabeth — even she has conceived a son in her old age, and this is the sixth month for her who was called childless. [37] For nothing will be impossible with God."

[38] "I am the Lord's servant," said Mary. "May it be done to me according to your word." Then the angel left her.

[39] In those days Mary set out and hurried to a town in the hill country of Judah [40] where she entered Zechariah's house and greeted Elizabeth. [41] When Elizabeth heard Mary's greeting, the baby leaped inside her, and Elizabeth was filled with the Holy Spirit. [42] Then she exclaimed with a loud cry: "Blessed are you among women, and your child will be blessed! [43] How could this happen to me, that the mother of my Lord should come to me? [44] For you see, when the sound of your greeting reached my ears, the baby leaped for joy inside me. [45] Blessed is she who has believed that the Lord would fulfill what he has spoken to her!"

[46] And Mary said:

My soul praises the greatness of the Lord,
[47]   and my spirit rejoices in God my Savior,
[48]   because he has looked with favor
    on the humble condition of his servant.
    Surely, from now on all generations
    will call me blessed,
[49]   because the Mighty One
    has done great things for me,
    and his name is holy.
[50]   His mercy is from generation to generation
    on those who fear him.
[51]   He has done a mighty deed with his arm;
    he has scattered the proud
    because of the thoughts of their hearts;
[52]   he has toppled the mighty from their thrones
    and exalted the lowly.
[53]   He has satisfied the hungry with good things
    and sent the rich away empty.

MATTHEW   MARK   LUKE   JOHN

⁵⁴ He has helped his servant Israel,
     remembering his mercy
⁵⁵ to Abraham and his descendants forever,
     just as he spoke to our ancestors.

⁵⁶ And Mary stayed with her about three months; then she returned to her home.

THE BIRTH AND NAMING OF JOHN

⁵⁷ Now the time had come for Elizabeth to give birth, and she had a son. ⁵⁸ Then her neighbors and relatives heard that the Lord had shown her his great mercy, and they rejoiced with her.

⁵⁹ When they came to circumcise the child on the eighth day, they were going to name him Zechariah, after his father. ⁶⁰ But his mother responded, "No. He will be called John."

⁶¹ Then they said to her, "None of your relatives has that name." ⁶² So they motioned to his father to find out what he wanted him to be called. ⁶³ He asked for a writing tablet and wrote: "His name is John." And they were all amazed. ⁶⁴ Immediately his mouth was opened and his tongue set free, and he began to speak, praising God. ⁶⁵ Fear came on all those who lived around them, and all these things were being talked about throughout the hill country of Judea. ⁶⁶ All who heard about him took it to heart, saying, "What then will this child become?" For, indeed, the Lord's hand was with him.

ZECHARIAH'S PROPHECY

⁶⁷ Then his father Zechariah was filled with the Holy Spirit and prophesied:
⁶⁸   Blessed is the Lord, the God of Israel,
     because he has visited
     and provided redemption for his people.
⁶⁹   He has raised up a horn of salvation for us
     in the house of his servant David,
⁷⁰   just as he spoke by the mouth
     of his holy prophets in ancient times;
⁷¹   salvation from our enemies
     and from the hand of those who hate us.
⁷²   He has dealt mercifully with our fathers
     and remembered his holy covenant —
⁷³   the oath that he swore to our father Abraham.
     He has given us the privilege,
⁷⁴   since we have been rescued
     from the hand of our enemies,
     to serve him without fear
⁷⁵   in holiness and righteousness
     in his presence all our days.
⁷⁶   And you, child, will be called
     a prophet of the Most High,
     for you will go before the Lord
     to prepare his ways,

> [77] to give his people knowledge of salvation
> through the forgiveness of their sins.
> [78] Because of our God's merciful compassion,
> the dawn from on high will visit us
> [79] to shine on those who live in darkness
> and the shadow of death,
> to guide our feet into the way of peace.

[80] The child grew up and became spiritually strong, and he was in the wilderness until the day of his public appearance to Israel.

THE BIRTH OF JESUS

MT 1:18-25   LK 2:1-7

In light of their respective introductions, one begins to develop an expectation for how a Gospel writer might narrate an event such as the birth of Jesus. Matthew seeks to show the cohesion between Jesus's birth and OT prophecy through his many "fulfillment" quotations (1:22-23). Luke, however, gives an account of the events that triggered the pilgrimage of Joseph and Mary from Nazareth to Bethlehem as a means of placing Jesus's birth in the context of Greco-Roman history. Chronologically, Luke's account could fit seamlessly between Matthew 1:25 and 2:1.

[18] The birth of Jesus Christ came about this way: After his mother Mary had been engaged to Joseph, it was discovered before they came together that she was pregnant from the Holy Spirit. [19] So her husband Joseph, being a righteous man, and not wanting to disgrace her publicly, decided to divorce her secretly.

[20] But after he had considered these things, an angel of the Lord appeared to him in a dream, saying, "Joseph, son of David, don't be afraid to take Mary as your wife, because what has been conceived in her is from the Holy Spirit. [21] She will give birth to a son, and you are to name him Jesus, because he will save his people from their sins."

[22] Now all this took place to fulfill what was spoken by the Lord through the prophet:

[23] **See, the virgin will become pregnant**
and give birth to a son,
and they will name him Immanuel,

which is translated "God is with us."

[24] When Joseph woke up, he did as the Lord's angel had commanded him. He married her [25] but did not have sexual relations with her until she gave birth to a son. And he named him Jesus.

[1] In those days a decree went out from Caesar Augustus that the whole empire should be registered. [2] This first registration took place while Quirinius was governing Syria. [3] So everyone went to be registered, each to his own town.

[4] Joseph also went up from the town of Nazareth in Galilee, to Judea, to the city of David, which is called Bethlehem, because he was of the house and family line of David, [5] to be registered along with Mary, who was engaged to him and was pregnant. [6] While they were there, the time came for her to give birth. [7] Then she gave birth to her firstborn Son, and she wrapped him tightly in cloth and laid him in a manger, because there was no guest room available for them.

THE SHEPHERDS AND THE ANGELS

LK 2:8-20

[8] In the same region, shepherds were staying out in the fields and keeping watch at night over their flock. [9] Then an angel of the Lord stood before them, and the glory of the Lord shone around them, and they were terrified. [10] But the angel said to them, "Don't be afraid, for look, I proclaim to you good news of great joy that will be for all the people: [11] Today in the city of David a Savior was born for you, who is the Messiah, the Lord. [12] This will be the sign for you: You will find a baby wrapped tightly in cloth and lying in a manger."

[13] Suddenly there was a multitude of the heavenly host with the angel, praising God and saying:

¹⁴ Glory to God in the highest heaven,
and peace on earth to people he favors!

¹⁵ When the angels had left them and returned to heaven, the shepherds said to one another, "Let's go straight to Bethlehem and see what has happened, which the Lord has made known to us."

¹⁶ They hurried off and found both Mary and Joseph, and the baby who was lying in the manger. ¹⁷ After seeing them, they reported the message they were told about this child, ¹⁸ and all who heard it were amazed at what the shepherds said to them. ¹⁹ But Mary was treasuring up all these things in her heart and meditating on them. ²⁰ The shepherds returned, glorifying and praising God for all the things they had seen and heard, which were just as they had been told.

INFANT JESUS AT THE TEMPLE

LK 2:21-38

²¹ When the eight days were completed for his circumcision, he was named Jesus—the name given by the angel before he was conceived. ²² And when the days of their purification according to the law of Moses were finished, they brought him up to Jerusalem to present him to the Lord ²³ (just as it is written in the law of the Lord, **Every firstborn male will be dedicated to the Lord**) ²⁴ and to offer a sacrifice (according to what is stated in the law of the Lord, **a pair of turtledoves or two young pigeons**).

²⁵ There was a man in Jerusalem whose name was Simeon. This man was righteous and devout, looking forward to Israel's consolation, and the Holy Spirit was on him. ²⁶ It had been revealed to him by the Holy Spirit that he would not see death before he saw the Lord's Messiah. ²⁷ Guided by the Spirit, he entered the temple. When the parents brought in the child Jesus to perform for him what was customary under the law, ²⁸ Simeon took him up in his arms, praised God, and said,

²⁹ Now, Master,
you can dismiss your servant in peace,
as you promised.
³⁰ For my eyes have seen your salvation.
³¹ You have prepared it
in the presence of all peoples—
³² a light for revelation to the Gentiles
and glory to your people Israel.

³³ His father and mother were amazed at what was being said about him. ³⁴ Then Simeon blessed them and told his mother Mary: "Indeed, this child is destined to cause the fall and rise of many in Israel and to be a sign that will be opposed— ³⁵ and a sword will pierce your own soul—that the thoughts of many hearts may be revealed."

³⁶ There was also a prophetess, Anna, a daughter of Phanuel, of the tribe of Asher. She was well along in years, having lived with her husband seven years after her marriage, ³⁷ and was a widow for eighty-four years. She did not leave the temple, serving God night and day with fasting and prayers. ³⁸ At that very moment, she came up and began to thank God and to speak about him to all who were looking forward to the redemption of Jerusalem.

[1] After Jesus was born in Bethlehem of Judea in the days of King Herod, wise men from the east arrived in Jerusalem, [2] saying, "Where is he who has been born king of the Jews? For we saw his star at its rising and have come to worship him."

[3] When King Herod heard this, he was deeply disturbed, and all Jerusalem with him. [4] So he assembled all the chief priests and scribes of the people and asked them where the Christ would be born.

[5] "In Bethlehem of Judea," they told him, "because this is what was written by the prophet:

[6] **And you, Bethlehem,** in the land of Judah,
   are by no means **least among the rulers of Judah:**
   Because out of you will come a ruler
   who will shepherd my people Israel."

[7] Then Herod secretly summoned the wise men and asked them the exact time the star appeared. [8] He sent them to Bethlehem and said, "Go and search carefully for the child. When you find him, report back to me so that I too can go and worship him."

[9] After hearing the king, they went on their way. And there it was — the star they had seen at its rising. It led them until it came and stopped above the place where the child was. [10] When they saw the star, they were overwhelmed with joy. [11] Entering the house, they saw the child with Mary his mother, and falling to their knees, they worshiped him. Then they opened their treasures and presented him with gifts: gold, frankincense, and myrrh. [12] And being warned in a dream not to go back to Herod, they returned to their own country by another route.

FLIGHT FROM HEROD THE GREAT

[13] After they were gone, an angel of the Lord appeared to Joseph in a dream, saying, "Get up! Take the child and his mother, flee to Egypt, and stay there until I tell you. For Herod is about to search for the child to kill him." [14] So he got up, took the child and his mother during the night, and escaped to Egypt. [15] He stayed there until Herod's death, so that what was spoken by the Lord through the prophet might be fulfilled: **Out of Egypt I called my Son.**

[16] Then Herod, when he realized that he had been outwitted by the wise men, flew into a rage. He gave orders to massacre all the boys in and around Bethlehem who were two years old and under, in keeping with the time he had learned from the wise men. [17] Then what was spoken through Jeremiah the prophet was fulfilled:

[18] **A voice was heard in Ramah,**
   weeping, and great mourning,
   Rachel weeping for her children;
   and she refused to be consoled,
   because they are no more.

[19] After Herod died, an angel of the Lord appeared in a dream to Joseph in Egypt, [20] saying, "Get up, take the child and his mother, and go to the land of Israel, because those who intended to kill the child are dead." [21] So he got up, took the child and his mother, and entered the land of Israel. [22] But when he heard that Archelaus was ruling over Judea in place of his father Herod, he was afraid to go there. And being warned in a dream, he withdrew to the region of Galilee.

²³ Then he went and settled in a town called Nazareth to fulfill what was spoken through the prophets, that he would be called a Nazarene.

³⁹ When they had completed everything according to the law of the Lord, they returned to Galilee, to their own town of Nazareth. ⁴⁰ The boy grew up and became strong, filled with wisdom, and God's grace was on him.

⁴¹ Every year his parents traveled to Jerusalem for the Passover Festival. ⁴² When he was twelve years old, they went up according to the custom of the festival. ⁴³ After those days were over, as they were returning, the boy Jesus stayed behind in Jerusalem, but his parents did not know it. ⁴⁴ Assuming he was in the traveling party, they went a day's journey. Then they began looking for him among their relatives and friends. ⁴⁵ When they did not find him, they returned to Jerusalem to search for him. ⁴⁶ After three days, they found him in the temple sitting among the teachers, listening to them and asking them questions. ⁴⁷ And all those who heard him were astounded at his understanding and his answers. ⁴⁸ When his parents saw him, they were astonished, and his mother said to him, "Son, why have you treated us like this? Your father and I have been anxiously searching for you."

⁴⁹ "Why were you searching for me?" he asked them. "Didn't you know that it was necessary for me to be in my Father's house?" ⁵⁰ But they did not understand what he said to them.

⁵¹ Then he went down with them and came to Nazareth and was obedient to them. His mother kept all these things in her heart. ⁵² And Jesus increased in wisdom and stature, and in favor with God and with people.

JOHN THE BAPTIST PREPARES THE WAY   MT 3:1-12   MK 1:2-8   LK 3:1-18   JN 1:19-28

The account of John the Baptist is a good example of how the four Gospel writers showcase their unique literary nuances, relative to their purpose and style, without compromising the historical core of the event. In all four Gospels, John is described in relation to both the OT Scriptures and to Jesus. He is, on the one hand, the forerunner of the Messiah as foretold by Isaiah (Is 40:3). On the other hand, he must defer to the emerging mission of Jesus defined as baptism by "fire."

It is where the Gospel writers diverge, however, that proves most helpful in filling in some of the historical and theological gaps for the reader. Mark, as is often the case, gives only the essential details. But a comparison of Matthew and Luke is quite insightful. Matthew singles out the Pharisees and Sadducees as the central recipients of Jesus's scathing rebuke. These religious leaders will emerge as the antagonists as his story unfolds. Luke, though, applies Jesus's rebuke more broadly to the "multitude." Moreover, by highlighting John's reply to the repeated question, "What then should we do?" from various groups, Luke shows a number of his own social concerns. John's account has some affinities with Matthew in how he singles out the religious officials who will play a similar antagonistic role in his Gospel. Yet, in John, the discussion of the Baptist's identity is a response to the badgering inquisition of the religious leaders.

¹ In those days John the Baptist came, preaching in the wilderness of Judea ² and saying, "Repent, because the kingdom of heaven has come near!" ³ For he is the one spoken of through the prophet Isaiah, who said:

A voice of one crying out
  in the wilderness:
Prepare the way for the Lord;
  make his paths straight!

¹ In the fifteenth year of the reign of Tiberius Caesar, while Pontius Pilate was governor of Judea, Herod was tetrarch of Galilee, his brother Philip tetrarch of the region of Iturea and Trachonitis, and Lysanias tetrarch of Abilene, ² during the high priesthood of Annas and Caiaphas, God's word came to John the son of Zechariah in the wilderness. ³ He went into all the vicinity of the Jordan, proclaiming a baptism of

¹⁹ This was John's testimony when the Jews from Jerusalem sent priests and Levites to ask him, "Who are you?"

²⁰ He didn't deny it but confessed: "I am not the Messiah."

²¹ "What then?" they asked him. "Are you Elijah?"

"I am not," he said.

"Are you the Prophet?"

⁴ Now John had a camel-hair garment with a leather belt around his waist, and his food was locusts and wild honey. ⁵ Then people from Jerusalem, all Judea, and all the vicinity of the Jordan were going out to him, ⁶ and they were baptized by him in the Jordan River, confessing their sins.

⁷ When he saw many of the Pharisees and Sadducees coming to his baptism, he said to them, "Brood of vipers! Who warned you to flee from the coming wrath? ⁸ Therefore produce fruit consistent with repentance. ⁹ And don't presume to say to yourselves, 'We have Abraham as our father.' For I tell you that God is able to raise up children for Abraham from these stones. ¹⁰ The ax is already at the root of the trees. Therefore, every tree that doesn't produce good fruit will be cut down and thrown into the fire.

¹¹ "I baptize you with water for repentance, but the one who is coming after me is more powerful than I. I am not worthy to remove his sandals. He himself will baptize you with the Holy Spirit and fire. ¹² His winnowing shovel is in his hand, and he will clear his threshing floor and gather his wheat into the barn. But the chaff he will burn with fire that never goes out."

² As it is written in Isaiah the prophet:

See, I am sending
my messenger ahead
of you;
he will prepare your way.
³ A voice of one crying out
in the wilderness:
Prepare the way
for the Lord;
make his paths straight!

⁴ John came baptizing in the wilderness and proclaiming a baptism of repentance for the forgiveness of sins. ⁵ The whole Judean countryside and all the people of Jerusalem were going out to him, and they were baptized by him in the Jordan River, confessing their sins. ⁶ John wore a camel-hair garment with a leather belt around his waist and ate locusts and wild honey.

⁷ He proclaimed, "One who is more powerful than I am is coming after me. I am not worthy to stoop down and untie the strap of his sandals. ⁸ I baptize you with water, but he will baptize you with the Holy Spirit."

repentance for the forgiveness of sins, ⁴ as it is written in the book of the words of the prophet Isaiah:

A voice of one crying out
in the wilderness:
Prepare the way for the Lord;
make his paths straight!
⁵ Every valley will be filled,
and every mountain and hill
will be made low;
the crooked
will become straight,
the rough ways smooth,
⁶ and everyone will see
the salvation of God.

⁷ He then said to the crowds who came out to be baptized by him, "Brood of vipers! Who warned you to flee from the coming wrath? ⁸ Therefore produce fruit consistent with repentance. And don't start saying to yourselves, 'We have Abraham as our father,' for I tell you that God is able to raise up children for Abraham from these stones. ⁹ The ax is already at the root of the trees. Therefore, every tree that doesn't produce good fruit will be cut down and thrown into the fire."

¹⁰ "What then should we do?" the crowds were asking him.

¹¹ He replied to them, "The one who has two shirts must share with someone who has none, and the one who has food must do the same."

¹² Tax collectors also came to be baptized, and they asked him, "Teacher, what should we do?"

¹³ He told them, "Don't collect any more than what you have been authorized."

¹⁴ Some soldiers also questioned him, "What should we do?"

He said to them, "Don't take money from anyone by force or false accusation, and be satisfied with your wages."

¹⁵ Now the people were waiting expectantly, and all of them were questioning in their hearts whether John might be the Messiah. ¹⁶ John answered them all, "I baptize you with water, but one who is more powerful than I am is coming. I am not worthy to untie the strap of his sandals. He will baptize you with the Holy Spirit and fire. ¹⁷ His winnowing shovel is in his hand to clear his threshing floor and gather the wheat into his barn, but the chaff he will burn with fire that never goes out." ¹⁸ Then, along with many other exhortations, he proclaimed good news to the people.

"No," he answered.
²² "Who are you, then?" they asked. "We need to give an answer to those who sent us. What can you tell us about yourself?"

²³ He said, "I am a **voice of one crying out in the wilderness: Make straight the way of the Lord** —just as Isaiah the prophet said."

²⁴ Now they had been sent from the Pharisees. ²⁵ So they asked him, "Why then do you baptize if you aren't the Messiah, or Elijah, or the Prophet?"

²⁶ "I baptize with water," John answered them. "Someone stands among you, but you don't know him. ²⁷ He is the one coming after me, whose sandal strap I'm not worthy to untie." ²⁸ All this happened in Bethany across the Jordan, where John was baptizing.

There is little divergence among the Gospel writers regarding Jesus's baptism, especially in the Synoptic Gospels (i.e., Matthew, Mark, and Luke) and their unanimous testimony about the voice from heaven that affirms Jesus as "my beloved Son." Nevertheless, some peculiarities warrant comment. Matthew, for example, highlights the important shift from John's role to Jesus's mission, a transition that will "fulfill all righteousness." This is the first of seven distinctive uses of the term "righteousness" in Matthew that highlights the author's burden to show Jesus's conformity to a moral norm, namely the Jewish law. John's account of Jesus's baptism is also unique, yet it fits his primary intent to "testify" to the truthfulness of Jesus's identity, a governing purpose made explicit at the end of his Gospel (cf. 21:24).

13 Then Jesus came from Galilee to John at the Jordan, to be baptized by him. **14** But John tried to stop him, saying, "I need to be baptized by you, and yet you come to me?"
15 Jesus answered him, "Allow it for now, because this is the way for us to fulfill all righteousness." Then John allowed him to be baptized.
16 When Jesus was baptized, he went up immediately from the water. The heavens suddenly opened for him, and he saw the Spirit of God descending like a dove and coming down on him. **17** And a voice from heaven said: "This is my beloved Son, with whom I am well-pleased."

9 In those days Jesus came from Nazareth in Galilee and was baptized in the Jordan by John. **10** As soon as he came up out of the water, he saw the heavens being torn open and the Spirit descending on him like a dove. **11** And a voice came from heaven: "You are my beloved Son; with you I am well-pleased."

21 When all the people were baptized, Jesus also was baptized. As he was praying, heaven opened, **22** and the Holy Spirit descended on him in a physical appearance like a dove. And a voice came from heaven: "You are my beloved Son; with you I am well-pleased."

29 The next day John saw Jesus coming toward him and said, "Here is the Lamb of God, who takes away the sin of the world! **30** This is the one I told you about: 'After me comes a man who ranks ahead of me, because he existed before me.' **31** I didn't know him, but I came baptizing with water so he might be revealed to Israel." **32** And John testified, "I saw the Spirit descending from heaven like a dove, and he rested on him. **33** I didn't know him, but he who sent me to baptize with water told me, 'The one you see the Spirit descending and resting on — he is the one who baptizes with the Holy Spirit.' **34** I have seen and testified that this is the Son of God."

Mark's account of the temptation of Jesus offers, once again, only the bare essentials of the event. Matthew and Luke, however, are more expansive. A comparison of the two reveals a discrepancy related to the order of the three temptations. The last two temptations are reversed: Matthew = bread → temple → mountain; Luke = bread → mountain → temple. The simplest explanation is that Matthew's order is chronological and Luke's is thematic. As such, Luke preferred to end his account with the temple scene given the significance of the temple for his unfolding story of Jesus's mission. Yet the acceptability of this explanation rests upon one's ability to distinguish between strict chronology and historicity. In other words, the historical accuracy of an account is not necessarily compromised if the events are presented in a different chronological order. Both authors, it should be noted, are driven primarily by thematic concerns. The original chronology, it seems, fits Matthew's literary and theological purposes. Yet Luke deviates from strict chronology to make a theological point, but he retains the historical core of the event.

1 Then Jesus was led up by the Spirit into the wilderness to be tempted by the devil. **2** After he had fasted forty days and forty nights, he was hungry. **3** Then the tempter approached

12 Immediately the Spirit drove him into the wilderness. **13** He was in the wilderness forty days, being tempted by Satan. He was with the wild animals, and the angels were serving him.

1 Then Jesus left the Jordan, full of the Holy Spirit, and was led by the Spirit in the wilderness **2** for forty days to be tempted by the devil. He ate nothing during those days, and when

him and said, "If you are the Son of God, tell these stones to become bread."

[4] He answered, "It is written: **Man must not live on bread alone but on every word that comes from the mouth of God.**"

[5] Then the devil took him to the holy city, had him stand on the pinnacle of the temple, [6] and said to him, "If you are the Son of God, throw yourself down. For it is written:

> **He will give his angels orders concerning you**,
> and **they will support you with their hands**
> so that you will not strike
> your foot against a stone."

[7] Jesus told him, "It is also written: **Do not test the Lord your God.**"

[8] Again, the devil took him to a very high mountain and showed him all the kingdoms of the world and their splendor. [9] And he said to him, "I will give you all these things if you will fall down and worship me."

[10] Then Jesus told him, "Go away, Satan! For it is written: **Worship the Lord your God, and serve only him.**"

[11] Then the devil left him, and angels came and began to serve him.

they were over, he was hungry. [3] The devil said to him, "If you are the Son of God, tell this stone to become bread."

[4] But Jesus answered him, "It is written: **Man must not live on bread alone.**"

[5] So he took him up and showed him all the kingdoms of the world in a moment of time. [6] The devil said to him, "I will give you their splendor and all this authority, because it has been given over to me, and I can give it to anyone I want. [7] If you, then, will worship me, all will be yours."

[8] And Jesus answered him, "It is written: **Worship the Lord your God, and serve him only.**"

[9] So he took him to Jerusalem, had him stand on the pinnacle of the temple, and said to him, "If you are the Son of God, throw yourself down from here. [10] For it is written:

> **He will give his angels orders concerning you,**
> **to protect you,** [11] and
> **they will support you with their hands,**
> **so that you will not strike**
> **your foot against a stone.**"

[12] And Jesus answered him, "It is said: **Do not test the Lord your God.**"

[13] After the devil had finished every temptation, he departed from him for a time.

THE BEGINNING OF JESUS'S MINISTRY

³⁵ The next day, John was standing with two of his disciples. ³⁶ When he saw Jesus passing by, he said, "Look, the Lamb of God!"

³⁷ The two disciples heard him say this and followed Jesus. ³⁸ When Jesus turned and noticed them following him, he asked them, "What are you looking for?"

They said to him, "Rabbi" (which means "Teacher"), "where are you staying?"

³⁹ "Come and you'll see," he replied. So they went and saw where he was staying, and they stayed with him that day. It was about four in the afternoon.

⁴⁰ Andrew, Simon Peter's brother, was one of the two who heard John and followed him. ⁴¹ He first found his own brother Simon and told him, "We have found the Messiah" (which is translated "the Christ"), ⁴² and he brought Simon to Jesus.

When Jesus saw him, he said, "You are Simon, son of John. You will be called Cephas" (which is translated "Peter").

⁴³ The next day Jesus decided to leave for Galilee. He found Philip and told him, "Follow me."

⁴⁴ Now Philip was from Bethsaida, the hometown of Andrew and Peter. ⁴⁵ Philip found Nathanael and told him, "We have found the one Moses wrote about in the law (and so did the prophets): Jesus the son of Joseph, from Nazareth."

⁴⁶ "Can anything good come out of Nazareth?" Nathanael asked him.

"Come and see," Philip answered.

⁴⁷ Then Jesus saw Nathanael coming toward him and said about him, "Here truly is an Israelite in whom there is no deceit."

⁴⁸ "How do you know me?" Nathanael asked.

"Before Philip called you, when you were under the fig tree, I saw you," Jesus answered.

⁴⁹ "Rabbi," Nathanael replied, "You are the Son of God; you are the King of Israel!"

⁵⁰ Jesus responded to him, "Do you believe because I told you I saw you under the fig tree? You will see greater things than this." ⁵¹ Then he said, "Truly I tell you, you will see heaven opened and the angels of God ascending and descending on the Son of Man."

¹ On the third day a wedding took place in Cana of Galilee. Jesus's mother was there, and ² Jesus and his disciples were invited to the wedding as well. ³ When the wine ran out, Jesus's mother told him, "They don't have any wine."

⁴ "What does that have to do with you and me, woman?" Jesus asked. "My hour has not yet come."

⁵ "Do whatever he tells you," his mother told the servants.

⁶ Now six stone water jars had been set there for Jewish purification. Each contained twenty or thirty gallons.

⁷ "Fill the jars with water," Jesus told them. So they filled them to the brim. ⁸ Then he said to them, "Now draw some out and take it to the headwaiter." And they did.

⁹ When the headwaiter tasted the water (after it had become wine), he did not know where it came from — though the servants who had drawn the water knew. He called the groom ¹⁰ and told him, "Everyone sets out the fine wine first, then, after people are drunk, the inferior. But you have kept the fine wine until now."

¹¹ Jesus did this, the first of his signs, in Cana of Galilee. He revealed his glory, and his disciples believed in him.

¹² After this, he went down to Capernaum, together with his mother, his brothers, and his disciples, and they stayed there only a few days.

THE CLEANSING OF THE TEMPLE
JN 2:13-22

¹³ The Jewish Passover was near, and so Jesus went up to Jerusalem. ¹⁴ In the temple he found people selling oxen, sheep, and doves, and he also found the money changers sitting there. ¹⁵ After making a whip out of cords, he drove everyone out of the temple with their sheep and oxen. He also poured out the money changers' coins and overturned the tables. ¹⁶ He told those who were selling doves, "Get these things out of here! Stop turning my Father's house into a marketplace!"

¹⁷ And his disciples remembered that it is written: **Zeal for your house will consume me**.

¹⁸ So the Jews replied to him, "What sign will you show us for doing these things?"

¹⁹ Jesus answered, "Destroy this temple, and I will raise it up in three days."

²⁰ Therefore the Jews said, "This temple took forty-six years to build, and will you raise it up in three days?"

²¹ But he was speaking about the temple of his body. ²² So when he was raised from the dead, his disciples remembered that he had said this, and they believed the Scripture and the statement Jesus had made.

JESUS AND NICODEMUS
JN 2:23–3:21

²³ While he was in Jerusalem during the Passover Festival, many believed in his name when they saw the signs he was doing. ²⁴ Jesus, however, would not entrust himself to them, since he knew them all ²⁵ and because he did not need anyone to testify about man; for he himself knew what was in man.

¹ There was a man from the Pharisees named Nicodemus, a ruler of the Jews. ² This man came to him at night and said, "Rabbi, we know that you are a teacher who has come from God, for no one could perform these signs you do unless God were with him."

³ Jesus replied, "Truly I tell you, unless someone is born again, he cannot see the kingdom of God."

⁴ "How can anyone be born when he is old?" Nicodemus asked him. "Can he enter his mother's womb a second time and be born?"

⁵ Jesus answered, "Truly I tell you, unless someone is born of water and the Spirit, he cannot enter the kingdom of God. ⁶ Whatever is born of the flesh is flesh, and whatever is born of the

Spirit is spirit. [7] Do not be amazed that I told you that you must be born again. [8] The wind blows where it pleases, and you hear its sound, but you don't know where it comes from or where it is going. So it is with everyone born of the Spirit."

[9] "How can these things be?" asked Nicodemus.

[10] "Are you a teacher of Israel and don't know these things?" Jesus replied. [11] "Truly I tell you, we speak what we know and we testify to what we have seen, but you do not accept our testimony. [12] If I have told you about earthly things and you don't believe, how will you believe if I tell you about heavenly things? [13] No one has ascended into heaven except the one who descended from heaven — the Son of Man.

[14] "Just as Moses lifted up the snake in the wilderness, so the Son of Man must be lifted up, [15] so that everyone who believes in him may have eternal life. [16] For God loved the world in this way: He gave his one and only Son, so that everyone who believes in him will not perish but have eternal life. [17] For God did not send his Son into the world to condemn the world, but to save the world through him. [18] Anyone who believes in him is not condemned, but anyone who does not believe is already condemned, because he has not believed in the name of the one and only Son of God. [19] This is the judgment: The light has come into the world, and people loved darkness rather than the light because their deeds were evil. [20] For everyone who does evil hates the light and avoids it, so that his deeds may not be exposed. [21] But anyone who lives by the truth comes to the light, so that his works may be shown to be accomplished by God."

THE TESTIMONY OF JOHN THE BAPTIST

JN 3:22-36

[22] After this, Jesus and his disciples went to the Judean countryside, where he spent time with them and baptized.

[23] John also was baptizing in Aenon near Salim, because there was plenty of water there. People were coming and being baptized, [24] since John had not yet been thrown into prison.

[25] Then a dispute arose between John's disciples and a Jew about purification. [26] So they came to John and told him, "Rabbi, the one you testified about, and who was with you across the Jordan, is baptizing — and everyone is going to him."

[27] John responded, "No one can receive anything unless it has been given to him from heaven. [28] You yourselves can testify that I said, 'I am not the Messiah, but I've been sent ahead of him.' [29] He who has the bride is the groom. But the groom's friend, who stands by and listens for him, rejoices greatly at the groom's voice. So this joy of mine is complete. [30] He must increase, but I must decrease."

[31] The one who comes from above is above all. The one who is from the earth is earthly and speaks in earthly terms. The one who comes from heaven is above all. [32] He testifies to what he has seen and heard, and yet no one accepts his testimony. [33] The one who has accepted his testimony has affirmed that God is true. [34] For the one whom God sent speaks God's words, since he gives the Spirit without measure. [35] The Father loves the Son and has given all things into his hands. [36] The one who believes in the Son has eternal life, but the one who rejects the Son will not see life; instead, the wrath of God remains on him.

[19] But when John rebuked Herod the tetrarch because of Herodias, his brother's wife, and all the evil things he had done, [20] Herod added this to everything else — he locked up John in prison.

JESUS IN SAMARIA   JN 4:1-42

[1] When Jesus learned that the Pharisees had heard he was making and baptizing more disciples than John [2] (though Jesus himself was not baptizing, but his disciples were), [3] he left Judea and went again to Galilee. [4] He had to travel through Samaria; [5] so he came to a town of Samaria called Sychar near the property that Jacob had given his son Joseph. [6] Jacob's well was there, and Jesus, worn out from his journey, sat down at the well. It was about noon.

[7] A woman of Samaria came to draw water.

"Give me a drink," Jesus said to her, [8] because his disciples had gone into town to buy food.

[9] "How is it that you, a Jew, ask for a drink from me, a Samaritan woman?" she asked him. For Jews do not associate with Samaritans.

[10] Jesus answered, "If you knew the gift of God, and who is saying to you, 'Give me a drink,' you would ask him, and he would give you living water."

[11] "Sir," said the woman, "you don't even have a bucket, and the well is deep. So where do you get this 'living water'? [12] You aren't greater than our father Jacob, are you? He gave us the well and drank from it himself, as did his sons and livestock."

[13] Jesus said, "Everyone who drinks from this water will get thirsty again. [14] But whoever drinks from the water that I will give him will never get thirsty again. In fact, the water I will give him will become a well of water springing up in him for eternal life."

[15] "Sir," the woman said to him, "give me this water so that I won't get thirsty and come here to draw water."

[16] "Go call your husband," he told her, "and come back here."

[17] "I don't have a husband," she answered.

"You have correctly said, 'I don't have a husband,'" Jesus said. [18] "For you've had five husbands, and the man you now have is not your husband. What you have said is true."

[19] "Sir," the woman replied, "I see that you are a prophet. [20] Our fathers worshiped on this mountain, but you Jews say that the place to worship is in Jerusalem."

[21] Jesus told her, "Believe me, woman, an hour is coming when you will worship the Father neither on this mountain nor in Jerusalem. [22] You Samaritans worship what you do not know. We worship what we do know, because salvation is from the Jews. [23] But an hour is coming, and is now here, when the true worshipers will worship the Father in Spirit and in truth. Yes, the Father wants such people to worship him. [24] God is spirit, and those who worship him must worship in Spirit and in truth."

[25] The woman said to him, "I know that the Messiah is coming" (who is called Christ). "When he comes, he will explain everything to us."

[26] Jesus told her, "I, the one speaking to you, am he."

[27] Just then his disciples arrived, and they were amazed that he was talking with a woman. Yet no one said, "What do you want?" or "Why are you talking with her?"

²⁸ Then the woman left her water jar, went into town, and told the people, ²⁹ "Come, see a man who told me everything I ever did. Could this be the Messiah? " ³⁰ They left the town and made their way to him.

³¹ In the meantime the disciples kept urging him, "Rabbi, eat something."

³² But he said, "I have food to eat that you don't know about."

³³ The disciples said to one another, "Could someone have brought him something to eat? "

³⁴ "My food is to do the will of him who sent me and to finish his work," Jesus told them. ³⁵ "Don't you say, 'There are still four more months, and then comes the harvest'? Listen to what I'm telling you: Open your eyes and look at the fields, because they are ready for harvest. ³⁶ The reaper is already receiving pay and gathering fruit for eternal life, so that the sower and reaper can rejoice together. ³⁷ For in this case the saying is true: 'One sows and another reaps.' ³⁸ I sent you to reap what you didn't labor for; others have labored, and you have benefited from their labor."

³⁹ Now many Samaritans from that town believed in him because of what the woman said when she testified, "He told me everything I ever did." ⁴⁰ So when the Samaritans came to him, they asked him to stay with them, and he stayed there two days. ⁴¹ Many more believed because of what he said. ⁴² And they told the woman, "We no longer believe because of what you said, since we have heard for ourselves and know that this really is the Savior of the world."

JESUS COMES TO GALILEE

MT 4:12-17   MK 1:14-15   LK 4:14-15   JN 4:43-45

The four slightly nuanced accounts of Jesus's move from Nazareth to Galilee demonstrate that no event is theologically neutral. Matthew, for example, links the event with yet another fulfillment quote from the prophet Isaiah (Is 9:1-2), marking the shift from the preparation phase to the ministry phase. For Matthew, this is nothing less than the in-breaking of the "kingdom of heaven," a phrase unique to the his Gospel. Mark agrees but prefers the more common designation, "kingdom of God." Matthew's deviation here can only be fully understood in light of his pervasive use of "heaven" language across his Gospel. Luke and John have less interest in this statement but, instead, highlight Jesus's fame across Galilee. Only John points out that this fame was at the expense of his reputation in his hometown of Nazareth.

¹² When he heard that John had been arrested, he withdrew into Galilee. ¹³ He left Nazareth and went to live in Capernaum by the sea, in the region of Zebulun and Naphtali. ¹⁴ This was to fulfill what was spoken through the prophet Isaiah:

¹⁵   Land of Zebulun and land of Naphtali,
     along the road by the sea, beyond the Jordan,
     Galilee of the Gentiles.

¹⁶   The people who live in darkness
     have seen a great light,
     and for those living in the land of the shadow of death,
     a light has dawned.

¹⁷ From then on Jesus began to preach, "Repent, because the kingdom of heaven has come near."

¹⁴ After John was arrested, Jesus went to Galilee, proclaiming the good news of God: ¹⁵ "The time is fulfilled, and the kingdom of God has come near. Repent and believe the good news! "

¹⁴ Then Jesus returned to Galilee in the power of the Spirit, and news about him spread throughout the entire vicinity. ¹⁵ He was teaching in their synagogues, being praised by everyone.

⁴³ After two days he left there for Galilee. ⁴⁴ (Jesus himself had testified that a prophet has no honor in his own country.) ⁴⁵ When they entered Galilee, the Galileans welcomed him because they had seen everything he did in Jerusalem during the festival. For they also had gone to the festival.

⁴⁶ He went again to Cana of Galilee, where he had turned the water into wine. There was a certain royal official whose son was ill at Capernaum. ⁴⁷ When this man heard that Jesus had come from Judea into Galilee, he went to him and pleaded with him to come down and heal his son, since he was about to die.

⁴⁸ Jesus told him, "Unless you people see signs and wonders, you will not believe."

⁴⁹ "Sir," the official said to him, "come down before my boy dies."

⁵⁰ "Go," Jesus told him, "your son will live." The man believed what Jesus said to him and departed.

⁵¹ While he was still going down, his servants met him saying that his boy was alive. ⁵² He asked them at what time he got better. "Yesterday at one in the afternoon the fever left him," they answered. ⁵³ The father realized this was the very hour at which Jesus had told him, "Your son will live." So he himself believed, along with his whole household.

⁵⁴ Now this was also the second sign Jesus performed after he came from Judea to Galilee.

THE CALLING OF FOUR FISHERMEN

MT 4:18-22   MK 1:16-20   LK 5:1-11

Matthew and Mark are clearly drawing from the same tradition, whether oral or written, with regard to the calling of the first disciples. Luke, however, expands the account and focuses on Peter to highlight Jesus's holiness and sovereignty. Mark and Luke also differ in that Mark places this event before Jesus's trip to Capernaum, and Luke places it after. For this reason, some have suggested that Luke's account of Peter's call is a different event. To be sure, there could have been multiple callings of the same disciples. In such a case, Luke would be narrating a subsequent, and certainly more profound, encounter between Jesus and Peter where instead of only forsaking their "nets," as in Matthew and Mark, they have now forsaken "all." Alternatively, as in the account of the temptation, Luke could be deviating from a strict chronology to make a theological point. Either way, the historical core remains intact and the two accounts remain compatible since both Mark and Luke have Peter with Jesus in Capernaum.

¹⁸ As he was walking along the Sea of Galilee, he saw two brothers, Simon (who is called Peter), and his brother Andrew. They were casting a net into the sea — for they were fishermen. ¹⁹ "Follow me," he told them, "and I will make you fish for people." ²⁰ Immediately they left their nets and followed him.

²¹ Going on from there, he saw two other brothers, James the son of Zebedee, and his brother John. They were in a boat with Zebedee their father, preparing their nets, and he called them. ²² Immediately they left the boat and their father and followed him.

¹⁶ As he passed alongside the Sea of Galilee, he saw Simon and Andrew, Simon's brother, casting a net into the sea — for they were fishermen. ¹⁷ "Follow me," Jesus told them, "and I will make you fish for people." ¹⁸ Immediately they left their nets and followed him. ¹⁹ Going on a little farther, he saw James the son of Zebedee and his brother John in a boat putting their nets in order. ²⁰ Immediately he called them, and they left their father Zebedee in the boat with the hired men and followed him.

¹ As the crowd was pressing in on Jesus to hear God's word, he was standing by Lake Gennesaret. ² He saw two boats at the edge of the lake; the fishermen had left them and were washing their nets. ³ He got into one of the boats, which belonged to Simon, and asked him to put out a little from the land. Then he sat down and was teaching the crowds from the boat.

⁴ When he had finished speaking, he said to Simon, "Put out into deep water and let down your nets for a catch."

⁵ "Master," Simon replied, "we've worked hard all night long and caught nothing. But if you say so, I'll let down the nets."

⁶ When they did this, they caught a great number of fish, and their nets began to tear. ⁷ So they signaled to their partners in the other boat to come and help them; they came and filled both boats so full that they began to sink.

[8] When Simon Peter saw this, he fell at Jesus's knees and said, "Go away from me, because I'm a sinful man, Lord!" [9] For he and all those with him were amazed at the catch of fish they had taken, [10] and so were James and John, Zebedee's sons, who were Simon's partners.

"Don't be afraid," Jesus told Simon. "From now on you will be catching people." [11] Then they brought the boats to land, left everything, and followed him.

THE EXORCISM AT THE SYNAGOGUE IN CAPERNAUM

MK 1:21-28   LK 4:31-37

Mark and Luke are almost in verbatim agreement about Jesus's exorcism in Capernaum. Yet Luke's placement of this event prior to the calling of the disciples, but subsequent to Jesus's near-death experience in Nazareth, makes it a fitting illustration of the liberating work described in Luke's quotation of Isaiah (Lk 4:18-19).

[21] They went into Capernaum, and right away he entered the synagogue on the Sabbath and began to teach. [22] They were astonished at his teaching because he was teaching them as one who had authority, and not like the scribes.

[23] Just then a man with an unclean spirit was in their synagogue. He cried out, [24] "What do you have to do with us, Jesus of Nazareth? Have you come to destroy us? I know who you are — the Holy One of God!"

[25] Jesus rebuked him saying, "Be silent, and come out of him!" [26] And the unclean spirit threw him into convulsions, shouted with a loud voice, and came out of him.

[27] They were all amazed, and so they began to ask each other: "What is this? A new teaching with authority! He commands even the unclean spirits, and they obey him." [28] At once the news about him spread throughout the entire vicinity of Galilee.

[31] Then he went down to Capernaum, a town in Galilee, and was teaching them on the Sabbath. [32] They were astonished at his teaching because his message had authority. [33] In the synagogue there was a man with an unclean demonic spirit who cried out with a loud voice, [34] "Leave us alone! What do you have to do with us, Jesus of Nazareth? Have you come to destroy us? I know who you are — the Holy One of God!"

[35] But Jesus rebuked him and said, "Be silent and come out of him!" And throwing him down before them, the demon came out of him without hurting him at all.

[36] Amazement came over them all, and they were saying to one another, "What is this message? For he commands the unclean spirits with authority and power, and they come out!" [37] And news about him began to go out to every place in the vicinity.

HEALINGS AT CAPERNAUM

MT 8:14-17   MK 1:29-34   LK 4:38-41

The three Synoptic Gospels are in essential agreement about the initial healings of Jesus in Capernaum. The exorcism and the healing of Peter's mother-in-law were not isolated events but the first of many such healings, and Matthew supports this aspect of Jesus's ministry with another fulfillment quotation from Isaiah (Is 53:4). Furthermore, Matthew places this event after Jesus's first lengthy discourse (Mt 5-7) and at the beginning of a new section dedicated to showing how the in-breaking of the kingdom of heaven is manifest through Jesus's healing. This is one instance where Mark is actually longer than Matthew. Both Mark and Luke note how Jesus silences the demons, which will be a recurring pattern as their stories unfold.

[14] Jesus went into Peter's house and saw his mother-in-law lying in bed with a fever. [15] So he touched her hand, and the fever left her. Then she got up and began to serve him. [16] When evening came, they brought to him many who were demon-possessed. He drove out the spirits with a word and healed all who were sick, [17] so that what was spoken through the prophet Isaiah might be fulfilled:

[29] As soon as they left the synagogue, they went into Simon and Andrew's house with James and John. [30] Simon's mother-in-law was lying in bed with a fever, and they told him about her at once. [31] So he went to her, took her by the hand, and raised her up. The fever left her, and she began to serve them.

[32] When evening came, after the sun had set, they brought to him all those who were sick

[38] After he left the synagogue, he entered Simon's house. Simon's mother-in-law was suffering from a high fever, and they asked him about her. [39] So he stood over her and rebuked the fever, and it left her. She got up immediately and began to serve them.

[40] When the sun was setting, all those who had anyone sick with various diseases brought them to him. As he laid his hands on each

He himself took our weaknesses
and carried our diseases.

and demon-possessed. [33] The whole town was assembled at the door, [34] and he healed many who were sick with various diseases and drove out many demons. And he would not permit the demons to speak, because they knew him.

one of them, he healed them. [41] Also, demons were coming out of many, shouting and saying, "You are the Son of God!" But he rebuked them and would not allow them to speak, because they knew he was the Christ.

JESUS PREACHES THROUGHOUT GALILEE

MT 4:23-25   MK 1:35-39   LK 4:42-44

For the Synoptic writers, this account serves as a programmatic statement of the central purpose of Jesus's mission. But it functions slightly differently for each author. Matthew places it as a hinge between his early accounts of Jesus's life and his public ministry. He also includes the task of teaching and the mission of healing. Together, these tasks serve as the structure for Matthew's unfolding story of Jesus, centered around five major discourses. For Mark and Luke, the account is more closely tied to the preceding events at Capernaum. His fame there notwithstanding, the message about the kingdom of God, according to Luke, must be unleashed.

[23] Now Jesus began to go all over Galilee, teaching in their synagogues, preaching the good news of the kingdom, and healing every disease and sickness among the people. [24] Then the news about him spread throughout Syria. So they brought to him all those who were afflicted, those suffering from various diseases and intense pains, the demon-possessed, the epileptics, and the paralytics. And he healed them. [25] Large crowds followed him from Galilee, the Decapolis, Jerusalem, Judea, and beyond the Jordan.

[35] Very early in the morning, while it was still dark, he got up, went out, and made his way to a deserted place; and there he was praying. [36] Simon and his companions searched for him, [37] and when they found him they said, "Everyone is looking for you."

[38] And he said to them, "Let's go on to the neighboring villages so that I may preach there too. This is why I have come."

[39] He went into all of Galilee, preaching in their synagogues and driving out demons.

[42] When it was day, he went out and made his way to a deserted place. But the crowds were searching for him. They came to him and tried to keep him from leaving them. [43] But he said to them, "It is necessary for me to proclaim the good news about the kingdom of God to the other towns also, because I was sent for this purpose." [44] And he was preaching in the synagogues of Judea.

CLEANSING OF THE LEPROUS MAN

MT 8:1-4   MK 1:40-45   LK 5:12-16

Matthew, Mark, and Luke are similar in their account of this healing. Matthew is surprisingly the shortest, omitting Jesus's command for the leper to remain silent. But Mark and Luke retain this detail, a pattern that scholars have come to label the "messianic secret." This command for silence is a pattern in Mark and Luke and so also is the refusal to obey, resulting in increased fame among Jesus's followers. By this "messianic secret," the authors create for the reader what the characters missed—that is, an appreciation for a more profound messianic identity of Jesus, one marked by sacrificial suffering.

[1] When he came down from the mountain, large crowds followed him. [2] Right away a man with leprosy came up and knelt before him, saying, "Lord, if you are willing, you can make me clean." [3] Reaching out his hand, Jesus touched him, saying, "I am willing; be made clean." Immediately his leprosy was cleansed. [4] Then Jesus told him, "See that you don't tell anyone; but go, show yourself to the priest, and offer the gift that Moses commanded, as a testimony to them."

[40] Then a man with leprosy came to him and, on his knees, begged him: "If you are willing, you can make me clean." [41] Moved with compassion, Jesus reached out his hand and touched him. "I am willing," he told him. "Be made clean." [42] Immediately the leprosy left him, and he was made clean. [43] Then he sternly warned him and sent him away at once, [44] telling him, "See that you say nothing to anyone; but go and show yourself to

[12] While he was in one of the towns, a man was there who had leprosy all over him. He saw Jesus, fell facedown, and begged him: "Lord, if you are willing, you can make me clean."

[13] Reaching out his hand, Jesus touched him, saying, "I am willing; be made clean," and immediately the leprosy left him. [14] Then he ordered him to tell no one: "But go and show yourself to the priest, and offer what Moses commanded for your cleansing as a testimony to them."

MATTHEW   MARK   LUKE   JOHN

the priest, and offer what Moses commanded for your cleansing, as a testimony to them." **45** Yet he went out and began to proclaim it widely and to spread the news, with the result that Jesus could no longer enter a town openly. But he was out in deserted places, and they came to him from everywhere.

15 But the news about him spread even more, and large crowds would come together to hear him and to be healed of their sicknesses. **16** Yet he often withdrew to deserted places and prayed.

HEALING OF THE PARALYTIC MAN

MT 9:1-8   MK 2:1-12   LK 5:17-26

The Synoptic authors agree about the essential core of this healing event. Matthew omits the details of the paralytic's adventurous entry into the house, which Mark and Luke have retained. More importantly, all three highlight an important development in Jesus's ministry—namely, that the aim of healing reaches far beyond physical restoration to spiritual restoration and forgiveness.

1 So he got into a boat, crossed over, and came to his own town. **2** Just then some men brought to him a paralytic lying on a stretcher. Seeing their faith, Jesus told the paralytic, "Have courage, son, your sins are forgiven."

3 At this, some of the scribes said to themselves, "He's blaspheming!"

4 Perceiving their thoughts, Jesus said, "Why are you thinking evil things in your hearts? **5** For which is easier: to say, 'Your sins are forgiven,' or to say, 'Get up and walk'? **6** But so that you may know that the Son of Man has authority on earth to forgive sins" — then he told the paralytic, "Get up, take your stretcher, and go home." **7** So he got up and went home. **8** When the crowds saw this, they were awestruck and gave glory to God, who had given such authority to men.

1 When he entered Capernaum again after some days, it was reported that he was at home. **2** So many people gathered together that there was no more room, not even in the doorway, and he was speaking the word to them. **3** They came to him bringing a paralytic, carried by four of them. **4** Since they were not able to bring him to Jesus because of the crowd, they removed the roof above him, and after digging through it, they lowered the mat on which the paralytic was lying. **5** Seeing their faith, Jesus told the paralytic, "Son, your sins are forgiven."

6 But some of the scribes were sitting there, questioning in their hearts: **7** "Why does he speak like this? He's blaspheming! Who can forgive sins but God alone?"

8 Right away Jesus perceived in his spirit that they were thinking like this within themselves and said to them, "Why are you thinking these things in your hearts? **9** Which is easier: to say to the paralytic, 'Your sins are forgiven,' or to say, 'Get up, take your mat, and walk'? **10** But so that you may know that the Son of Man has authority on earth to forgive sins" — he told the paralytic — **11** "I tell you: get up, take your mat, and go home."

12 Immediately he got up, took the mat, and went out in front of everyone. As a result, they were all astounded and gave glory to God, saying, "We have never seen anything like this!"

17 On one of those days while he was teaching, Pharisees and teachers of the law were sitting there who had come from every village of Galilee and Judea, and also from Jerusalem. And the Lord's power to heal was in him. **18** Just then some men came, carrying on a stretcher a man who was paralyzed. They tried to bring him in and set him down before him. **19** Since they could not find a way to bring him in because of the crowd, they went up on the roof and lowered him on the stretcher through the roof tiles into the middle of the crowd before Jesus.

20 Seeing their faith he said, "Friend, your sins are forgiven."

21 Then the scribes and the Pharisees began to think to themselves: "Who is this man who speaks blasphemies? Who can forgive sins but God alone?"

22 But perceiving their thoughts, Jesus replied to them, "Why are you thinking this in your hearts? **23** Which is easier: to say, 'Your sins are forgiven you,' or to say, 'Get up and walk'? **24** But so that you may know that the Son of Man has authority on earth to forgive sins" — he told the paralyzed man, "I tell you: Get up, take your stretcher, and go home."

25 Immediately he got up before them, picked up what he had been lying on, and went home glorifying God. **26** Then everyone was astounded, and they were giving glory to God. And they were filled with awe and said, "We have seen incredible things today."

The account of the call of Matthew/Levi serves a similar theological function in each of the Synoptic Gospels, showing the deeper reality of Jesus's mission to save unworthy sinners. The "doctor" metaphor helps the reader connect those dots. While one might be sympathetic toward the paralytic in the previous passage, within a first-century Jewish social and religious context, the restoration of a "tax collector and sinner" was unthinkable.

9 As Jesus went on from there, he saw a man named Matthew sitting at the toll booth, and he said to him, "Follow me," and he got up and followed him.

10 While he was reclining at the table in the house, many tax collectors and sinners came to eat with Jesus and his disciples. 11 When the Pharisees saw this, they asked his disciples, "Why does your teacher eat with tax collectors and sinners?"

12 Now when he heard this, he said, "It is not those who are well who need a doctor, but those who are sick. 13 Go and learn what this means: **I desire mercy and not sacrifice.** For I didn't come to call the righteous, but sinners."

13 Jesus went out again beside the sea. The whole crowd was coming to him, and he was teaching them. 14 Then, passing by, he saw Levi the son of Alphaeus sitting at the toll booth, and he said to him, "Follow me," and he got up and followed him.

15 While he was reclining at the table in Levi's house, many tax collectors and sinners were eating with Jesus and his disciples, for there were many who were following him. 16 When the scribes who were Pharisees saw that he was eating with sinners and tax collectors, they asked his disciples, "Why does he eat with tax collectors and sinners?"

17 When Jesus heard this, he told them, "It is not those who are well who need a doctor, but those who are sick. I didn't come to call the righteous, but sinners."

27 After this, Jesus went out and saw a tax collector named Levi sitting at the tax office, and he said to him, "Follow me." 28 So, leaving everything behind, he got up and began to follow him.

29 Then Levi hosted a grand banquet for him at his house. Now there was a large crowd of tax collectors and others who were guests with them. 30 But the Pharisees and their scribes were complaining to his disciples, "Why do you eat and drink with tax collectors and sinners?"

31 Jesus replied to them, "It is not those who are healthy who need a doctor, but those who are sick. 32 I have not come to call the righteous, but sinners to repentance."

QUESTION ABOUT FASTING   MT 9:14-17   MK 2:18-22   LK 5:33-39

Matthew, Mark, and Luke are in essential agreement on the core components of this account. There are slight differences in how each author recounts the three parables of the bridegroom, the garment, and the wineskins, yet all three make the same general point about the relationship of the Jewish law to the mission of Jesus. One might have hoped for a more explicit propositional statement by Jesus on this important issue instead of analogies. Yet the authors strategically leave the reader with only a glimpse of how the old and new relate in light of Jesus's ministry. The reader must read on.

14 Then John's disciples came to him, saying, "Why do we and the Pharisees fast often, but your disciples do not fast?"

15 Jesus said to them, "Can the wedding guests be sad while the groom is with them? The time will come when the groom will be taken away from them, and then they will fast. 16 No one patches an old garment with unshrunk cloth, because the patch pulls away from the garment and makes the tear worse. 17 And no one puts new wine into old wineskins. Otherwise, the skins burst, the wine spills out, and the skins are ruined. No, they

18 Now John's disciples and the Pharisees were fasting. People came and asked him, "Why do John's disciples and the Pharisees' disciples fast, but your disciples do not fast?"

19 Jesus said to them, "The wedding guests cannot fast while the groom is with them, can they? As long as they have the groom with them, they cannot fast. 20 But the time will come when the groom will be taken away from them, and then they will fast on that day. 21 No one sews a patch of unshrunk cloth on an old garment. Otherwise, the new patch pulls away from the old cloth, and a worse tear is

33 Then they said to him, "John's disciples fast often and say prayers, and those of the Pharisees do the same, but yours eat and drink."

34 Jesus said to them, "You can't make the wedding guests fast while the groom is with them, can you? 35 But the time will come when the groom will be taken away from them — then they will fast in those days."

36 He also told them a parable: "No one tears a patch from a new garment and puts it on an old garment. Otherwise, not only will he tear the new, but also the piece from the new

put new wine into fresh wineskins, and both are preserved."

made. [22] And no one puts new wine into old wineskins. Otherwise, the wine will burst the skins, and the wine is lost as well as the skins. No, new wine is put into fresh wineskins."

garment will not match the old. [37] And no one puts new wine into old wineskins. Otherwise, the new wine will burst the skins, it will spill, and the skins will be ruined. [38] No, new wine is put into fresh wineskins. [39] And no one, after drinking old wine, wants new, because he says, 'The old is better.' "

JESUS RETURNS TO JERUSALEM AND HEALS A LAME MAN

JN 5:1-15

[1] After this, a Jewish festival took place, and Jesus went up to Jerusalem. [2] By the Sheep Gate in Jerusalem there is a pool, called Bethesda in Aramaic, which has five colonnades. [3] Within these lay a large number of the disabled—blind, lame, and paralyzed.

[5] One man was there who had been disabled for thirty-eight years. [6] When Jesus saw him lying there and realized he had already been there a long time, he said to him, "Do you want to get well?"

[7] "Sir," the disabled man answered, "I have no one to put me into the pool when the water is stirred up, but while I'm coming, someone goes down ahead of me."

[8] "Get up," Jesus told him, "pick up your mat and walk." [9] Instantly the man got well, picked up his mat, and started to walk.

Now that day was the Sabbath, [10] and so the Jews said to the man who had been healed, "This is the Sabbath. The law prohibits you from picking up your mat."

[11] He replied, "The man who made me well told me, 'Pick up your mat and walk.' "

[12] "Who is this man who told you, 'Pick up your mat and walk'?" they asked. [13] But the man who was healed did not know who it was, because Jesus had slipped away into the crowd that was there.

[14] After this, Jesus found him in the temple and said to him, "See, you are well. Do not sin anymore, so that something worse doesn't happen to you." [15] The man went and reported to the Jews that it was Jesus who had made him well.

THE JEWS OFFENDED BY JESUS'S DEEDS AND WORDS

JN 5:16-47

[16] Therefore, the Jews began persecuting Jesus because he was doing these things on the Sabbath.

[17] Jesus responded to them, "My Father is still working, and I am working also." [18] This is why the Jews began trying all the more to kill him: Not only was he breaking the Sabbath, but he was even calling God his own Father, making himself equal to God.

[19] Jesus replied, "Truly I tell you, the Son is not able to do anything on his own, but only what he sees the Father doing. For whatever the Father does, the Son likewise does these things. [20] For the Father loves the Son and shows him everything he is doing, and he will show him greater works than these so that you will be amazed. [21] And just as the Father raises the dead and gives them life, so the Son also gives life to whom he wants. [22] The Father, in fact, judges no one but has given all judgment to the Son, [23] so that all people may honor the Son just as they honor the Father. Anyone who does not honor the Son does not honor the Father who sent him.

[24] "Truly I tell you, anyone who hears my word and believes him who sent me has eternal life and will not come under judgment but has passed from death to life.

²⁵ "Truly I tell you, an hour is coming, and is now here, when the dead will hear the voice of the Son of God, and those who hear will live. ²⁶ For just as the Father has life in himself, so also he has granted to the Son to have life in himself. ²⁷ And he has granted him the right to pass judgment, because he is the Son of Man. ²⁸ Do not be amazed at this, because a time is coming when all who are in the graves will hear his voice ²⁹ and come out — those who have done good things, to the resurrection of life, but those who have done wicked things, to the resurrection of condemnation.

³⁰ "I can do nothing on my own. I judge only as I hear, and my judgment is just, because I do not seek my own will, but the will of him who sent me.

³¹ "If I testify about myself, my testimony is not true. ³² There is another who testifies about me, and I know that the testimony he gives about me is true. ³³ You sent messengers to John, and he testified to the truth. ³⁴ I don't receive human testimony, but I say these things so that you may be saved. ³⁵ John was a burning and shining lamp, and you were willing to rejoice for a while in his light.

³⁶ "But I have a greater testimony than John's because of the works that the Father has given me to accomplish. These very works I am doing testify about me that the Father has sent me. ³⁷ The Father who sent me has himself testified about me. You have not heard his voice at any time, and you haven't seen his form. ³⁸ You don't have his word residing in you, because you don't believe the one he sent. ³⁹ You pore over the Scriptures because you think you have eternal life in them, and yet they testify about me. ⁴⁰ But you are not willing to come to me so that you may have life.

⁴¹ "I do not accept glory from people, ⁴² but I know you — that you have no love for God within you. ⁴³ I have come in my Father's name, and yet you don't accept me. If someone else comes in his own name, you will accept him. ⁴⁴ How can you believe, since you accept glory from one another but don't seek the glory that comes from the only God? ⁴⁵ Do not think that I will accuse you to the Father. Your accuser is Moses, on whom you have set your hope. ⁴⁶ For if you believed Moses, you would believe me, because he wrote about me. ⁴⁷ But if you don't believe what he wrote, how will you believe my words?"

THE DISCIPLES PICKING GRAIN ON THE SABBATH

MT 12:1-8   MK 2:23-28   LK 6:1-5

Aside from a few minor differences, the Synoptic accounts of this first Sabbath controversy are quite consistent. All three include Jesus's unequivocal declaration of his lordship over the Sabbath. Jesus does not deny that the ceremonial law was broken but only that, by analogy to the OT, such regulations should give way to a higher moral standard—in this case human need. Mark is more explicit on this point, adding that the Sabbath was "made for man." Matthew records an expanded version of the event that includes not only Jesus's relationship to the Sabbath but also to the temple, a theme that will become increasingly important in his Gospel. All three authors help the reader see how the "old" relates to the "new," a topic introduced in the fasting controversy above.

¹ At that time Jesus passed through the grainfields on the Sabbath. His disciples were hungry and began to pick and eat some heads of grain. ² When the Pharisees saw this, they said to him, "See, your disciples are doing what is not lawful to do on the Sabbath."

²³ On the Sabbath he was going through the grainfields, and his disciples began to make their way, picking some heads of grain. ²⁴ The Pharisees said to him, "Look, why are they doing what is not lawful on the Sabbath?"
²⁵ He said to them, "Have you never read what David and those who were with him did

¹ On a Sabbath, he passed through the grainfields. His disciples were picking heads of grain, rubbing them in their hands, and eating them. ² But some of the Pharisees said, "Why are you doing what is not lawful on the Sabbath?"
³ Jesus answered them, "Haven't you read what David and those who were with him did

MATTHEW   MARK   LUKE   JOHN

³ He said to them, "Haven't you read what David did when he and those who were with him were hungry: ⁴ how he entered the house of God, and they ate the bread of the Presence — which is not lawful for him or for those with him to eat, but only for the priests? ⁵ Or haven't you read in the law that on Sabbath days the priests in the temple violate the Sabbath and are innocent? ⁶ I tell you that something greater than the temple is here. ⁷ If you had known what this means, **I desire mercy and not sacrifice**, you would not have condemned the innocent. ⁸ For the Son of Man is Lord of the Sabbath."

when he was in need and hungry — ²⁶ how he entered the house of God in the time of Abiathar the high priest and ate the bread of the Presence — which is not lawful for anyone to eat except the priests — and also gave some to his companions?" ²⁷ Then he told them, "The Sabbath was made for man and not man for the Sabbath. ²⁸ So then, the Son of Man is Lord even of the Sabbath."

when he was hungry — ⁴ how he entered the house of God and took and ate the bread of the Presence, which is not lawful for any but the priests to eat? He even gave some to those who were with him." ⁵ Then he told them, "The Son of Man is Lord of the Sabbath."

JESUS HEALS A MAN WITH A PARALYZED HAND   MT 12:9-14   MK 3:1-6   LK 6:6-11

This second Sabbath controversy reinforces the point of the first one above—namely, that doing good is intrinsic to the Sabbath regulation. Matthew enhances the point with an analogy of saving a sheep on the Sabbath. In addition, all three agree that this is a turning point in the relationship between Jesus and the religious officials who are now bent on destroying him. The only significant variation in the Synoptic accounts is that Luke places the event on a subsequent Sabbath while Matthew, and perhaps Mark, imply that it occurred on the same day as the first Sabbath controversy. This, again, calls for a careful distinction between historicity and strict chronology.

⁹ Moving on from there, he entered their synagogue. ¹⁰ There he saw a man who had a shriveled hand, and in order to accuse him they asked him, "Is it lawful to heal on the Sabbath?"

¹¹ He replied to them, "Who among you, if he had a sheep that fell into a pit on the Sabbath, wouldn't take hold of it and lift it out? ¹² A person is worth far more than a sheep; so it is lawful to do what is good on the Sabbath."

¹³ Then he told the man, "Stretch out your hand." So he stretched it out, and it was restored, as good as the other. ¹⁴ But the Pharisees went out and plotted against him, how they might kill him.

¹ Jesus entered the synagogue again, and a man was there who had a shriveled hand. ² In order to accuse him, they were watching him closely to see whether he would heal him on the Sabbath. ³ He told the man with the shriveled hand, "Stand before us." ⁴ Then he said to them, "Is it lawful to do good on the Sabbath or to do evil, to save life or to kill?" But they were silent. ⁵ After looking around at them with anger, he was grieved at the hardness of their hearts and told the man, "Stretch out your hand." So he stretched it out, and his hand was restored. ⁶ Immediately the Pharisees went out and started plotting with the Herodians against him, how they might kill him.

⁶ On another Sabbath he entered the synagogue and was teaching. A man was there whose right hand was shriveled. ⁷ The scribes and Pharisees were watching him closely, to see if he would heal on the Sabbath, so that they could find a charge against him. ⁸ But he knew their thoughts and told the man with the shriveled hand, "Get up and stand here." So he got up and stood there. ⁹ Then Jesus said to them, "I ask you: Is it lawful to do good on the Sabbath or to do evil, to save life or to destroy it?" ¹⁰ After looking around at them all, he told him, "Stretch out your hand." He did, and his hand was restored. ¹¹ They, however, were filled with rage and started discussing with one another what they might do to Jesus.

It was not uncommon in antiquity for an individual to have more than one name, which accounts for the variation in the twelve disciples in Mark and Luke. Luke's "Judas the son of James" is usually associated with "Thaddeus" in Mark (see also Mt 10:2-4). There are other lists of disciples in the NT, all of which have Peter at the head and Judas Iscariot, the traitor, at the end. It is fitting that Mark and Luke would place this selection after the Sabbath controversy. Given the mounting hostility of the religious officials, the authors hint that Jesus's mission will endure through this new community.

[13] Jesus went up the mountain and summoned those he wanted, and they came to him. [14] He appointed twelve, whom he also named apostles, to be with him, to send them out to preach, [15] and to have authority to drive out demons. [16] He appointed the Twelve: To Simon, he gave the name Peter; [17] and to James the son of Zebedee, and to his brother John, he gave the name "Boanerges" (that is, "Sons of Thunder"); [18] Andrew; Philip and Bartholomew; Matthew and Thomas; James the son of Alphaeus, and Thaddaeus; Simon the Zealot, [19] and Judas Iscariot, who also betrayed him.

[12] During those days he went out to the mountain to pray and spent all night in prayer to God. [13] When daylight came, he summoned his disciples, and he chose twelve of them, whom he also named apostles: [14] Simon, whom he also named Peter, and Andrew his brother; James and John; Philip and Bartholomew; [15] Matthew and Thomas; James the son of Alphaeus, and Simon called the Zealot; [16] Judas the son of James, and Judas Iscariot, who became a traitor.

JESUS'S MINISTRY IN GALILEE

There are a number of summary statements like this across the four Gospels. They generally follow the movements of Jesus's ministry through Galilee, Judea, and ultimately to Jerusalem. There are a few differences among these accounts but none that prove historically challenging. Mark adds the incidental detail about the boat, and Matthew highlights how Jesus's ministry fulfilled OT prophecy. More significant is the relative placement of this in the storyline of each author. Matthew notably connects his summary to the mounting hostility resulting from the Sabbath controversies.

[15] Jesus was aware of this and withdrew. Large crowds followed him, and he healed them all. [16] He warned them not to make him known, [17] so that what was spoken through the prophet Isaiah might be fulfilled:
[18]   Here is my servant whom I have chosen,
        my beloved in whom I delight;
        I will put my Spirit on him,
        and he will proclaim justice
            to the nations.
[19]   He will not argue or shout,
        and no one will hear his voice
            in the streets.
[20]   He will not break a bruised reed,
        and he will not put out
            a smoldering wick,
        until he has led justice to victory.
[21]   The nations will put their hope
            in his name.

[7] Jesus departed with his disciples to the sea, and a large crowd followed from Galilee, and a large crowd followed from Judea, [8] Jerusalem, Idumea, beyond the Jordan, and around Tyre and Sidon. The large crowd came to him because they heard about everything he was doing. [9] Then he told his disciples to have a small boat ready for him, so that the crowd wouldn't crush him. [10] Since he had healed many, all who had diseases were pressing toward him to touch him. [11] Whenever the unclean spirits saw him, they fell down before him and cried out, "You are the Son of God!" [12] And he would strongly warn them not to make him known.

[17] After coming down with them, he stood on a level place with a large crowd of his disciples and a great number of people from all Judea and Jerusalem and from the seacoast of Tyre and Sidon. [18] They came to hear him and to be healed of their diseases; and those tormented by unclean spirits were made well. [19] The whole crowd was trying to touch him, because power was coming out from him and healing them all.

The Beatitudes serve as an introduction to two similar, yet distinct, discourses in Matthew (Sermon on the Mount) and Luke (Sermon on the Plain). The variances between them are easily explained once one realizes that Jesus would likely have preached a number of sermons at different times that shared similar themes. It would have been, as Walter Liefeld and David Pao ("Luke" in *The Expositor's Bible Commentary*) suggest, something like a "keynote" address.

[1] When he saw the crowds, he went up on the mountain, and after he sat down, his disciples came to him. [2] Then he began to teach them, saying:
[3]   "Blessed are the poor in spirit,
       for the kingdom of heaven is theirs.

[20] Then looking up at his disciples, he said:
       Blessed are you who are poor,
       because the kingdom of God is yours.
[21]   Blessed are you who are now hungry,
       because you will be filled.

4 Blessed are those who mourn,
    for they will be comforted.
5 Blessed are the humble,
    for they will inherit the earth.
6 Blessed are those who hunger and thirst for righteousness,
    for they will be filled.
7 Blessed are the merciful,
    for they will be shown mercy.
8 Blessed are the pure in heart,
    for they will see God.
9 Blessed are the peacemakers,
    for they will be called sons of God.
10 Blessed are those who are persecuted because of righteousness,
    for the kingdom of heaven is theirs.

11 "You are blessed when they insult you and persecute you and falsely say every kind of evil against you because of me. 12 Be glad and rejoice, because your reward is great in heaven. For that is how they persecuted the prophets who were before you."

Blessed are you who weep now,
    because you will laugh.
22 Blessed are you when people hate you,
    when they exclude you, insult you,
    and slander your name as evil
    because of the Son of Man.
23 "Rejoice in that day and leap for joy. Take note — your reward is great in heaven, for this is the way their ancestors used to treat the prophets.
24 But woe to you who are rich,
    for you have received your comfort.
25 Woe to you who are now full,
    for you will be hungry.
    Woe to you who are now laughing,
    for you will mourn and weep.
26 Woe to you
    when all people speak well of you,
    for this is the way their ancestors
    used to treat the false prophets."

JESUS TEACHES THE MULTITUDES

MT 5:13-42

13 "You are the salt of the earth. But if the salt should lose its taste, how can it be made salty? It's no longer good for anything but to be thrown out and trampled under people's feet.

14 "You are the light of the world. A city situated on a hill cannot be hidden. 15 No one lights a lamp and puts it under a basket, but rather on a lampstand, and it gives light for all who are in the house. 16 In the same way, let your light shine before others, so that they may see your good works and give glory to your Father in heaven.

17 "Don't think that I came to abolish the Law or the Prophets. I did not come to abolish but to fulfill. 18 For truly I tell you, until heaven and earth pass away, not the smallest letter or one stroke of a letter will pass away from the law until all things are accomplished. 19 Therefore, whoever breaks one of the least of these commands and teaches others to do the same will be called least in the kingdom of heaven. But whoever does and teaches these commands will be called great in the kingdom of heaven. 20 For I tell you, unless your righteousness surpasses that of the scribes and Pharisees, you will never get into the kingdom of heaven.

21 "You have heard that it was said to our ancestors, **Do not murder**, and whoever murders will be subject to judgment. 22 But I tell you, everyone who is angry with his brother or sister will be subject to judgment. Whoever insults his brother or sister, will be subject to the court. Whoever says, 'You fool!' will be subject to hellfire. 23 So if you are offering your gift on the altar, and there you remember that your brother or sister has something against you, 24 leave your gift there in front of the altar. First go and be reconciled with your brother or sister, and then come and offer your gift. 25 Reach a settlement quickly with your adversary while you're on the way with him to the court, or your adversary will hand you over to the judge, and the judge to the officer, and you will be thrown into prison. 26 Truly I tell you, you will never get out of there until you have paid the last penny.

27 "You have heard that it was said, **Do not commit adultery.** 28 But I tell you, everyone who looks at a woman lustfully has already committed adultery with her in his heart. 29 If your right eye causes you to sin, gouge it out and throw it away. For it is better that you lose one of the parts of your body than for your whole body to be thrown into hell. 30 And if your right hand causes you to sin, cut it off and throw it away. For it is better that you lose one of the parts of your body than for your whole body to go into hell.

31 "It was also said, **Whoever divorces his wife must give her a written notice of divorce.** 32 But I tell you, everyone who divorces his wife, except in a case of sexual immorality, causes her to commit adultery. And whoever marries a divorced woman commits adultery.

33 "Again, you have heard that it was said to our ancestors, **You must not break your oath, but you must keep your oaths to the Lord.** 34 But I tell you, don't take an oath at all: either by heaven, because it is God's throne; 35 or by the earth, because it is his footstool; or by Jerusalem, because it is the city of the great King. 36 Do not swear by your head, because you cannot make a single hair white or black. 37 But let your 'yes' mean 'yes,' and your 'no' mean 'no.' Anything more than this is from the evil one.

38 "You have heard that it was said, **An eye for an eye** and **a tooth for a tooth.** 39 But I tell you, don't resist an evildoer. On the contrary, if anyone slaps you on your right cheek, turn the other to him also. 40 As for the one who wants to sue you and take away your shirt, let him have your coat as well. 41 And if anyone forces you to go one mile, go with him two. 42 Give to the one who asks you, and don't turn away from the one who wants to borrow from you."

JESUS TEACHES ABOUT LOVE

MT 5:43-48   LK 6:27-36

Jesus's teaching on love in Matthew is one of five carefully crafted "antitheses" within the Sermon on the Mount. In his version of the sermon, however, Luke combines the core of two of these antitheses—loving one's enemies and retribution—and expands them under the one theme of love. As with the Beatitudes, each account could simply be a different version of a popular sermon. Yet one should not overlook how fitting each rendition is to the governing literary and theological aim of each author. Matthew is seeking to set out a "righteousness [that] surpasses that of the scribes and Pharisees" (5:20); therefore, he presents Jesus's teaching over against a distortion of the OT. Luke, however, offers only the positive command, highlighting the Golden Rule, an axiom Matthew will appeal to later (cp. 7:12).

43 "You have heard that it was said, **Love your neighbor** and hate your enemy. 44 But I tell you, love your enemies and pray for those who persecute you, 45 so that you may be children of your Father in heaven. For he causes his sun to rise on the evil and the good, and sends rain on the righteous and the unrighteous. 46 For if you love those who love you, what reward will you have? Don't even the tax collectors do the same? 47 And if you greet only your brothers and sisters, what are you doing out of the ordinary? Don't even the Gentiles do the same? 48 Be perfect, therefore, as your heavenly Father is perfect."

27 "But I say to you who listen: Love your enemies, do what is good to those who hate you, 28 bless those who curse you, pray for those who mistreat you. 29 If anyone hits you on the cheek, offer the other also. And if anyone takes away your coat, don't hold back your shirt either. 30 Give to everyone who asks you, and from someone who takes your things, don't ask for them back. 31 Just as you want others to do for you, do the same for them. 32 If you love those who love you, what credit is that to you? Even sinners love those who love them. 33 If you do what is good to those who are good to you, what credit is that to you? Even sinners do that. 34 And if you lend to those from whom you expect to receive, what credit is that to you? Even sinners lend to sinners to be repaid in full. 35 But love your enemies, do what is good, and lend, expecting nothing in return. Then your reward will be great, and you will be children of the Most High. For he is gracious to the ungrateful and evil. 36 Be merciful, just as your Father also is merciful."

---

[1] "Be careful not to practice your righteousness in front of others to be seen by them. Otherwise, you have no reward with your Father in heaven. [2] So whenever you give to the poor, don't sound a trumpet before you, as the hypocrites do in the synagogues and on the streets, to be applauded by people. Truly I tell you, they have their reward. [3] But when you give to the poor, don't let your left hand know what your right hand is doing, [4] so that your giving may be in secret. And your Father who sees in secret will reward you.

[5] "Whenever you pray, you must not be like the hypocrites, because they love to pray standing in the synagogues and on the street corners to be seen by people. Truly I tell you, they have their reward. [6] But when you pray, go into your private room, shut your door, and pray to your Father who is in secret. And your Father who sees in secret will reward you. [7] When you pray, don't babble like the Gentiles, since they imagine they'll be heard for their many words. [8] Don't be like them, because your Father knows the things you need before you ask him.

[9] "Therefore, you should pray like this:

Our Father in heaven,
your name be honored as holy.
[10] Your kingdom come.
Your will be done
on earth as it is in heaven.
[11] Give us today our daily bread.
[12] And forgive us our debts,
as we also have forgiven our debtors.
[13] And do not bring us into temptation,
but deliver us from the evil one.

[14] "For if you forgive others their offenses, your heavenly Father will forgive you as well. [15] But if you don't forgive others, your Father will not forgive your offenses.

[16] "Whenever you fast, don't be gloomy like the hypocrites. For they make their faces unattractive so that their fasting is obvious to people. Truly I tell you, they have their reward. [17] But when you fast, put oil on your head and wash your face, [18] so that your fasting isn't obvious to others but to your Father who is in secret. And your Father who sees in secret will reward you.

[19] "Don't store up for yourselves treasures on earth, where moth and rust destroy and where thieves break in and steal. [20] But store up for yourselves treasures in heaven, where neither moth nor rust destroys, and where thieves don't break in and steal. [21] For where your treasure is, there your heart will be also.

[22] "The eye is the lamp of the body. If your eye is healthy, your whole body will be full of light. [23] But if your eye is bad, your whole body will be full of darkness. So if the light within you is darkness, how deep is that darkness!

[24] "No one can serve two masters, since either he will hate one and love the other, or he will be devoted to one and despise the other. You cannot serve both God and money.

[25] "Therefore I tell you: Don't worry about your life, what you will eat or what you will drink; or about your body, what you will wear. Isn't life more than food and the body more than clothing? [26] Consider the birds of the sky: They don't sow or reap or gather into barns, yet your heavenly Father feeds them. Aren't you worth more than they? [27] Can any of you add one moment to his life-span by worrying? [28] And why do you worry about clothes? Observe how

MATTHEW   MARK   LUKE   JOHN

the wildflowers of the field grow: They don't labor or spin thread. **29** Yet I tell you that not even Solomon in all his splendor was adorned like one of these. **30** If that's how God clothes the grass of the field, which is here today and thrown into the furnace tomorrow, won't he do much more for you—you of little faith? **31** So don't worry, saying, 'What will we eat?' or 'What will we drink?' or 'What will we wear?' **32** For the Gentiles eagerly seek all these things, and your heavenly Father knows that you need them. **33** But seek first the kingdom of God and his righteousness, and all these things will be provided for you. **34** Therefore don't worry about tomorrow, because tomorrow will worry about itself. Each day has enough trouble of its own."

JESUS TEACHES ABOUT JUDGING

MT 7:1-5 LK 6:37-42

Both Matthew and Luke preserve the core of Jesus's teaching on judging but include a few unique details relative to their own purposes. Such details are perhaps best understood when read within the context of each Gospel. Nevertheless, these variances would be expected if Jesus were to have given the speech on numerous occasions and in a variety of contexts.

1 "Do not judge, so that you won't be judged. **2** For you will be judged by the same standard with which you judge others, and you will be measured by the same measure you use. **3** Why do you look at the splinter in your brother's eye but don't notice the beam of wood in your own eye? **4** Or how can you say to your brother, 'Let me take the splinter out of your eye,' and look, there's a beam of wood in your own eye? **5** Hypocrite! First take the beam of wood out of your eye, and then you will see clearly to take the splinter out of your brother's eye."

37 "Do not judge, and you will not be judged. Do not condemn, and you will not be condemned. Forgive, and you will be forgiven. **38** Give, and it will be given to you; a good measure—pressed down, shaken together, and running over—will be poured into your lap. For with the measure you use, it will be measured back to you."

39 He also told them a parable: "Can the blind guide the blind? Won't they both fall into a pit? **40** A disciple is not above his teacher, but everyone who is fully trained will be like his teacher.

41 "Why do you look at the splinter in your brother's eye, but don't notice the beam of wood in your own eye? **42** Or how can you say to your brother, 'Brother, let me take out the splinter that is in your eye,' when you yourself don't see the beam of wood in your eye? Hypocrite! First take the beam of wood out of your eye, and then you will see clearly to take out the splinter in your brother's eye."

JESUS TEACHES THE MULTITUDES

MT 7:6-14

6 Don't give what is holy to dogs or toss your pearls before pigs, or they will trample them under their feet, turn, and tear you to pieces.

7 "Ask, and it will be given to you. Seek, and you will find. Knock, and the door will be opened to you. **8** For everyone who asks receives, and the one who seeks finds, and to the one who knocks, the door will be opened. **9** Who among you, if his son asks him for bread, will give him a stone? **10** Or if he asks for a fish, will give him a snake? **11** If you then, who are evil, know how to give good gifts to your children, how much more will your Father in heaven give good things to those who ask him. **12** Therefore, whatever you want others to do for you, do also the same for them, for this is the Law and the Prophets.

13 "Enter through the narrow gate. For the gate is wide and the road broad that leads to destruction, and there are many who go through it. **14** How narrow is the gate and difficult the road that leads to life, and few find it."

Matthew and Luke, again, are remarkably similar in their presentations of this teaching of Jesus. Matthew is more expansive given the addition of vv. 21-23 which casts a reproachful tone across his version. Yet this is understandable given the sharp transition he makes to the topic of false prophets. There is less of a reproachful tone in Luke perhaps because his account is not directed at any particular opponent but more closely follows the previous section.

[15] "Be on your guard against false prophets who come to you in sheep's clothing but inwardly are ravaging wolves. [16] You'll recognize them by their fruit. Are grapes gathered from thornbushes or figs from thistles? [17] In the same way, every good tree produces good fruit, but a bad tree produces bad fruit. [18] A good tree can't produce bad fruit; neither can a bad tree produce good fruit. [19] Every tree that doesn't produce good fruit is cut down and thrown into the fire. [20] So you'll recognize them by their fruit.

[21] "Not everyone who says to me, 'Lord, Lord,' will enter the kingdom of heaven, but only the one who does the will of my Father in heaven. [22] On that day many will say to me, 'Lord, Lord, didn't we prophesy in your name, drive out demons in your name, and do many miracles in your name?' [23] Then I will announce to them, 'I never knew you. **Depart from me, you lawbreakers!**'

[24] "Therefore, everyone who hears these words of mine and acts on them will be like a wise man who built his house on the rock. [25] The rain fell, the rivers rose, and the winds blew and pounded that house. Yet it didn't collapse, because its foundation was on the rock. [26] But everyone who hears these words of mine and doesn't act on them will be like a foolish man who built his house on the sand. [27] The rain fell, the rivers rose, the winds blew and pounded that house, and it collapsed. It collapsed with a great crash."

[43] "A good tree doesn't produce bad fruit; on the other hand, a bad tree doesn't produce good fruit. [44] For each tree is known by its own fruit. Figs aren't gathered from thornbushes, or grapes picked from a bramble bush. [45] A good person produces good out of the good stored up in his heart. An evil person produces evil out of the evil stored up in his heart, for his mouth speaks from the overflow of the heart.

[46] "Why do you call me 'Lord, Lord,' and don't do the things I say? [47] I will show you what someone is like who comes to me, hears my words, and acts on them: [48] He is like a man building a house, who dug deep and laid the foundation on the rock. When the flood came, the river crashed against that house and couldn't shake it, because it was well built. [49] But the one who hears and does not act is like a man who built a house on the ground without a foundation. The river crashed against it, and immediately it collapsed. And the destruction of that house was great."

REACTION TO JESUS'S SERMON   MT 7:28-29

[28] When Jesus had finished saying these things, the crowds were astonished at his teaching, [29] because he was teaching them like one who had authority, and not like their scribes.

THE FAITH OF THE CENTURION   MT 8:5-13   LK 7:1-10

The significance of this encounter between Jesus and a high-ranking Gentile is relative to each author's unfolding story. Matthew gives passing hints at Jesus's Gentile mission but focuses mainly on Israel until after Jesus's death and resurrection. For Luke, though, this event marks a significant shift in his narrative. It is for this reason that Luke offers a fuller account that focuses on the character of the centurion. Important to this character development is the fact that it was his sense of unworthiness that led him to send emissaries on his behalf to Jesus. Yet Matthew's condensed version represents the centurion's petition as if he were there in person. It should be noted, however, that while it is clear from Luke's version that the centurion was not actually physically present, the way he tells the story makes it seem as though he was. In the end, it is best to allow ancient authors some freedom with regard to recording secondhand dialogue.

[5] When he entered Capernaum, a centurion came to him, pleading with him, [6] "Lord, my servant is lying at home paralyzed, in terrible agony."

[1] When he had concluded saying all this to the people who were listening, he entered Capernaum. [2] A centurion's servant, who was highly

[7] He said to him, "Am I to come and heal him?"

[8] "Lord," the centurion replied, "I am not worthy to have you come under my roof. But just say the word, and my servant will be healed. [9] For I too am a man under authority, having soldiers under my command. I say to this one, 'Go,' and he goes; and to another, 'Come,' and he comes; and to my servant, 'Do this!' and he does it."

[10] Hearing this, Jesus was amazed and said to those following him, "Truly I tell you, I have not found anyone in Israel with so great a faith. [11] I tell you that many will come from east and west to share the banquet with Abraham, Isaac, and Jacob in the kingdom of heaven. [12] But the sons of the kingdom will be thrown into the outer darkness where there will be weeping and gnashing of teeth." [13] Then Jesus told the centurion, "Go. As you have believed, let it be done for you." And his servant was healed that very moment.

valued by him, was sick and about to die. [3] When the centurion heard about Jesus, he sent some Jewish elders to him, requesting him to come and save the life of his servant. [4] When they reached Jesus, they pleaded with him earnestly, saying, "He is worthy for you to grant this, [5] because he loves our nation and has built us a synagogue."

[6] Jesus went with them, and when he was not far from the house, the centurion sent friends to tell him, "Lord, don't trouble yourself, since I am not worthy to have you come under my roof. [7] That is why I didn't even consider myself worthy to come to you. But say the word, and my servant will be healed. [8] For I too am a man placed under authority, having soldiers under my command. I say to this one, 'Go,' and he goes; and to another, 'Come,' and he comes; and to my servant, 'Do this,' and he does it."

[9] Jesus heard this and was amazed at him, and turning to the crowd following him, he said, "I tell you, I have not found so great a faith even in Israel." [10] When those who had been sent returned to the house, they found the servant in good health.

JESUS RAISES THE SON OF NAIN'S WIDOW
LK 7:11-17

[11] Afterward he was on his way to a town called Nain. His disciples and a large crowd were traveling with him. [12] Just as he neared the gate of the town, a dead man was being carried out. He was his mother's only son, and she was a widow. A large crowd from the city was also with her. [13] When the Lord saw her, he had compassion on her and said, "Don't weep." [14] Then he came up and touched the open coffin, and the pallbearers stopped. And he said, "Young man, I tell you, get up!"

[15] The dead man sat up and began to speak, and Jesus gave him to his mother. [16] Then fear came over everyone, and they glorified God, saying, "A great prophet has risen among us," and "God has visited his people." [17] This report about him went throughout Judea and all the vicinity.

JESUS ANSWERS THE QUESTION FROM JOHN THE BAPTIST
MT 11:1-19   LK 7:18-35

The essence of this lengthy account of Jesus's teaching on John the Baptist is retained by both Matthew and Luke with only a few incidental details added relative to their style and purposes. In both cases, the exchange affords each author the opportunity to clarify the mission of Jesus, as one who inaugurates the "new," relative to John who represents the "old." Yet the comparison extends beyond John and Jesus to include those who are "least in the kingdom of heaven."

[1] When Jesus had finished giving instructions to his twelve disciples, he moved on from there to teach and preach in their towns. [2] Now when John heard in prison what the Christ was doing, he sent a message through his disciples [3] and asked him, "Are you the one who is to come, or should we expect someone else?"

[4] Jesus replied to them, "Go and report to John what you hear and see: [5] The blind receive their sight, the lame walk, those with leprosy are cleansed, the deaf hear, the dead are raised, and the poor are

[18] Then John's disciples told him about all these things. So John summoned two of his disciples [19] and sent them to the Lord, asking, "Are you the one who is to come, or should we expect someone else?"

[20] When the men reached him, they said, "John the Baptist sent us to ask you, 'Are you the one who is to come, or should we expect someone else?'"

[21] At that time Jesus healed many people of diseases, afflictions, and evil spirits, and he granted sight to many blind people. [22] He replied to

told the good news, **6** and blessed is the one who isn't offended by me."

7 As these men were leaving, Jesus began to speak to the crowds about John: "What did you go out into the wilderness to see? A reed swaying in the wind? **8** What then did you go out to see? A man dressed in soft clothes? See, those who wear soft clothes are in royal palaces. **9** What then did you go out to see? A prophet? Yes, I tell you, and more than a prophet. **10** This is the one about whom it is written:

> **See, I am sending my messenger ahead of you;**
> **he will prepare your way before you.**

11 "Truly I tell you, among those born of women no one greater than John the Baptist has appeared, but the least in the kingdom of heaven is greater than he. **12** From the days of John the Baptist until now, the kingdom of heaven has been suffering violence, and the violent have been seizing it by force. **13** For all the prophets and the law prophesied until John. **14** And if you're willing to accept it, he is the Elijah who is to come. **15** Let anyone who has ears listen.

16 "To what should I compare this generation? It's like children sitting in the marketplaces who call out to other children:

17
> We played the flute for you,
> but you didn't dance;
> we sang a lament,
> but you didn't mourn!

18 For John came neither eating nor drinking, and they say, 'He has a demon!' **19** The Son of Man came eating and drinking, and they say, 'Look, a glutton and a drunkard, a friend of tax collectors and sinners!' Yet wisdom is vindicated by her deeds."

them, "Go and report to John what you have seen and heard: The blind receive their sight, the lame walk, those with leprosy are cleansed, the deaf hear, the dead are raised, and the poor are told the good news, **23** and blessed is the one who isn't offended by me."

24 After John's messengers left, he began to speak to the crowds about John: "What did you go out into the wilderness to see? A reed swaying in the wind? **25** What then did you go out to see? A man dressed in soft clothes? See, those who are splendidly dressed and live in luxury are in royal palaces. **26** What then did you go out to see? A prophet? Yes, I tell you, and more than a prophet. **27** This is the one about whom it is written:

> **See, I am sending my messenger**
> **ahead of you;**
> **he will prepare your way before you.**

28 I tell you, among those born of women no one is greater than John, but the least in the kingdom of God is greater than he."

29 (And when all the people, including the tax collectors, heard this, they acknowledged God's way of righteousness, because they had been baptized with John's baptism. **30** But since the Pharisees and experts in the law had not been baptized by him, they rejected the plan of God for themselves.)

31 "To what then should I compare the people of this generation, and what are they like? **32** They are like children sitting in the marketplace and calling to each other:

> We played the flute for you,
> but you didn't dance;
> we sang a lament,
> but you didn't weep!

33 For John the Baptist did not come eating bread or drinking wine, and you say, 'He has a demon!' **34** The Son of Man has come eating and drinking, and you say, 'Look, a glutton and a drunkard, a friend of tax collectors and sinners!' **35** Yet wisdom is vindicated by all her children."

JESUS REBUKES CITIES AND PROMISES REST

MT 11:20-30

20 Then he proceeded to denounce the towns where most of his miracles were done, because they did not repent: **21** "Woe to you, Chorazin! Woe to you, Bethsaida! For if the miracles that were done in you had been done in Tyre and Sidon, they would have repented in sackcloth and ashes long ago. **22** But I tell you, it will be more tolerable for Tyre and Sidon on the day of judgment than for you. **23** And you, Capernaum, will you be exalted to heaven? No, you will go down to Hades. For if the miracles that were done in you had been done in Sodom, it would have remained until today. **24** But I tell you, it will be more tolerable for the land of Sodom on the day of judgment than for you."

25 At that time Jesus said, "I praise you, Father, Lord of heaven and earth, because you have hidden these things from the wise and intelligent and revealed them to infants. **26** Yes, Father, because this was your good pleasure. **27** All things have been entrusted to me by my Father. No one knows the Son except the Father, and no one knows the Father except the Son and anyone to whom the Son desires to reveal him.

²⁸ "Come to me, all of you who are weary and burdened, and I will give you rest. ²⁹ Take up my yoke and learn from me, because I am lowly and humble in heart, and you will find rest for your souls. ³⁰ For my yoke is easy and my burden is light."

THE SINFUL WOMAN IN THE HOUSE OF SIMON THE PHARISEE

LK 7:36-50

³⁶ Then one of the Pharisees invited him to eat with him. He entered the Pharisee's house and reclined at the table. ³⁷ And a woman in the town who was a sinner found out that Jesus was reclining at the table in the Pharisee's house. She brought an alabaster jar of perfume ³⁸ and stood behind him at his feet, weeping, and began to wash his feet with her tears. She wiped his feet with her hair, kissing them and anointing them with the perfume.

³⁹ When the Pharisee who had invited him saw this, he said to himself, "This man, if he were a prophet, would know who and what kind of woman this is who is touching him — she's a sinner!"

⁴⁰ Jesus replied to him, "Simon, I have something to say to you."

He said, "Say it, teacher."

⁴¹ "A creditor had two debtors. One owed five hundred denarii, and the other fifty. ⁴² Since they could not pay it back, he graciously forgave them both. So, which of them will love him more?"

⁴³ Simon answered, "I suppose the one he forgave more."

"You have judged correctly," he told him. ⁴⁴ Turning to the woman, he said to Simon, "Do you see this woman? I entered your house; you gave me no water for my feet, but she, with her tears, has washed my feet and wiped them with her hair. ⁴⁵ You gave me no kiss, but she hasn't stopped kissing my feet since I came in. ⁴⁶ You didn't anoint my head with olive oil, but she has anointed my feet with perfume. ⁴⁷ Therefore I tell you, her many sins have been forgiven; that's why she loved much. But the one who is forgiven little, loves little." ⁴⁸ Then he said to her, "Your sins are forgiven."

⁴⁹ Those who were at the table with him began to say among themselves, "Who is this man who even forgives sins?"

⁵⁰ And he said to the woman, "Your faith has saved you. Go in peace."

THE WOMEN FOLLOWING JESUS AND HIS DISCIPLES

LK 8:1-3

¹ Afterward he was traveling from one town and village to another, preaching and telling the good news of the kingdom of God. The Twelve were with him, ² and also some women who had been healed of evil spirits and sicknesses: Mary, called Magdalene (seven demons had come out of her); ³ Joanna the wife of Chuza, Herod's steward; Susanna; and many others who were supporting them from their possessions.

The minor variations between the Synoptic accounts of Jesus and Beelzebul are best explained by the respective literary position in each account. This placement is most visible in Mark who situates the account just after the calling of the disciples. Much has happened in Matthew and Luke, however, since that event. Mathew and Mark draw attention to the religious official as the central antagonist in the debate while Luke remains neutral. In addition, Luke leaves out the puzzling remark about the "unforgivable sin" of blasphemy against the Spirit. None of these variations prove incompatible; together they offer a full picture of the event and its significance.

[22] Then a demon-possessed man who was blind and unable to speak was brought to him. He healed him, so that the man could both speak and see. [23] All the crowds were astounded and said, "Could this be the Son of David?"

[24] When the Pharisees heard this, they said, "This man drives out demons only by Beelzebul, the ruler of the demons."

[25] Knowing their thoughts, he told them: "Every kingdom divided against itself is headed for destruction, and no city or house divided against itself will stand. [26] If Satan drives out Satan, he is divided against himself. How then will his kingdom stand? [27] And if I drive out demons by Beelzebul, by whom do your sons drive them out? For this reason they will be your judges. [28] If I drive out demons by the Spirit of God, then the kingdom of God has come upon you. [29] How can someone enter a strong man's house and steal his possessions unless he first ties up the strong man? Then he can plunder his house. [30] Anyone who is not with me is against me, and anyone who does not gather with me scatters. [31] Therefore, I tell you, people will be forgiven every sin and blasphemy, but the blasphemy against the Spirit will not be forgiven. [32] Whoever speaks a word against the Son of Man, it will be forgiven him; but whoever speaks against the Holy Spirit, it will not be forgiven him, either in this age or in the one to come."

[20] Jesus entered a house, and the crowd gathered again so that they were not even able to eat. [21] When his family heard this, they set out to restrain him, because they said, "He's out of his mind."

[22] The scribes who had come down from Jerusalem said, "He is possessed by Beelzebul," and, "He drives out demons by the ruler of the demons."

[23] So he summoned them and spoke to them in parables: "How can Satan drive out Satan? [24] If a kingdom is divided against itself, that kingdom cannot stand. [25] If a house is divided against itself, that house cannot stand. [26] And if Satan opposes himself and is divided, he cannot stand but is finished. [27] But no one can enter a strong man's house and plunder his possessions unless he first ties up the strong man. Then he can plunder his house.

[28] "Truly I tell you, people will be forgiven for all sins and whatever blasphemies they utter. [29] But whoever blasphemes against the Holy Spirit never has forgiveness, but is guilty of an eternal sin" — [30] because they were saying, "He has an unclean spirit."

[14] Now he was driving out a demon that was mute. When the demon came out, the man who had been mute spoke, and the crowds were amazed. [15] But some of them said, "He drives out demons by Beelzebul, the ruler of the demons." [16] And others, as a test, were demanding of him a sign from heaven.

[17] Knowing their thoughts, he told them, "Every kingdom divided against itself is headed for destruction, and a house divided against itself falls. [18] If Satan also is divided against himself, how will his kingdom stand? For you say I drive out demons by Beelzebul. [19] And if I drive out demons by Beelzebul, by whom do your sons drive them out? For this reason they will be your judges. [20] If I drive out demons by the finger of God, then the kingdom of God has come upon you. [21] When a strong man, fully armed, guards his estate, his possessions are secure. [22] But when one stronger than he attacks and overpowers him, he takes from him all his weapons he trusted in, and divides up his plunder. [23] Anyone who is not with me is against me, and anyone who does not gather with me scatters."

[33] "Either make the tree good and its fruit will be good, or make the tree bad and its fruit will be bad; for a tree is known by its fruit. [34] Brood of vipers! How can you speak good things when you are evil? For the mouth speaks from the overflow of the heart. [35] A good person produces good things from his storeroom of good, and an evil person produces evil things from his storeroom

of evil. [36] I tell you that on the day of judgment people will have to account for every careless word they speak. [37] For by your words you will be acquitted, and by your words you will be condemned."

THE RETURN OF THE UNCLEAN SPRIT
MT 12:43-45   LK 11:24-28

See "Sign of Jonah" below.

[43] "When an unclean spirit comes out of a person, it roams through waterless places looking for rest but doesn't find any. [44] Then it says, 'I'll go back to my house that I came from.' Returning, it finds the house vacant, swept, and put in order. [45] Then it goes and brings with it seven other spirits more evil than itself, and they enter and settle down there. As a result, that person's last condition is worse than the first. That's how it will also be with this evil generation."

[24] "When an unclean spirit comes out of a person, it roams through waterless places looking for rest, and not finding rest, it then says, 'I'll go back to my house that I came from.' [25] Returning, it finds the house swept and put in order. [26] Then it goes and brings seven other spirits more evil than itself, and they enter and settle down there. As a result, that person's last condition is worse than the first."

[27] As he was saying these things, a woman from the crowd raised her voice and said to him, "Blessed is the womb that bore you and the one who nursed you!"

[28] He said, "Rather, blessed are those who hear the word of God and keep it."

THE SIGN OF JONAH
MT 12:38-42   LK 11:29-32

Matthew and Luke reverse the order of Jesus's teaching on the "Sign of Jonah" and the "Return of the Unclean Spirit." Yet the variances in these two accounts are best explained in light of the flow of each narrative reaching back to the account of "Jesus and Beelzebul." Luke's account flows seamlessly from the latter, maintaining the theme of "unclean spirits." Matthew, on the other hand, has chosen to shift topics while retaining the focus on the scribes and Pharisees as those who represent an "evil and adulterous generation." They are the ones who, for Matthew, demand a "sign." With this in mind, the switch proves to be quite fitting given each author's respective literary and theological purposes.

[38] Then some of the scribes and Pharisees said to him, "Teacher, we want to see a sign from you."

[39] He answered them, "An evil and adulterous generation demands a sign, but no sign will be given to it except the sign of the prophet Jonah. [40] For as Jonah was in the belly of the huge fish three days and three nights, so the Son of Man will be in the heart of the earth three days and three nights. [41] The men of Nineveh will stand up at the judgment with this generation and condemn it, because they repented at Jonah's preaching; and look — something greater than Jonah is here. [42] The queen of the south will rise up at the judgment with this generation and condemn it, because she came from the ends of the earth to hear the wisdom of Solomon; and look — something greater than Solomon is here."

[29] As the crowds were increasing, he began saying: "This generation is an evil generation. It demands a sign, but no sign will be given to it except the sign of Jonah. [30] For just as Jonah became a sign to the people of Nineveh, so also the Son of Man will be to this generation. [31] The queen of the south will rise up at the judgment with the men of this generation and condemn them, because she came from the ends of the earth to hear the wisdom of Solomon, and look — something greater than Solomon is here. [32] The men of Nineveh will stand up at the judgment with this generation and condemn it, because they repented at Jonah's preaching, and look — something greater than Jonah is here."

MATTHEW   MARK   LUKE   JOHN   JESUS'S MINISTRY IN GALILEE   43

All three Synoptics recall Jesus's identification of his true family, and there are only minor differences among the accounts. In Matthew the focus is on the disciples as Jesus's true family, while Jesus's comment in Luke and Mark is more general. All three, though, make the same point about the nature of true discipleship. More significant, perhaps, is Luke's placement of the account relative to Mathew and Mark who place it after the Beelzebul controversy for thematic reasons.

[46] While he was still speaking with the crowds, his mother and brothers were standing outside wanting to speak to him. [47] Someone told him, "Look, your mother and your brothers are standing outside, wanting to speak to you."

[48] He replied to the one who was speaking to him, "Who is my mother and who are my brothers?" [49] Stretching out his hand toward his disciples, he said, "Here are my mother and my brothers! [50] For whoever does the will of my Father in heaven is my brother and sister and mother."

[31] His mother and his brothers came, and standing outside, they sent word to him and called him. [32] A crowd was sitting around him and told him, "Look, your mother, your brothers, and your sisters are outside asking for you."

[33] He replied to them, "Who are my mother and my brothers?" [34] Looking at those sitting in a circle around him, he said, "Here are my mother and my brothers! [35] Whoever does the will of God is my brother and sister and mother."

[19] Then his mother and brothers came to him, but they could not meet with him because of the crowd. [20] He was told, "Your mother and your brothers are standing outside, wanting to see you."

[21] But he replied to them, "My mother and my brothers are those who hear and do the word of God."

THE PARABLE OF THE SOWER

The parable is probably Jesus's most popular teaching tool. Yet it is also his most perplexing. Like his sermons, he would no doubt have taught the same parable on a number of occasions and in various versions, which would account for the slight deviations between the Synoptic accounts of the Parable of the Sower. Apart from Luke's notable brevity, Matthew is unique, first, in how he gathers Jesus's parables into the third of Jesus's five major discourses. Second, Matthew connects Jesus's rationale for using parables with the prophet Isaiah in yet another fulfillment quotation (Is 6:9-10). Besides these differences, the three accounts are very similar.

[1] On that day Jesus went out of the house and was sitting by the sea. [2] Such large crowds gathered around him that he got into a boat and sat down, while the whole crowd stood on the shore.

[3] Then he told them many things in parables, saying: "Consider the sower who went out to sow. [4] As he sowed, some seed fell along the path, and the birds came and devoured them. [5] Other seed fell on rocky ground where it didn't have much soil, and it grew up quickly since the soil wasn't deep. [6] But when the sun came up, it was scorched, and since it had no root, it withered away. [7] Other seed fell among thorns, and the thorns came up and choked it. [8] Still other seed fell on good ground and produced fruit: some a hundred,

[1] Again he began to teach by the sea, and a very large crowd gathered around him. So he got into a boat on the sea and sat down, while the whole crowd was by the sea on the shore. [2] He taught them many things in parables, and in his teaching he said to them: [3] "Listen! Consider the sower who went out to sow. [4] As he sowed, some seed fell along the path, and the birds came and devoured it. [5] Other seed fell on rocky ground where it didn't have much soil, and it grew up quickly, since the soil wasn't deep. [6] When the sun came up, it was scorched, and since it had no root, it withered away. [7] Other seed fell among thorns, and the thorns came up and choked it, and it didn't produce fruit. [8] Still other seed fell on good ground and it grew up, producing fruit that increased

[4] As a large crowd was gathering, and people were coming to Jesus from every town, he said in a parable: [5] "A sower went out to sow his seed. As he sowed, some seed fell along the path; it was trampled on, and the birds of the sky devoured it. [6] Other seed fell on the rock; when it grew up, it withered away, since it lacked moisture. [7] Other seed fell among thorns; the thorns grew up with it and choked it. [8] Still other seed fell on good ground; when it grew up, it produced fruit: a hundred times what was sown." As he said this, he called out, "Let anyone who has ears to hear listen."

[9] Then his disciples asked him, "What does this parable mean?" [10] So he said, "The secrets of the kingdom of God have been given for

some sixty, and some thirty times what was sown. [9] Let anyone who has ears listen."

[10] Then the disciples came up and asked him, "Why are you speaking to them in parables?"

[11] He answered, "Because the secrets of the kingdom of heaven have been given for you to know, but it has not been given to them. [12] For whoever has, more will be given to him, and he will have more than enough; but whoever does not have, even what he has will be taken away from him. [13] That is why I speak to them in parables, because looking they do not see, and hearing they do not listen or understand. [14] Isaiah's prophecy is fulfilled in them, which says:

> You will listen and listen,
> but never understand;
> you will look and look,
> but never perceive.
> [15]   For this people's heart has grown callous;
>   their ears are hard of hearing,
>   and they have shut their eyes;
>   otherwise they might see with their eyes,
>   and hear with their ears, and
>   understand with their hearts,
>   and turn back —
>   and I would heal them.

[16] "Blessed are your eyes because they do see, and your ears because they do hear. [17] For truly I tell you, many prophets and righteous people longed to see the things you see but didn't see them, to hear the things you hear but didn't hear them.

[18] "So listen to the parable of the sower: [19] When anyone hears the word about the kingdom and doesn't understand it, the evil one comes and snatches away what was sown in his heart. This is the one sown along the path. [20] And the one sown on rocky ground — this is one who hears the word and immediately receives it with joy. [21] But he has no root and is short-lived. When distress or persecution comes because of the word, immediately he falls away. [22] Now the one sown among the thorns — this is one who hears the word, but the worries of this age and the deceitfulness of wealth choke the word, and it becomes unfruitful. [23] But the one sown on the good ground — this is one who hears and understands the word, who does produce fruit and yields: some a hundred, some sixty, some thirty times what was sown."

thirty, sixty, and a hundred times." [9] Then he said, "Let anyone who has ears to hear listen."

[10] When he was alone, those around him with the Twelve, asked him about the parables. [11] He answered them, "The secret of the kingdom of God has been given to you, but to those outside, everything comes in parables [12] so that

> they may indeed look,
> and yet not perceive;
> they may indeed listen,
> and yet not understand;
> otherwise, they might
>   turn back
> and be forgiven."

[13] Then he said to them: "Don't you understand this parable? How then will you understand all of the parables? [14] The sower sows the word. [15] Some are like the word sown on the path. When they hear, immediately Satan comes and takes away the word sown in them. [16] And others are like seed sown on rocky ground. When they hear the word, immediately they receive it with joy. [17] But they have no root; they are short-lived. When distress or persecution comes because of the word, they immediately fall away. [18] Others are like seed sown among thorns; these are the ones who hear the word, [19] but the worries of this age, the deceitfulness of wealth, and the desires for other things enter in and choke the word, and it becomes unfruitful. [20] And those like seed sown on good ground hear the word, welcome it, and produce fruit thirty, sixty, and a hundred times what was sown."

you to know, but to the rest it is in parables, so that

> **Looking they may not see,
> and hearing they may
>   not understand.**

[11] "This is the meaning of the parable: The seed is the word of God. [12] The seed along the path are those who have heard and then the devil comes and takes away the word from their hearts, so that they may not believe and be saved. [13] And the seed on the rock are those who, when they hear, receive the word with joy. Having no root, these believe for a while and fall away in a time of testing. [14] As for the seed that fell among thorns, these are the ones who, when they have heard, go on their way and are choked with worries, riches, and pleasures of life, and produce no mature fruit. [15] But the seed in the good ground — these are the ones who, having heard the word with an honest and good heart, hold on to it and by enduring, produce fruit."

Mark and Luke include similar versions of this parable, while Matthew places a version of it in a totally different context (cp. Mt 5:15). Such literary decisions reflect the degree to which parables were remembered differently and placed in different contexts relative to an author's theological purposes.

[21] He also said to them, "Is a lamp brought in to be put under a basket or under a bed? Isn't it to be put on a lampstand? [22] For there is nothing hidden that will not be revealed, and nothing concealed that will not be brought to light. [23] If anyone has ears to hear, let him listen." [24] And he said to them, "Pay attention to what you hear. By the measure you use, it will be measured to you — and more will be added to you. [25] For whoever has, more will be given to him, and whoever does not have, even what he has will be taken away from him."

[16] "No one, after lighting a lamp, covers it with a basket or puts it under a bed, but puts it on a lampstand so that those who come in may see its light. [17] For nothing is concealed that won't be revealed, and nothing hidden that won't be made known and brought to light. [18] Therefore take care how you listen. For whoever has, more will be given to him; and whoever does not have, even what he thinks he has will be taken away from him."

THE PARABLE OF THE SEED GROWING SECRETLY

[26] "The kingdom of God is like this," he said. "A man scatters seed on the ground. [27] He sleeps and rises night and day; the seed sprouts and grows, although he doesn't know how. [28] The soil produces a crop by itself — first the blade, then the head, and then the full grain on the head. [29] As soon as the crop is ready, he sends for the sickle, because the harvest has come."

THE PARABLE OF THE WEEDS

[24] He presented another parable to them: "The kingdom of heaven may be compared to a man who sowed good seed in his field. [25] But while people were sleeping, his enemy came, sowed weeds among the wheat, and left. [26] When the plants sprouted and produced grain, then the weeds also appeared. [27] The landowner's servants came to him and said, 'Master, didn't you sow good seed in your field? Then where did the weeds come from?'
[28] "'An enemy did this,' he told them.
"'So, do you want us to go and pull them up?' the servants asked him.
[29] "'No,' he said. 'When you pull up the weeds, you might also uproot the wheat with them. [30] Let both grow together until the harvest. At harvest time I'll tell the reapers: Gather the weeds first and tie them in bundles to burn them, but collect the wheat in my barn.'"

THE PARABLE OF THE MUSTARD SEED

Individual parables of Jesus were collected and ordered differently by the Gospel writers depending on their literary and theological purposes. For Matthew, the Parable of the Mustard Seed is one of three parables within a larger discourse (with the Parable of the Weeds and the Parable of the Yeast) that addresses the theme of the growth of the kingdom. Mark contextualizes Jesus's parables similarly to Matthew—that is, within a teaching context—but he includes fewer parables and has a less apparent structure than found in Matthew. Luke pairs this parable with the Parable of the Yeast. Instead of including them in a teaching context, he links them with the preceding account of the healing of the woman on the Sabbath (13:10-17). Yet, regardless of the context in each Gospel, the core of the parable is preserved by each Synoptic author. One should also note that Matthew prefers the designation "kingdom of heaven" rather than the more common "kingdom of God" in Mark and Luke. It is likely that Jesus used these designations interchangeably in different versions of the same parable. However, the fact that Matthew consistently uses "heaven" language in his Gospel alerts the reader to a special theological emphasis.

[31] He presented another parable to them: "The kingdom of heaven is like a mustard seed that a man took and sowed in his field. [32] It's the smallest of all the seeds, but when grown, it's taller than the garden plants and becomes a tree, so that the birds of the sky come and nest in its branches."

[30] And he said, "With what can we compare the kingdom of God, or what parable can we use to describe it? [31] It's like a mustard seed that, when sown upon the soil, is the smallest of all the seeds on the ground. [32] And when sown, it comes up and grows taller than all the garden plants, and produces large branches, so that the birds of the sky can nest in its shade."

[18] He said, therefore, "What is the kingdom of God like, and what can I compare it to? [19] It's like a mustard seed that a man took and sowed in his garden. It grew and became a tree, and the birds of the sky nested in its branches."

THE PARABLE OF THE LEAVEN

MT 13:33   LK 13:20-21

See "Parable of the Mustard Seed" on p. 46.

[33] He told them another parable: "The kingdom of heaven is like leaven that a woman took and mixed into fifty pounds of flour until all of it was leavened."

[20] Again he said, "What can I compare the kingdom of God to? [21] It's like leaven that a woman took and mixed into fifty pounds of flour until all of it was leavened."

JESUS EXPLAINS WHY HE USES PARABLES

MT 13:34-35   MK 4:33-34

Matthew and Mark agree on Jesus's rationale for using parables. Mark's account functions as the culmination of a collection of parables. In Matthew, the careful reader will recall a similar explanation in the Parable of the Sower above (13:1-23) that opened the parable discourse.

[34] Jesus told the crowds all these things in parables, and he did not tell them anything without a parable, [35] so that what was spoken through the prophet might be fulfilled:

I will open my mouth in parables;
I will declare things kept secret
from the foundation of the world.

[33] He was speaking the word to them with many parables like these, as they were able to understand. [34] He did not speak to them without a parable. Privately, however, he explained everything to his own disciples.

JESUS EXPLAINS THE PARABLE OF THE WEEDS

MT 13:36-43

[36] Then he left the crowds and went into the house. His disciples approached him and said, "Explain to us the parable of the weeds in the field."
[37] He replied: "The one who sows the good seed is the Son of Man; [38] the field is the world; and the good seed — these are the children of the kingdom. The weeds are the children of the evil one, [39] and the enemy who sowed them is the devil. The harvest is the end of the age, and the harvesters are angels. [40] Therefore, just as the weeds are gathered and burned in the fire, so it will be at the end of the age. [41] The Son of Man will send out his angels, and they will gather from his kingdom all who cause sin and those guilty of lawlessness. [42] They will throw them into the blazing furnace where there will be weeping and gnashing of teeth. [43] Then the righteous will shine like the sun in their Father's kingdom. Let anyone who has ears listen."

44 "The kingdom of heaven is like treasure, buried in a field, that a man found and reburied. Then in his joy he goes and sells everything he has and buys that field.

45 "Again, the kingdom of heaven is like a merchant in search of fine pearls. 46 When he found one priceless pearl, he went and sold everything he had and bought it.

47 "Again, the kingdom of heaven is like a large net thrown into the sea. It collected every kind of fish, 48 and when it was full, they dragged it ashore, sat down, and gathered the good fish into containers, but threw out the worthless ones. 49 So it will be at the end of the age. The angels will go out, separate the evil people from the righteous, 50 and throw them into the blazing furnace, where there will be weeping and gnashing of teeth.

51 "Have you understood all these things?"

They answered him, "Yes."

52 "Therefore," he said to them, "every teacher of the law who has become a disciple in the kingdom of heaven is like the owner of a house who brings out of his storeroom treasures new and old."

JESUS STILLS THE STORM

MT 8:23-27 MK 4:35-41 LK 8:22-25

The three Synoptic accounts are very similar and include an almost verbatim response by the disciples. Mark and Luke describe the event in more vivid detail. But Matthew's abridged version fits nicely within a series of events that feature the in-breaking of the kingdom through Jesus's healings and miracles. Mark's version is the longest of the three serving a similar function as Matthew's. Yet while Mark is longer on this individual narrative, he includes far fewer illustrations of Jesus's healings and miracles. For Luke, this is the first time he has recorded Jesus's miraculous power toward an inanimate object rather than a person.

23 As he got into the boat, his disciples followed him. 24 Suddenly, a violent storm arose on the sea, so that the boat was being swamped by the waves — but Jesus kept sleeping. 25 So the disciples came and woke him up, saying, "Lord, save us! We're going to die!"

26 He said to them, "Why are you afraid, you of little faith?" Then he got up and rebuked the winds and the sea, and there was a great calm.

27 The men were amazed and asked, "What kind of man is this? Even the winds and the sea obey him!"

35 On that day, when evening had come, he told them, "Let's cross over to the other side of the sea." 36 So they left the crowd and took him along since he was in the boat. And other boats were with him. 37 A great windstorm arose, and the waves were breaking over the boat, so that the boat was already being swamped. 38 He was in the stern, sleeping on the cushion. So they woke him up and said to him, "Teacher! Don't you care that we're going to die?"

39 He got up, rebuked the wind, and said to the sea, "Silence! Be still!" The wind ceased, and there was a great calm. 40 Then he said to them, "Why are you afraid? Do you still have no faith?"

41 And they were terrified and asked one another, "Who then is this? Even the wind and the sea obey him!"

22 One day he and his disciples got into a boat, and he told them, "Let's cross over to the other side of the lake." So they set out, 23 and as they were sailing he fell asleep. Then a fierce windstorm came down on the lake; they were being swamped and were in danger. 24 They came and woke him up, saying, "Master, Master, we're going to die!"

Then he got up and rebuked the wind and the raging waves. So they ceased, and there was a calm. 25 He said to them, "Where is your faith?"

They were fearful and amazed, asking one another, "Who then is this? He commands even the winds and the waves, and they obey him!"

Apart from the more vivid detail provided by Mark and Luke, the most obvious variation among the three accounts is Matthew's recording of two demoniacs while Mark and Luke have only one. Of course, it's reasonable to suggest that Mark and Luke only highlight one of the two demoniacs present. After all, where there are two, there is certainly one. Thus, there is no necessary contradiction.

It is helpful to note, though, that scholars have observed Matthew's pattern for "doubles." Matthew may have a pressing theological reason for mentioning the presence of both demoniacs—what R. T. France refers to as "double vision." One compelling rationale, for example, might be Matthew's deference to the OT legal principle of "two or three witnesses" to validate one's testimony.

[28] When he had come to the other side, to the region of the Gadarenes, two demon-possessed men met him as they came out of the tombs. They were so violent that no one could pass that way. [29] Suddenly they shouted, "What do you have to do with us, Son of God? Have you come here to torment us before the time?"

[30] A long way off from them, a large herd of pigs was feeding. [31] "If you drive us out," the demons begged him, "send us into the herd of pigs."

[32] "Go!" he told them. So when they had come out, they entered the pigs, and the whole herd rushed down the steep bank into the sea and perished in the water. [33] Then the men who tended them fled. They went into the city and reported everything, especially what had happened to those who were demon-possessed. [34] At that, the whole town went out to meet Jesus. When they saw him, they begged him to leave their region.

[1] They came to the other side of the sea, to the region of the Gerasenes. [2] As soon as he got out of the boat, a man with an unclean spirit came out of the tombs and met him. [3] He lived in the tombs, and no one was able to restrain him anymore—not even with a chain—[4] because he often had been bound with shackles and chains, but had torn the chains apart and smashed the shackles. No one was strong enough to subdue him. [5] Night and day among the tombs and on the mountains, he was always crying out and cutting himself with stones.

[6] When he saw Jesus from a distance, he ran and knelt down before him. [7] And he cried out with a loud voice, "What do you have to do with me, Jesus, Son of the Most High God? I beg you before God, don't torment me!" [8] For he had told him, "Come out of the man, you unclean spirit!"

[9] "What is your name?" he asked him.

"My name is Legion," he answered him, "because we are many." [10] And he begged him earnestly not to send them out of the region.

[11] A large herd of pigs was there, feeding on the hillside. [12] The demons begged him, "Send us to the pigs, so that we may enter them." [13] So he gave them permission, and the unclean spirits came out and entered the pigs. The herd of about two thousand rushed down the steep bank into the sea and drowned there.

[14] The men who tended them ran off and reported it in the town and the countryside, and people went to see what had happened. [15] They came to Jesus and saw the man who had been demon-possessed, sitting there, dressed and in his right mind; and they were

[26] Then they sailed to the region of the Gerasenes, which is opposite Galilee. [27] When he got out on land, a demon-possessed man from the town met him. For a long time he had worn no clothes and did not stay in a house but in the tombs. [28] When he saw Jesus, he cried out, fell down before him, and said in a loud voice, "What do you have to do with me, Jesus, Son of the Most High God? I beg you, don't torment me!" [29] For he had commanded the unclean spirit to come out of the man. Many times it had seized him, and though he was guarded, bound by chains and shackles, he would snap the restraints and be driven by the demon into deserted places.

[30] "What is your name?" Jesus asked him.

"Legion," he said, because many demons had entered him. [31] And they begged him not to banish them to the abyss.

[32] A large herd of pigs was there, feeding on the hillside. The demons begged him to permit them to enter the pigs, and he gave them permission. [33] The demons came out of the man and entered the pigs, and the herd rushed down the steep bank into the lake and drowned.

[34] When the men who tended them saw what had happened, they ran off and reported it in the town and in the countryside. [35] Then people went out to see what had happened. They came to Jesus and found the man the demons had departed from, sitting at Jesus's feet, dressed and in his right mind. And they were afraid. [36] Meanwhile, the eyewitnesses reported to them how the demon-possessed man was delivered. [37] Then all the people of the Gerasene region asked him to leave them, because they were gripped by great fear. So getting into the boat, he returned.

MATTHEW   MARK   LUKE   JOHN

afraid. [16] Those who had seen it described to them what had happened to the demon-possessed man and told about the pigs. [17] Then they began to beg him to leave their region.

[18] As he was getting into the boat, the man who had been demon-possessed begged him earnestly that he might remain with him. [19] Jesus did not let him but told him, "Go home to your own people, and report to them how much the Lord has done for you and how he has had mercy on you." [20] So he went out and began to proclaim in the Decapolis how much Jesus had done for him, and they were all amazed.

[38] The man from whom the demons had departed begged him earnestly to be with him. But he sent him away and said, [39] "Go back to your home, and tell all that God has done for you." And off he went, proclaiming throughout the town how much Jesus had done for him.

JESUS HEALS A BLEEDING WOMAN AND RAISES A GIRL   MT 9:18-26   MK 5:21-43   LK 8:40-56

Matthew, Mark, and Luke all include the same essential aspects of these two healings. The two stories have been paired together by all three authors because of the common theme of salvation/healing by faith. There are, to be sure, some variations in secondary details and timing between the accounts. One could also scrutinize a given author's presentation of medical facts and terminology, yet one should resist the temptation to impose the expectations of modern medicine upon an ancient text. Mark's vivid details, including the inward thoughts of the bleeding woman, takes up almost three times the space as Matthew. Matthew's abbreviated version, however, allows him to cover a vast array of miraculous events across chaps. 8-9. Luke's version is about a third shorter than Mark's, but he adds a few notable details to his description (e.g., the girl is Jairus's "only" daughter). Overall, the stories are quite complementary.

[18] As he was telling them these things, suddenly one of the leaders came and knelt down before him, saying, "My daughter just died, but come and lay your hand on her, and she will live." [19] So Jesus and his disciples got up and followed him.

[20] Just then, a woman who had suffered from bleeding for twelve years approached from behind and touched the end of his robe, [21] for she said to herself, "If I can just touch his robe, I'll be made well."

[22] Jesus turned and saw her. "Have courage, daughter," he said. "Your faith has saved you." And the woman was made well from that moment.

[23] When Jesus came to the leader's house, he saw the flute players and a crowd lamenting loudly. [24] "Leave," he said, "because the girl is not dead but asleep." And they laughed at him. [25] After the crowd had been put outside, he went in and took her by the hand,

[21] When Jesus had crossed over again by boat to the other side, a large crowd gathered around him while he was by the sea. [22] One of the synagogue leaders, named Jairus, came, and when he saw Jesus, he fell at his feet [23] and begged him earnestly, "My little daughter is dying. Come and lay your hands on her so that she can get well and live." [24] So Jesus went with him, and a large crowd was following and pressing against him.

[25] Now a woman suffering from bleeding for twelve years [26] had endured much under many doctors. She had spent everything she had and was not helped at all. On the contrary, she became worse. [27] Having heard about Jesus, she came up behind him in the crowd and touched his clothing. [28] For she said, "If I just touch his clothes, I'll be made well." [29] Instantly her flow of blood ceased, and she sensed in her body that she was healed of her affliction.

[30] At once Jesus realized in himself that power had gone out from him. He turned around in the crowd and said, "Who touched my clothes?"

[31] His disciples said to him, "You see the crowd pressing against you, and yet you say, 'Who touched me?'"

[32] But he was looking around to see who had done this. [33] The woman, with fear and trembling, knowing what had happened to her, came and fell down before him, and told him the whole truth. [34] "Daughter," he said to her, "your faith has saved you. Go in peace and be healed from your affliction."

[35] While he was still speaking, people came from the synagogue leader's house and said, "Your daughter is dead. Why bother the teacher anymore?"

[36] When Jesus overheard what was said, he told the synagogue leader, "Don't be afraid. Only believe." [37] He did not let anyone accompany him

[40] When Jesus returned, the crowd welcomed him, for they were all expecting him. [41] Just then, a man named Jairus came. He was a leader of the synagogue. He fell down at Jesus's feet and pleaded with him to come to his house, [42] because he had an only daughter about twelve years old, and she was dying.

While he was going, the crowds were nearly crushing him. [43] A woman suffering from bleeding for twelve years, who had spent all she had on doctors and yet could not be healed by any, [44] approached from behind and touched the end of his robe. Instantly her bleeding stopped.

[45] "Who touched me?" Jesus asked.

When they all denied it, Peter said, "Master, the crowds are hemming you in and pressing against you."

[46] "Someone did touch me," said Jesus. "I know that power has gone out from me." [47] When the

---

and the girl got up. **26** Then news of this spread throughout that whole area.

except Peter, James, and John, James's brother. **38** They came to the leader's house, and he saw a commotion—people weeping and wailing loudly. **39** He went in and said to them, "Why are you making a commotion and weeping? The child is not dead but asleep." **40** They laughed at him, but he put them all outside. He took the child's father, mother, and those who were with him, and entered the place where the child was. **41** Then he took the child by the hand and said to her, *"Talitha koum"* (which is translated, "Little girl, I say to you, get up"). **42** Immediately the girl got up and began to walk. (She was twelve years old.) At this they were utterly astounded. **43** Then he gave them strict orders that no one should know about this and told them to give her something to eat.

woman saw that she was discovered, she came trembling and fell down before him. In the presence of all the people, she declared the reason she had touched him and how she was instantly healed. **48** "Daughter," he said to her, "your faith has saved you. Go in peace."

49 While he was still speaking, someone came from the synagogue leader's house and said, "Your daughter is dead. Don't bother the teacher anymore."

50 When Jesus heard it, he answered him, "Don't be afraid. Only believe, and she will be saved." **51** After he came to the house, he let no one enter with him except Peter, John, James, and the child's father and mother. **52** Everyone was crying and mourning for her. But he said, "Stop crying, because she is not dead but asleep."

53 They laughed at him, because they knew she was dead. **54** So he took her by the hand and called out, "Child, get up!" **55** Her spirit returned, and she got up at once. Then he gave orders that she be given something to eat. **56** Her parents were astounded, but he instructed them to tell no one what had happened.

JESUS HEALS BLIND AND MUTE MEN

27 As Jesus went on from there, two blind men followed him, calling out, "Have mercy on us, Son of David!"

28 When he entered the house, the blind men approached him, and Jesus said to them, "Do you believe that I can do this?"

They said to him, "Yes, Lord."

29 Then he touched their eyes, saying, "Let it be done for you according to your faith." **30** And their eyes were opened. Then Jesus warned them sternly, "Be sure that no one finds out." **31** But they went out and spread the news about him throughout that whole area.

32 Just as they were going out, a demon-possessed man who was unable to speak was brought to him. **33** When the demon had been driven out, the man who had been mute spoke, and the crowds were amazed, saying, "Nothing like this has ever been seen in Israel!"

34 But the Pharisees said, "He drives out demons by the ruler of the demons."

JESUS IS REJECTED IN HIS HOMETOWN
MT 13:53-58   MK 6:1-6   LK 4:16-30

Matthew and Mark are quite similar in their accounts of Jesus's rejection in Nazareth. Compared to Luke, however, it seems that they have included only the essentials of this event. Yet their point is well made—namely, that unbelief was pervasive among those who knew Jesus best. Luke's expanded version calls for some comment. Its length compared to the others is due in large part to its role in marking the beginning of Jesus's public ministry. As

MATTHEW   MARK   LUKE   JOHN   **JESUS'S MINISTRY IN GALILEE** 51 we have seen often in Matthew's Gospel, Luke connects Jesus to OT prophecy with a fulfillment quote. However, it is Jesus himself who makes the connection, not the narrator. It is also clear from Luke's account that the response to Jesus was far more volatile than one might have realized from Matthew or Mark's account. Together the three offer a cohesive, though slightly nuanced, account.

53 When Jesus had finished these parables, he left there. **54** He went to his hometown and began to teach them in their synagogue, so that they were astonished and said, "Where did this man get this wisdom and these miraculous powers? **55** Isn't this the carpenter's son? Isn't his mother called Mary, and his brothers James, Joseph, Simon, and Judas? **56** And his sisters, aren't they all with us? So where does he get all these things?" **57** And they were offended by him.

Jesus said to them, "A prophet is not without honor except in his hometown and in his household." **58** And he did not do many miracles there because of their unbelief.

1 He left there and came to his hometown, and his disciples followed him. **2** When the Sabbath came, he began to teach in the synagogue, and many who heard him were astonished. "Where did this man get these things?" they said. "What is this wisdom that has been given to him, and how are these miracles performed by his hands? **3** Isn't this the carpenter, the son of Mary, and the brother of James, Joses, Judas, and Simon? And aren't his sisters here with us?" So they were offended by him.

4 Jesus said to them, "A prophet is not without honor except in his hometown, among his relatives, and in his household." **5** He was not able to do a miracle there, except that he laid his hands on a few sick people and healed them. **6** And he was amazed at their unbelief.

16 He came to Nazareth, where he had been brought up. As usual, he entered the synagogue on the Sabbath day and stood up to read. **17** The scroll of the prophet Isaiah was given to him, and unrolling the scroll, he found the place where it was written:

18   **The Spirit of the Lord is on me,**
because he has anointed me
to preach good news to the poor.
He has sent me
to proclaim release to the captives
and recovery of sight to the blind,
to set free the oppressed,
19   **to proclaim the year of the Lord's favor.**

20 He then rolled up the scroll, gave it back to the attendant, and sat down. And the eyes of everyone in the synagogue were fixed on him. **21** He began by saying to them, "Today as you listen, this Scripture has been fulfilled."

22 They were all speaking well of him and were amazed by the gracious words that came from his mouth; yet they said, "Isn't this Joseph's son?"

23 Then he said to them, "No doubt you will quote this proverb to me: 'Doctor, heal yourself. What we've heard that took place in Capernaum, do here in your hometown also.'"

24 He also said, "Truly I tell you, no prophet is accepted in his hometown. **25** But I say to you, there were certainly many widows in Israel in Elijah's days, when the sky was shut up for three years and six months while a great famine came over all the land. **26** Yet Elijah was not sent to any of them except a widow at Zarephath in Sidon. **27** And in the prophet Elisha's time, there were many in Israel who had leprosy, and yet not one of them was cleansed except Naaman the Syrian."

28 When they heard this, everyone in the synagogue was enraged. **29** They got up, drove him out of town, and brought him to the edge of the hill that their town was built on, intending to hurl him over the cliff. **30** But he passed right through the crowd and went on his way.

THE LORD OF THE HARVEST   MT 9:35-38

35 Jesus continued going around to all the towns and villages, teaching in their synagogues, preaching the good news of the kingdom, and healing every disease and every sickness. **36** When he saw the crowds, he felt compassion for them, because they were distressed and dejected, like sheep without a shepherd. **37** Then he said to his disciples, "The harvest is abundant, but the workers are few. **38** Therefore, pray to the Lord of the harvest to send out workers into his harvest."

The core features of this event are retained in each of the Synoptic accounts. The length of Matthew's account relative to Mark and Luke is due in large measure to the fact that he has included this important event within one of his five major discourses (the mission discourse, Mt 10:1-42). Mark and Luke have already named the disciples elsewhere (cp. Mk 3:13-19; Lk 6:12-16 above), which accounts for the omission here. These variations notwithstanding, the three accounts are very similar if slightly nuanced.

¹ Summoning his twelve disciples, he gave them authority over unclean spirits, to drive them out and to heal every disease and sickness. ² These are the names of the twelve apostles: First, Simon, who is called Peter, and Andrew his brother; James the son of Zebedee, and John his brother; ³ Philip and Bartholomew; Thomas and Matthew the tax collector; James the son of Alphaeus, and Thaddaeus; ⁴ Simon the Zealot, and Judas Iscariot, who also betrayed him.

⁵ Jesus sent out these twelve after giving them instructions: "Don't take the road that leads to the Gentiles, and don't enter any Samaritan town. ⁶ Instead, go to the lost sheep of the house of Israel. ⁷ As you go, proclaim: 'The kingdom of heaven has come near.' ⁸ Heal the sick, raise the dead, cleanse those with leprosy, drive out demons. Freely you received, freely give. ⁹ Don't acquire gold, silver, or copper for your money-belts. ¹⁰ Don't take a traveling bag for the road, or an extra shirt, sandals, or a staff, for the worker is worthy of his food. ¹¹ When you enter any town or village, find out who is worthy, and stay there until you leave. ¹² Greet a household when you enter it, ¹³ and if the household is worthy, let your peace be on it; but if it is unworthy, let your peace return to you. ¹⁴ If anyone does not welcome you or listen to your words, shake the dust off your feet when you leave that house or town. ¹⁵ Truly I tell you, it will be more tolerable on the day of judgment for the land of Sodom and Gomorrah than for that town."

He was going around the villages teaching.

⁷ He summoned the Twelve and began to send them out in pairs and gave them authority over unclean spirits. ⁸ He instructed them to take nothing for the road except a staff—no bread, no traveling bag, no money in their belts, ⁹ but to wear sandals and not put on an extra shirt. ¹⁰ He said to them, "Whenever you enter a house, stay there until you leave that place. ¹¹ If any place does not welcome you or listen to you, when you leave there, shake the dust off your feet as a testimony against them." ¹² So they went out and preached that people should repent. ¹³ They drove out many demons, anointed many sick people with oil and healed them.

¹ Summoning the Twelve, he gave them power and authority over all the demons and to heal diseases. ² Then he sent them to proclaim the kingdom of God and to heal the sick.

³ "Take nothing for the road," he told them, "no staff, no traveling bag, no bread, no money; and don't take an extra shirt. ⁴ Whatever house you enter, stay there and leave from there. ⁵ If they do not welcome you, when you leave that town, shake off the dust from your feet as a testimony against them." ⁶ So they went out and traveled from village to village, proclaiming the good news and healing everywhere.

¹⁶ "Look, I'm sending you out like sheep among wolves. Therefore be as shrewd as serpents and as innocent as doves. ¹⁷ Beware of them, because they will hand you over to local courts and flog you in their synagogues. ¹⁸ You will even be brought before governors and kings because of me, to bear witness to them and to the Gentiles. ¹⁹ But when they hand you over, don't worry about how or what you are to speak. For you will be given what to say at that hour, ²⁰ because it isn't you speaking, but the Spirit of your Father is speaking through you.

²¹ "Brother will betray brother to death, and a father his child. Children will rise up against parents and have them put to death. ²² You will be hated by everyone because of my name. But the one who endures to the end will be saved. ²³ When they persecute you in one town, flee to another. For truly I tell you, you will not have gone through the towns of Israel before the Son of Man comes. ²⁴ A disciple is not above his teacher, or a slave above his master. ²⁵ It is enough for a disciple to become like his teacher and a slave like his master. If they called the head of the house 'Beelzebul,' how much more the members of his household!

26 "Therefore, don't be afraid of them, since there is nothing covered that won't be uncovered and nothing hidden that won't be made known. **27** What I tell you in the dark, speak in the light. What you hear in a whisper, proclaim on the housetops. **28** Don't fear those who kill the body but are not able to kill the soul; rather, fear him who is able to destroy both soul and body in hell. **29** Aren't two sparrows sold for a penny? Yet not one of them falls to the ground without your Father's consent. **30** But even the hairs of your head have all been counted. **31** So don't be afraid; you are worth more than many sparrows.

32 "Therefore, everyone who will acknowledge me before others, I will also acknowledge him before my Father in heaven. **33** But whoever denies me before others, I will also deny him before my Father in heaven. **34** Don't assume that I came to bring peace on the earth. I did not come to bring peace, but a sword. **35** For I came to turn

> **a man against his father,**
> **a daughter against her mother,**
> **a daughter-in-law against her mother-in-law;**
> **36** **and a man's enemies will be**
> **the members of his household.**

37 The one who loves a father or mother more than me is not worthy of me; the one who loves a son or daughter more than me is not worthy of me. **38** And whoever doesn't take up his cross and follow me is not worthy of me. **39** Anyone who finds his life will lose it, and anyone who loses his life because of me will find it.

40 "The one who welcomes you welcomes me, and the one who welcomes me welcomes him who sent me. **41** Anyone who welcomes a prophet because he is a prophet will receive a prophet's reward. And anyone who welcomes a righteous person because he's righteous will receive a righteous person's reward. **42** And whoever gives even a cup of cold water to one of these little ones because he is a disciple, truly I tell you, he will never lose his reward."

HEROD IS INTERESTED IN JESUS 　　　　　　　　MT 14:1-2　　　MK 6:14-16　　　LK 9:7-9

Characters are important to any story, and Herod is no different. To be sure, the historicity of such people is important, but equally significant is the role they play in the narrative of each Gospel. For Matthew and Mark the focus on Herod and John has at least two functions. First, Herod represents the hostility of the "kingdoms of the world" that is an affront to the kingdom of heaven/God.

Second, John's fate foreshadows the suffering of Jesus. For Luke, Herod's query about the identity of Jesus ("Who is this?") serves as a literary device that invites the reader to ask the same question. Consequently, Luke will revisit the same question with the disciples later in verse 18. For all three authors, the identity of Jesus is at the center of the narrative.

1 At that time Herod the tetrarch heard the report about Jesus. **2** "This is John the Baptist," he told his servants. "He has been raised from the dead, and that's why miraculous powers are at work in him."

14 King Herod heard about it, because Jesus's name had become well known. Some said, "John the Baptist has been raised from the dead, and that's why miraculous powers are at work in him." **15** But others said, "He's Elijah." Still others said, "He's a prophet, like one of the prophets from long ago." **16** When Herod heard of it, he said, "John, the one I beheaded, has been raised!"

7 Herod the tetrarch heard about everything that was going on. He was perplexed, because some said that John had been raised from the dead, **8** some that Elijah had appeared, and others that one of the ancient prophets had risen. **9** "I beheaded John," Herod said, "but who is this I hear such things about?" And he wanted to see him.

Regarding the role of Herod and John in each Gospel, see the preceding entry. Luke does not include the account of Herod's ruthless execution of John. For Matthew and Mark, such details reinforce the hostility of Herod and the kingdom he represents.

³ For Herod had arrested John, chained him, and put him in prison on account of Herodias, his brother Philip's wife, ⁴ since John had been telling him, "It's not lawful for you to have her." ⁵ Though Herod wanted to kill John, he feared the crowd since they regarded John as a prophet. ⁶ When Herod's birthday celebration came, Herodias's daughter danced before them and pleased Herod. ⁷ So he promised with an oath to give her whatever she asked. ⁸ Prompted by her mother, she answered, "Give me John the Baptist's head here on a platter." ⁹ Although the king regretted it, he commanded that it be granted because of his oaths and his guests. ¹⁰ So he sent orders and had John beheaded in the prison. ¹¹ His head was brought on a platter and given to the girl, who carried it to her mother. ¹² Then his disciples came, removed the corpse, buried it, and went and reported to Jesus.

¹⁷ For Herod himself had given orders to arrest John and to chain him in prison on account of Herodias, his brother Philip's wife, because he had married her. ¹⁸ John had been telling Herod, "It is not lawful for you to have your brother's wife." ¹⁹ So Herodias held a grudge against him and wanted to kill him. But she could not, ²⁰ because Herod feared John and protected him, knowing he was a righteous and holy man. When Herod heard him he would be very perplexed, and yet he liked to listen to him. ²¹ An opportune time came on his birthday, when Herod gave a banquet for his nobles, military commanders, and the leading men of Galilee. ²² When Herodias's own daughter came in and danced, she pleased Herod and his guests. The king said to the girl, "Ask me whatever you want, and I'll give it to you." ²³ He promised her with an oath: "Whatever you ask me I will give you, up to half my kingdom."

²⁴ She went out and said to her mother, "What should I ask for?"

"John the Baptist's head," she said.

²⁵ At once she hurried to the king and said, "I want you to give me John the Baptist's head on a platter immediately." ²⁶ Although the king was deeply distressed, because of his oaths and the guests he did not want to refuse her. ²⁷ The king immediately sent for an executioner and commanded him to bring John's head. So he went and beheaded him in prison, ²⁸ brought his head on a platter, and gave it to the girl. Then the girl gave it to her mother. ²⁹ When John's disciples heard about it, they came and removed his corpse and placed it in a tomb.

JESUS FEEDS THE FIVE THOUSAND   MT 14:13-21   MK 6:30-44   LK 9:10-17   JN 6:1-15

This epic event is recorded in all four Gospels, and the central details are the same. For example, in all four there are about five thousand men who are fed by five loaves and two fish, after which time twelve baskets of leftovers are collected. Yet each Gospel sets this event in a slightly different narrative setting. In Mark and Luke, for example, it follows on the heels of the disciples' missionary journey, while in Matthew it follows the account of John the Baptist's death. In all three accounts the setting is a respite for Jesus, his disciples, or both. For John, it sets up the subsequent "bread of life discourse" in which Jesus proclaims the first of seven "I am" statements. In so doing, John makes his theological purposes more manifest by connecting the feeding to the manna of the OT.

¹³ When Jesus heard about it, he withdrew from there by boat to a remote place to be alone. When the crowds heard this, they followed him on foot from the towns. ¹⁴ When he went ashore, he saw a large crowd, had compassion on them, and healed their sick. ¹⁵ When evening came, the disciples approached him and said, "This place is deserted, and

³⁰ The apostles gathered around Jesus and reported to him all that they had done and taught. ³¹ He said to them, "Come away by yourselves to a remote place and rest for a while." For many people were coming and going, and they did not even have time to eat. ³² So they went away in the boat by themselves to a remote place, ³³ but many saw them leaving and

¹⁰ When the apostles returned, they reported to Jesus all that they had done. He took them along and withdrew privately to a town called Bethsaida. ¹¹ When the crowds found out, they followed him. He welcomed them, spoke to them about the kingdom of God, and healed those who needed healing.

¹ After this, Jesus crossed the Sea of Galilee (or Tiberias). ² A huge crowd was following him because they saw the signs that he was performing by healing the sick. ³ Jesus went up a mountain and sat down there with his disciples. ⁴ Now the Passover, a Jewish festival, was near. ⁵ So when Jesus looked up and noticed a huge crowd coming toward him, he

it is already late. Send the crowds away so that they can go into the villages and buy food for themselves."

¹⁶ "They don't need to go away," Jesus told them. "You give them something to eat."

¹⁷ "But we only have five loaves and two fish here," they said to him.

¹⁸ "Bring them here to me," he said. ¹⁹ Then he commanded the crowds to sit down on the grass. He took the five loaves and the two fish, and looking up to heaven, he blessed them. He broke the loaves and gave them to the disciples, and the disciples gave them to the crowds. ²⁰ Everyone ate and was satisfied. They picked up twelve baskets full of leftover pieces. ²¹ Now those who ate were about five thousand men, besides women and children.

recognized them, and they ran on foot from all the towns and arrived ahead of them.

³⁴ When he went ashore, he saw a large crowd and had compassion on them, because they were like sheep without a shepherd. Then he began to teach them many things.

³⁵ When it grew late, his disciples approached him and said, "This place is deserted, and it is already late. ³⁶ Send them away so that they can go into the surrounding countryside and villages to buy themselves something to eat."

³⁷ "You give them something to eat," he responded.

They said to him, "Should we go and buy two hundred denarii worth of bread and give them something to eat?"

³⁸ He asked them, "How many loaves do you have? Go and see."

When they found out they said, "Five, and two fish." ³⁹ Then he instructed them to have all the people sit down in groups on the green grass. ⁴⁰ So they sat down in groups of hundreds and fifties. ⁴¹ He took the five loaves and the two fish, and looking up to heaven, he blessed and broke the loaves. He kept giving them to his disciples to set before the people. He also divided the two fish among them all. ⁴² Everyone ate and was satisfied. ⁴³ They picked up twelve baskets full of pieces of bread and fish. ⁴⁴ Now those who had eaten the loaves were five thousand men.

¹² Late in the day, the Twelve approached and said to him, "Send the crowd away, so that they can go into the surrounding villages and countryside to find food and lodging, because we are in a deserted place here."

¹³ "You give them something to eat," he told them.

"We have no more than five loaves and two fish," they said, "unless we go and buy food for all these people." ¹⁴ (For about five thousand men were there.)

Then he told his disciples, "Have them sit down in groups of about fifty each." ¹⁵ They did what he said, and had them all sit down. ¹⁶ Then he took the five loaves and the two fish, and looking up to heaven, he blessed and broke them. He kept giving them to the disciples to set before the crowd. ¹⁷ Everyone ate and was filled. They picked up twelve baskets of leftover pieces.

asked Philip, "Where will we buy bread so that these people can eat?" ⁶ He asked this to test him, for he himself knew what he was going to do.

⁷ Philip answered him, "Two hundred denarii worth of bread wouldn't be enough for each of them to have a little."

⁸ One of his disciples, Andrew, Simon Peter's brother, said to him, ⁹ "There's a boy here who has five barley loaves and two fish— but what are they for so many?"

¹⁰ Jesus said, "Have the people sit down."

There was plenty of grass in that place; so they sat down. The men numbered about five thousand. ¹¹ Then Jesus took the loaves, and after giving thanks he distributed them to those who were seated—so also with the fish, as much as they wanted.

¹² When they were full, he told his disciples, "Collect the leftovers so that nothing is wasted." ¹³ So they collected them and filled twelve baskets with the pieces from the five barley loaves that were left over by those who had eaten.

¹⁴ When the people saw the sign he had done, they said, "This truly is the Prophet who is to come into the world."

¹⁵ Therefore, when Jesus realized that they were about to come and take him by force to make him king, he withdrew again to the mountain by himself.

In all three Gospels, the narrative of Jesus walking on the water follows the feeding of the five thousand. Only Matthew, however, includes the account of Peter's lack of faith while trying to emulate Jesus. Matthew takes a special interest in the role of Peter as a leader among the disciples. Yet, such a role is mainly symbolic, since Peter functions as a negative example in Matthew in addition to a positive one. Matthew makes a Christological point through an explicit comparison of Christ with a faithless Peter. For Mark and John, the point is made in comparison to the fearful disciples more generally.

[22] Immediately he made the disciples get into the boat and go ahead of him to the other side, while he dismissed the crowds. [23] After dismissing the crowds, he went up on the mountain by himself to pray. Well into the night, he was there alone. [24] Meanwhile, the boat was already some distance from land, battered by the waves, because the wind was against them. [25] Jesus came toward them walking on the sea very early in the morning. [26] When the disciples saw him walking on the sea, they were terrified. "It's a ghost!" they said, and they cried out in fear.

[27] Immediately Jesus spoke to them. "Have courage! It is I. Don't be afraid."

[28] "Lord, if it's you," Peter answered him, "command me to come to you on the water."

[29] He said, "Come."

And climbing out of the boat, Peter started walking on the water and came toward Jesus. [30] But when he saw the strength of the wind, he was afraid, and beginning to sink he cried out, "Lord, save me!"

[31] Immediately Jesus reached out his hand, caught hold of him, and said to him, "You of little faith, why did you doubt?"

[32] When they got into the boat, the wind ceased. [33] Then those in the boat worshiped him and said, "Truly you are the Son of God."

[45] Immediately he made his disciples get into the boat and go ahead of him to the other side, to Bethsaida, while he dismissed the crowd. [46] After he said good-bye to them, he went away to the mountain to pray. [47] Well into the night, the boat was in the middle of the sea, and he was alone on the land. [48] He saw them straining at the oars, because the wind was against them. Very early in the morning he came toward them walking on the sea and wanted to pass by them. [49] When they saw him walking on the sea, they thought it was a ghost and cried out, [50] because they all saw him and were terrified. Immediately he spoke with them and said, "Have courage! It is I. Don't be afraid." [51] Then he got into the boat with them, and the wind ceased. They were completely astounded, [52] because they had not understood about the loaves. Instead, their hearts were hardened.

[16] When evening came, his disciples went down to the sea, [17] got into a boat, and started across the sea to Capernaum. Darkness had already set in, but Jesus had not yet come to them. [18] A high wind arose, and the sea began to churn. [19] After they had rowed about three or four miles, they saw Jesus walking on the sea. He was coming near the boat, and they were afraid. [20] But he said to them, "It is I. Don't be afraid." [21] Then they were willing to take him on board, and at once the boat was at the shore where they were heading.

JESUS HEALS AT THE BANKS OF GENNESARET   MT 14:34-36   MK 6:53-56

Little needs to be said about the consistency between the two Gospels regarding this account, which functions for both Matthew and Mark as a summary of Jesus's pervasive healing ministry to all Israel regardless of social and religious status.

[34] When they had crossed over, they came to shore at Gennesaret. [35] When the men of that place recognized him, they alerted the whole vicinity and brought to him all who were sick. [36] They begged him that they might only touch the end of his robe, and as many as touched it were healed.

[53] When they had crossed over, they came to shore at Gennesaret and anchored there.

[54] As they got out of the boat, people immediately recognized him. [55] They hurried throughout that region and began to carry the sick on mats to wherever they heard he was. [56] Wherever he went, into

villages, towns, or the country, they laid the sick in the marketplaces and begged him that they might touch just the end of his robe. And everyone who touched it was healed.

22 The next day, the crowd that had stayed on the other side of the sea saw there had been only one boat. They also saw that Jesus had not boarded the boat with his disciples, but that his disciples had gone off alone. 23 Some boats from Tiberias came near the place where they had eaten the bread after the Lord had given thanks. 24 When the crowd saw that neither Jesus nor his disciples were there, they got into the boats and went to Capernaum looking for Jesus. 25 When they found him on the other side of the sea, they said to him, "Rabbi, when did you get here?"

26 Jesus answered, "Truly I tell you, you are looking for me, not because you saw the signs, but because you ate the loaves and were filled. 27 Don't work for the food that perishes but for the food that lasts for eternal life, which the Son of Man will give you, because God the Father has set his seal of approval on him."

28 "What can we do to perform the works of God?" they asked.

29 Jesus replied, "This is the work of God — that you believe in the one he has sent."

30 "What sign, then, are you going to do so we may see and believe you?" they asked. "What are you going to perform? 31 Our ancestors ate the manna in the wilderness, just as it is written: **He gave them bread from heaven to eat.**"

32 Jesus said to them, "Truly I tell you, Moses didn't give you the bread from heaven, but my Father gives you the true bread from heaven. 33 For the bread of God is the one who comes down from heaven and gives life to the world."

34 Then they said, "Sir, give us this bread always."

35 "I am the bread of life," Jesus told them. "No one who comes to me will ever be hungry, and no one who believes in me will ever be thirsty again. 36 But as I told you, you've seen me, and yet you do not believe. 37 Everyone the Father gives me will come to me, and the one who comes to me I will never cast out. 38 For I have come down from heaven, not to do my own will, but the will of him who sent me. 39 This is the will of him who sent me: that I should lose none of those he has given me but should raise them up on the last day. 40 For this is the will of my Father: that everyone who sees the Son and believes in him will have eternal life, and I will raise him up on the last day."

41 Therefore the Jews started complaining about him because he said, "I am the bread that came down from heaven." 42 They were saying, "Isn't this Jesus the son of Joseph, whose father and mother we know? How can he now say, 'I have come down from heaven'?"

43 Jesus answered them, "Stop complaining among yourselves. 44 No one can come to me unless the Father who sent me draws him, and I will raise him up on the last day. 45 It is written in the Prophets: **And they will all be taught by God.** Everyone who has listened to and learned from the Father comes to me — 46 not that anyone has seen the Father except the one who is from God. He has seen the Father.

47 "Truly I tell you, anyone who believes has eternal life. 48 I am the bread of life. 49 Your ancestors ate the manna in the wilderness, and they died. 50 This is the bread that comes down from heaven so that anyone may eat of it and not die. 51 I am the living bread that came down from heaven. If anyone eats of this bread he will live forever. The bread that I will give for the life of the world is my flesh."

⁵² At that, the Jews argued among themselves, "How can this man give us his flesh to eat?"

⁵³ So Jesus said to them, "Truly I tell you, unless you eat the flesh of the Son of Man and drink his blood, you do not have life in yourselves. ⁵⁴ The one who eats my flesh and drinks my blood has eternal life, and I will raise him up on the last day, ⁵⁵ because my flesh is true food and my blood is true drink. ⁵⁶ The one who eats my flesh and drinks my blood remains in me, and I in him. ⁵⁷ Just as the living Father sent me and I live because of the Father, so the one who feeds on me will live because of me. ⁵⁸ This is the bread that came down from heaven; it is not like the manna your ancestors ate — and they died. The one who eats this bread will live forever."

⁵⁹ He said these things while teaching in the synagogue in Capernaum.

REJECTION AND CONFESSION
JN 6:60-71

⁶⁰ Therefore, when many of his disciples heard this, they said, "This teaching is hard. Who can accept it?"

⁶¹ Jesus, knowing in himself that his disciples were complaining about this, asked them, "Does this offend you? ⁶² Then what if you were to observe the Son of Man ascending to where he was before? ⁶³ The Spirit is the one who gives life. The flesh doesn't help at all. The words that I have spoken to you are spirit and are life. ⁶⁴ But there are some among you who don't believe." (For Jesus knew from the beginning those who did not believe and the one who would betray him.) ⁶⁵ He said, "This is why I told you that no one can come to me unless it is granted to him by the Father."

⁶⁶ From that moment many of his disciples turned back and no longer accompanied him. ⁶⁷ So Jesus said to the Twelve, "You don't want to go away too, do you?"

⁶⁸ Simon Peter answered, "Lord, to whom will we go? You have the words of eternal life. ⁶⁹ We have come to believe and know that you are the Holy One of God."

⁷⁰ Jesus replied to them, "Didn't I choose you, the Twelve? Yet one of you is a devil." ⁷¹ He was referring to Judas, Simon Iscariot's son, one of the Twelve, because he was going to betray him.

OUTER AND INNER PURITY
MT 15:1-20   MK 7:1-23

Matthew and Mark are quite similar in their accounts of this controversy between Jesus and the religious officials about kosher laws. In both cases, Jesus claims that such traditions of the elders (or oral laws) actually infringe upon the law of Moses—specifically, the command to honor one's father and mother. That such delegates were "from Jerusalem" anticipates the mounting hostility that will climax with the religious leaders in Jerusalem. An irreversible rift has occurred here with Jesus's radical indictment of these officials.

¹ Then Jesus was approached by Pharisees and scribes from Jerusalem, who asked, ² "Why do your disciples break the tradition of the elders? For they don't wash their hands when they eat."

³ He answered them, "Why do you break God's commandment because of your tradition? ⁴ For God said: **Honor your father and your mother;** and, **Whoever speaks evil of father or mother must be put to death.** ⁵ But you say, 'Whoever tells his father or mother, "Whatever benefit you might have received from me is a gift committed to the temple," ⁶ he does not have to honor his father.' In this way, you have

¹ The Pharisees and some of the scribes who had come from Jerusalem gathered around him. ² They observed that some of his disciples were eating bread with unclean — that is, unwashed — hands. ³ (For the Pharisees and all the Jews do not eat unless they give their hands a ceremonial washing, keeping the tradition of the elders. ⁴ When they come from the marketplace, they do not eat unless they have washed. And there are many other customs they have received and keep, like the washing of cups, pitchers, kettles, and dining couches.) ⁵ So the Pharisees and the scribes asked him, "Why don't your disciples live

nullified the word of God because of your tradition. **7** Hypocrites! Isaiah prophesied correctly about you when he said:

8 **This people honors me with their lips,**
but their heart is far from me.
9 **They worship me in vain,**
teaching as doctrines human commands."

10 Summoning the crowd, he told them, "Listen and understand: **11** It's not what goes into the mouth that defiles a person, but what comes out of the mouth — this defiles a person."

12 Then the disciples came up and told him, "Do you know that the Pharisees took offense when they heard what you said?"

13 He replied, "Every plant that my heavenly Father didn't plant will be uprooted. **14** Leave them alone! They are blind guides. And if the blind guide the blind, both will fall into a pit."

15 Then Peter said, "Explain this parable to us."

16 "Do you still lack understanding?" he asked. **17** "Don't you realize that whatever goes into the mouth passes into the stomach and is eliminated? **18** But what comes out of the mouth comes from the heart, and this defiles a person. **19** For from the heart come evil thoughts, murders, adulteries, sexual immoralities, thefts, false testimonies, slander. **20** These are the things that defile a person; but eating with unwashed hands does not defile a person."

according to the tradition of the elders, instead of eating bread with ceremonially unclean hands?"

6 He answered them, "Isaiah prophesied correctly about you hypocrites, as it is written:

This people honors me with their lips,
but their heart is far from me.
7 **They worship me in vain,**
teaching as doctrines human commands.

8 Abandoning the command of God, you hold on to human tradition." **9** He also said to them, "You have a fine way of invalidating God's command in order to set up your tradition! **10** For Moses said: **Honor your father and your mother;** and **Whoever speaks evil of father or mother must be put to death. 11** But you say, 'If anyone tells his father or mother: Whatever benefit you might have received from me is *corban*'" (that is, an offering devoted to God), **12** "you no longer let him do anything for his father or mother. **13** You nullify the word of God by your tradition that you have handed down. And you do many other similar things."

14 Summoning the crowd again, he told them, "Listen to me, all of you, and understand: **15** Nothing that goes into a person from outside can defile him but the things that come out of a person are what defile him."

17 When he went into the house away from the crowd, his disciples asked him about the parable. **18** He said to them, "Are you also as lacking in understanding? Don't you realize that nothing going into a person from the outside can defile him? **19** For it doesn't go into his heart but into the stomach and is eliminated" (thus he declared all foods clean). **20** And he said, "What comes out of a person is what defiles him. **21** For from within, out of people's hearts, come evil thoughts, sexual immoralities, thefts, murders, **22** adulteries, greed, evil actions, deceit, self-indulgence, envy, slander, pride, and foolishness. **23** All these evil things come from within and defile a person."

EXORCISM AND HEALINGS BEYOND GALILEE
MT 15:21-31   MK 7:24-37

The slight variation between Matthew and Mark can be explained, in part, by their unique interest in casting the pagan women within a certain theological context. Matthew, for example, uses the OT place name of "Canaanite" in order to elicit memories of Israel's wars with the Canaanites in the days of Joshua. Matthew (vv. 29-31) offers another summary of Jesus's widespread

healings, whereas Mark includes a single healing of a deaf man. For Matthew, such a summary will serve as a fitting transition into a second epic feeding of mainly Gentile crowds—a counterpart to the feeding of the five thousand mainly Jewish people in Galilee.

21 When Jesus left there, he withdrew to the area of Tyre and Sidon. **22** Just then a Canaanite woman from that region came and kept crying out, "Have mercy on me, Lord, Son of David! My daughter is severely tormented by a demon."

24 He got up and departed from there to the region of Tyre. He entered a house and did not want anyone to know it, but he could not escape notice. **25** Instead, immediately after hearing about him, a woman whose little daughter had an unclean spirit came and fell at his feet.

---

23 Jesus did not say a word to her. His disciples approached him and urged him, "Send her away because she's crying out after us."

24 He replied, "I was sent only to the lost sheep of the house of Israel."

25 But she came, knelt before him, and said, "Lord, help me!"

26 He answered, "It isn't right to take the children's bread and throw it to the dogs."

27 "Yes, Lord," she said, "yet even the dogs eat the crumbs that fall from their masters' table."

28 Then Jesus replied to her, "Woman, your faith is great. Let it be done for you as you want." And from that moment her daughter was healed.

29 Moving on from there, Jesus passed along the Sea of Galilee. He went up on a mountain and sat there, **30** and large crowds came to him, including the lame, the blind, the crippled, those unable to speak, and many others. They put them at his feet, and he healed them. **31** So the crowd was amazed when they saw those unable to speak talking, the crippled restored, the lame walking, and the blind seeing, and they gave glory to the God of Israel.

26 The woman was a Gentile, a Syrophoenician by birth, and she was asking him to cast the demon out of her daughter. **27** He said to her, "Let the children be fed first, because it isn't right to take the children's bread and throw it to the dogs."

28 But she replied to him, "Lord, even the dogs under the table eat the children's crumbs."

29 Then he told her, "Because of this reply, you may go. The demon has left your daughter." **30** When she went back to her home, she found her child lying on the bed, and the demon was gone.

31 Again, leaving the region of Tyre, he went by way of Sidon to the Sea of Galilee, through the region of the Decapolis. **32** They brought to him a deaf man who had difficulty speaking and begged Jesus to lay his hand on him. **33** So he took him away from the crowd in private. After putting his fingers in the man's ears and spitting, he touched his tongue. **34** Looking up to heaven, he sighed deeply and said to him, *"Ephphatha!"* (that is, "Be opened!"). **35** Immediately his ears were opened, his tongue was loosened, and he began to speak clearly. **36** He ordered them to tell no one, but the more he ordered them, the more they proclaimed it.

37 They were extremely astonished and said, "He has done everything well. He even makes the deaf hear and the mute speak."

JESUS FEEDS THE FOUR THOUSAND

MT 15:32-39   MK 8:1-10

The questions surrounding the feeding of the four thousand have less to do with the compatibility of the accounts in Matthew and Mark (given the close similarities between them) and more to do with the fact that there were two such mass feedings in which the disciples manifest a lack of faith. However, as noted above, given the narrative setting outside of Galilee in mainly Gentile territory, this appears to be an event directed at Gentile crowds that serves as a fitting counterpart to the earlier feeding of the five thousand mainly Jewish crowds.

32 Jesus called his disciples and said, "I have compassion on the crowd, because they've already stayed with me three days and have nothing to eat. I don't want to send them away hungry, otherwise they might collapse on the way."

33 The disciples said to him, "Where could we get enough bread in this desolate place to feed such a crowd?"

34 "How many loaves do you have?" Jesus asked them.

"Seven," they said, "and a few small fish."

35 After commanding the crowd to sit down on the ground, **36** he took the seven loaves and the fish, gave thanks, broke them, and gave them to the disciples, and the disciples gave them to the crowds. **37** They all ate and were satisfied. They collected the leftover pieces — seven large baskets full. **38** Now there were four thousand men who had eaten, besides women and children. **39** After dismissing the crowds, he got into the boat and went to the region of Magadan.

1 In those days there was again a large crowd, and they had nothing to eat. He called the disciples and said to them, **2** "I have compassion on the crowd, because they've already stayed with me three days and have nothing to eat. **3** If I send them home hungry, they will collapse on the way, and some of them have come a long distance."

4 His disciples answered him, "Where can anyone get enough bread here in this desolate place to feed these people?"

5 "How many loaves do you have?" he asked them.

"Seven," they said. **6** He commanded the crowd to sit down on the ground. Taking the seven loaves, he gave thanks, broke them, and gave them to his disciples to set before the people. So they served them to the crowd. **7** They also had a few small fish, and after he had blessed them, he said these were to be served as well. **8** They ate and were satisfied. Then they collected seven large baskets of leftover pieces. **9** About four thousand were there. He dismissed them. **10** And he immediately got into the boat with his disciples and went to the district of Dalmanutha.

Compared to Matthew, Mark offers minimal details about the religious official's request for a sign. Matthew expands the account with Jesus's illustration about weather predictions that underscores the religious officials' inability to perceive even the most tangible signs of his authority (i.e., his miraculous power). Matthew's inclusion of the "sign of Jonah" (v. 4) serves as a thematic link to his reference to the same OT prophet earlier (12:39-41).

[1] The Pharisees and Sadducees approached, and tested him, asking him to show them a sign from heaven. [2] He replied, "When evening comes you say, 'It will be good weather because the sky is red.' [3] And in the morning, 'Today will be stormy because the sky is red and threatening.' You know how to read the appearance of the sky, but you can't read the signs of the times. [4] An evil and adulterous generation demands a sign, but no sign will be given to it except the sign of Jonah." Then he left them and went away.

[11] The Pharisees came and began to argue with him, demanding of him a sign from heaven to test him. [12] Sighing deeply in his spirit, he said, "Why does this generation demand a sign? Truly I tell you, no sign will be given to this generation." [13] Then he left them, got back into the boat, and went to the other side.

The placement of this story in the Gospel narratives is fitting, given the focus on the theme of bread. There are, though, a few notable differences between Matthew and Mark. Overall Mark is a bit more obscure than Matthew. This results in a far less positive assessment of the disciples, which fits Mark's interest in their lack of understanding. More perplexing, perhaps, is Mark's reference to the "leaven of Herod" in contrast to Matthew's "leaven of the . . . Sadducees." Craig Blomberg ("Matthew" in *The New American Commentary*) suggests that the two phrases mean essentially the same thing given the affiliation between the two groups (i.e., Herod and the Sadducees) within the political structure of the Roman Empire.

[5] The disciples reached the other shore, and they had forgotten to take bread. [6] Then Jesus told them, "Watch out and beware of the leaven of the Pharisees and Sadducees."
[7] They were discussing among themselves, "We didn't bring any bread."
[8] Aware of this, Jesus said, "You of little faith, why are you discussing among yourselves that you do not have bread? [9] Don't you understand yet? Don't you remember the five loaves for the five thousand and how many baskets you collected? [10] Or the seven loaves for the four thousand and how many large baskets you collected? [11] Why is it you don't understand that when I told you, 'Beware of the leaven of the Pharisees and Sadducees,' it wasn't about bread?" [12] Then they understood that he had not told them to beware of the leaven in bread, but of the teaching of the Pharisees and Sadducees.

[14] The disciples had forgotten to take bread and had only one loaf with them in the boat. [15] Then he gave them strict orders: "Watch out! Beware of the leaven of the Pharisees and the leaven of Herod." [16] They were discussing among themselves that they did not have any bread. [17] Aware of this, he said to them, "Why are you discussing the fact you have no bread? Don't you understand or comprehend? Do you have hardened hearts? [18] **Do you have eyes and not see; do you have ears and not hear?** And do you not remember? [19] When I broke the five loaves for the five thousand, how many baskets full of leftovers did you collect?"
"Twelve," they told him.
[20] "When I broke the seven loaves for the four thousand, how many baskets full of pieces did you collect?"
"Seven," they said.
[21] And he said to them, "Don't you understand yet?"

²² They came to Bethsaida. They brought a blind man to him and begged him to touch him.
²³ He took the blind man by the hand and brought him out of the village. Spitting on his eyes and laying his hands on him, he asked him, "Do you see anything?"

²⁴ He looked up and said, "I see people — they look like trees walking."

²⁵ Again Jesus placed his hands on the man's eyes. The man looked intently and his sight was restored and he saw everything clearly. ²⁶ Then he sent him home, saying, "Don't even go into the village."

All three Synoptics record the crucial moment when Peter confessed the identity of Jesus, a theme that has been the burden of all the Gospel writers from the beginning. Matthew takes further interest in Peter, as he has done previously (see "Jesus Walks on Water" on p. 57). Matthew's focus on Peter here underlines an important theological purpose: ecclesiology. It is here that the reader must remember that the Gospels are post-resurrection accounts of pre-resurrection events. With this in mind, Matthew is drawing attention to the central role that Peter will play in the "parting of ways" between the post-resurrection Christian community and Jewish community (see Ac 10–11).

¹³ When Jesus came to the region of Caesarea Philippi, he asked his disciples, "Who do people say that the Son of Man is?"

¹⁴ They replied, "Some say John the Baptist; others, Elijah; still others, Jeremiah or one of the prophets."

¹⁵ "But you," he asked them, "who do you say that I am?"

¹⁶ Simon Peter answered, "You are the Messiah, the Son of the living God."

¹⁷ Jesus responded, "Blessed are you, Simon son of Jonah, because flesh and blood did not reveal this to you, but my Father in heaven. ¹⁸ And I also say to you that you are Peter, and on this rock I will build my church, and the gates of Hades will not overpower it. ¹⁹ I will give you the keys of the kingdom of heaven, and whatever you bind on earth will have been bound in heaven, and whatever you loose on earth will have been loosed in heaven." ²⁰ Then he gave the disciples orders to tell no one that he was the Messiah.

²⁷ Jesus went out with his disciples to the villages of Caesarea Philippi. And on the road he asked his disciples, "Who do people say that I am?"

²⁸ They answered him, "John the Baptist; others, Elijah; still others, one of the prophets."

²⁹ "But you," he asked them, "who do you say that I am?"

Peter answered him, "You are the Messiah."

³⁰ And he strictly warned them to tell no one about him.

¹⁸ While he was praying in private and his disciples were with him, he asked them, "Who do the crowds say that I am?"

¹⁹ They answered, "John the Baptist; others, Elijah; still others, that one of the ancient prophets has come back."

²⁰ "But you," he asked them, "who do you say that I am?"

Peter answered, "God's Messiah."

²¹ But he strictly warned and instructed them to tell this to no one,

At the approximate center of all three Synoptic Gospels, the authors record a pivotal moment when the momentum of the narrative shifts towards the passion of Jesus. In addition, all three authors connect Jesus's approaching suffering to discipleship through his call for his disciples to "take up their cross." Matthew and Mark include the account of Peter's misguided rebuke of Jesus. In both cases, Jesus's counter-rebuke highlights the importance of embracing a comprehensive view of this suffering Messiah. In Matthew, the point is made all the more poignant by the comparison between Peter's Spirit-inspired confession in v. 16 and Satan-inspired rebuke in v. 22.

[21] From then on Jesus began to point out to his disciples that it was necessary for him to go to Jerusalem and suffer many things from the elders, chief priests, and scribes, be killed, and be raised the third day. [22] Peter took him aside and began to rebuke him, "Oh no, Lord! This will never happen to you!"

[23] Jesus turned and told Peter, "Get behind me, Satan! You are a hindrance to me because you're not thinking about God's concerns but human concerns."

[24] Then Jesus said to his disciples, "If anyone wants to follow after me, let him deny himself, take up his cross, and follow me. [25] For whoever wants to save his life will lose it, but whoever loses his life because of me will find it. [26] For what will it benefit someone if he gains the whole world yet loses his life? Or what will anyone give in exchange for his life? [27] For the Son of Man is going to come with his angels in the glory of his Father, and then he will reward each according to what he has done. [28] Truly I tell you, there are some standing here who will not taste death until they see the Son of Man coming in his kingdom."

[31] Then he began to teach them that it was necessary for the Son of Man to suffer many things and be rejected by the elders, chief priests, and scribes, be killed, and rise after three days. [32] He spoke openly about this. Peter took him aside and began to rebuke him. [33] But turning around and looking at his disciples, he rebuked Peter and said, "Get behind me, Satan! You are not thinking about God's concerns but human concerns."

[34] Calling the crowd along with his disciples, he said to them, "If anyone wants to follow after me, let him deny himself, take up his cross, and follow me. [35] For whoever wants to save his life will lose it, but whoever loses his life because of me and the gospel will save it. [36] For what does it benefit someone to gain the whole world and yet lose his life? [37] What can anyone give in exchange for his life? [38] For whoever is ashamed of me and my words in this adulterous and sinful generation, the Son of Man will also be ashamed of him when he comes in the glory of his Father with the holy angels."

[1] Then he said to them, "Truly I tell you, there are some standing here who will not taste death until they see the kingdom of God come in power."

[22] saying, "It is necessary that the Son of Man suffer many things and be rejected by the elders, chief priests, and scribes, be killed, and be raised the third day."

[23] Then he said to them all, "If anyone wants to follow after me, let him deny himself, take up his cross daily, and follow me. [24] For whoever wants to save his life will lose it, but whoever loses his life because of me will save it. [25] For what does it benefit someone if he gains the whole world, and yet loses or forfeits himself? [26] For whoever is ashamed of me and my words, the Son of Man will be ashamed of him when he comes in his glory and that of the Father and the holy angels. [27] Truly I tell you, there are some standing here who will not taste death until they see the kingdom of God."

The account of Jesus's transfiguration is a fitting follow up to the passion prediction given the focus of the three authors on the identity of Jesus and his imminent death. All three accounts are certainly compatible, yet there are some interesting variations. Matthew and Mark are similar in their accounts, noting the discussion between Jesus and his disciples about the way in which the fate of Elijah/John the Baptist foreshadowed the fate of Jesus himself. Luke, however, does not have this discussion but instead includes a comment about how Jesus's "departure" was the topic of his conversation with Moses and Elijah. The term used to refer to Jesus's "departure" is the Greek word *exodus*, which reminds the reader of the Lord's redemptive work delivering Israel from Egyptian slavery.

¹ After six days Jesus took Peter, James, and his brother John and led them up on a high mountain by themselves. ² He was transfigured in front of them, and his face shone like the sun; his clothes became as white as the light. ³ Suddenly, Moses and Elijah appeared to them, talking with him. ⁴ Then Peter said to Jesus, "Lord, it's good for us to be here. I will set up three shelters here: one for you, one for Moses, and one for Elijah."

⁵ While he was still speaking, suddenly a bright cloud covered them, and a voice from the cloud said: "This is my beloved Son, with whom I am well-pleased. Listen to him!"
⁶ When the disciples heard this, they fell facedown and were terrified.

⁷ Jesus came up, touched them, and said, "Get up; don't be afraid." ⁸ When they looked up they saw no one except Jesus alone.

⁹ As they were coming down the mountain, Jesus commanded them, "Don't tell anyone about the vision until the Son of Man is raised from the dead."

¹⁰ So the disciples asked him, "Why then do the scribes say that Elijah must come first?"

¹¹ "Elijah is coming and will restore everything," he replied. ¹² "But I tell you: Elijah has already come, and they didn't recognize him. On the contrary, they did whatever they pleased to him. In the same way the Son of Man is going to suffer at their hands." ¹³ Then the disciples understood that he had spoken to them about John the Baptist.

² After six days Jesus took Peter, James, and John and led them up a high mountain by themselves to be alone. He was transfigured in front of them, ³ and his clothes became dazzling — extremely white as no launderer on earth could whiten them. ⁴ Elijah appeared to them with Moses, and they were talking with Jesus. ⁵ Peter said to Jesus, "Rabbi, it's good for us to be here. Let us set up three shelters: one for you, one for Moses, and one for Elijah" —
⁶ because he did not know what to say, since they were terrified.

⁷ A cloud appeared, overshadowing them, and a voice came from the cloud: "This is my beloved Son; listen to him!"

⁸ Suddenly, looking around, they no longer saw anyone with them except Jesus.

⁹ As they were coming down the mountain, he ordered them to tell no one what they had seen until the Son of Man had risen from the dead. ¹⁰ They kept this word to themselves, questioning what "rising from the dead" meant.

¹¹ Then they asked him, "Why do the scribes say that Elijah must come first?"

¹² "Elijah does come first and restores all things," he replied. "Why then is it written that the Son of Man must suffer many things and be treated with contempt? ¹³ But I tell you that Elijah has come, and they did whatever they pleased to him, just as it is written about him."

²⁸ About eight days after this conversation, he took along Peter, John, and James and went up on the mountain to pray. ²⁹ As he was praying, the appearance of his face changed, and his clothes became dazzling white. ³⁰ Suddenly, two men were talking with him — Moses and Elijah. ³¹ They appeared in glory and were speaking of his departure, which he was about to accomplish in Jerusalem.

³² Peter and those with him were in a deep sleep, and when they became fully awake, they saw his glory and the two men who were standing with him. ³³ As the two men were departing from him, Peter said to Jesus, "Master, it's good for us to be here. Let us set up three shelters: one for you, one for Moses, and one for Elijah" — not knowing what he was saying.

³⁴ While he was saying this, a cloud appeared and overshadowed them. They became afraid as they entered the cloud. ³⁵ Then a voice came from the cloud, saying: "This is my Son, the Chosen One; listen to him!"

³⁶ After the voice had spoken, Jesus was found alone. They kept silent, and at that time told no one what they had seen.

THE EXORCISM OF A BOY

MT 17:14-21   MK 9:14-29   LK 9:37-42

Few healing stories rival this account of Jesus casting out an evil spirit from a young boy. All three Gospels include the main details of the event and draw attention to the inability of the disciples to heal the child. In Matthew (and to some extent in Luke), the omission of graphic details serves to highlight the lesson about faith while relegating the actual miracle to a position of secondary importance. As this is the last exorcism in Mark, the space he commits to it and the details he includes draw attention more evenly to both Jesus's power and the need for faith.

¹⁴ When they reached the crowd, a man approached and knelt down before him. ¹⁵ "Lord," he said, "have mercy on my son,

¹⁴ When they came to the disciples, they saw a large crowd around them and scribes disputing with them. ¹⁵ When the whole crowd saw him, they were amazed and ran to greet him. ¹⁶ He asked them, "What are you arguing with them about?"

³⁷ The next day, when they came down from the mountain, a large crowd met him. ³⁸ Just then a man from the crowd cried out,

because he has seizures and suffers terribly. He often falls into the fire and often into the water. [16] I brought him to your disciples, but they couldn't heal him."

[17] Jesus replied, "You unbelieving and perverse generation, how long will I be with you? How long must I put up with you? Bring him here to me." [18] Then Jesus rebuked the demon, and it came out of him, and from that moment the boy was healed.

[19] Then the disciples approached Jesus privately and said, "Why couldn't we drive it out?"

[20] "Because of your little faith," he told them. "For truly I tell you, if you have faith the size of a mustard seed, you will tell this mountain, 'Move from here to there,' and it will move. Nothing will be impossible for you."

[17] Someone from the crowd answered him, "Teacher, I brought my son to you. He has a spirit that makes him unable to speak. [18] Whenever it seizes him, it throws him down, and he foams at the mouth, grinds his teeth, and becomes rigid. I asked your disciples to drive it out, but they couldn't."

[19] He replied to them, "You unbelieving generation, how long will I be with you? How long must I put up with you? Bring him to me." [20] So they brought the boy to him. When the spirit saw him, it immediately threw the boy into convulsions. He fell to the ground and rolled around, foaming at the mouth. [21] "How long has this been happening to him?" Jesus asked his father.

"From childhood," he said. [22] "And many times it has thrown him into fire or water to destroy him. But if you can do anything, have compassion on us and help us."

[23] Jesus said to him, " 'If you can'? Everything is possible for the one who believes."

[24] Immediately the father of the boy cried out, "I do believe; help my unbelief!"

[25] When Jesus saw that a crowd was quickly gathering, he rebuked the unclean spirit, saying to it, "You mute and deaf spirit, I command you: Come out of him and never enter him again."

[26] Then it came out, shrieking and throwing him into terrible convulsions. The boy became like a corpse, so that many said, "He's dead." [27] But Jesus, taking him by the hand, raised him, and he stood up.

[28] After he had gone into the house, his disciples asked him privately, "Why couldn't we drive it out?"

[29] And he told them, "This kind can come out by nothing but prayer."

"Teacher, I beg you to look at my son, because he's my only child. [39] A spirit seizes him; suddenly he shrieks, and it throws him into convulsions until he foams at the mouth; severely bruising him, it scarcely ever leaves him. [40] I begged your disciples to drive it out, but they couldn't."

[41] Jesus replied, "You unbelieving and perverse generation, how long will I be with you and put up with you? Bring your son here."

[42] As the boy was still approaching, the demon knocked him down and threw him into severe convulsions. But Jesus rebuked the unclean spirit, healed the boy, and gave him back to his father.

JESUS'S SECOND PREDICTION OF HIS DEATH

MT 17:22-23   MK 9:30-32   LK 9:43-45

All three Gospel writers build upon the first prediction, creating momentum as Jesus makes his way toward Jerusalem and the cross. Perhaps the only significant variation is the way in which Mark and Luke more explicitly mention the inability of the disciples to understand such a claim.

[22] As they were gathering together in Galilee, Jesus told them, "The Son of Man is about to be betrayed into the hands of men. [23] They will kill him, and on the third day he will be raised up." And they were deeply distressed.

[30] Then they left that place and made their way through Galilee, but he did not want anyone to know it. [31] For he was teaching his disciples and telling them, "The Son of Man is going to be betrayed into the hands of men. They will kill him, and after he is killed, he will rise three days later." [32] But they did not understand this statement, and they were afraid to ask him.

[43] And they were all astonished at the greatness of God.

While everyone was amazed at all the things he was doing, he told his disciples, [44] "Let these words sink in: The Son of Man is about to be betrayed into the hands of men."

[45] But they did not understand this statement; it was concealed from them so that they could not grasp it, and they were afraid to ask him about it.

²⁴ When they came to Capernaum, those who collected the temple tax approached Peter and said, "Doesn't your teacher pay the temple tax?"

²⁵ "Yes," he said.

When he went into the house, Jesus spoke to him first, "What do you think, Simon? From whom do earthly kings collect tariffs or taxes? From their sons or from strangers?"

²⁶ "From strangers," he said.

"Then the sons are free," Jesus told him. ²⁷ "But, so we won't offend them, go to the sea, cast in a fishhook, and take the first fish that you catch. When you open its mouth you'll find a coin. Take it and give it to them for me and you."

THE ARGUMENT ABOUT BEING GREATEST

MT 18:1-5   MK 9:33-37   LK 9:46-48

In all three Gospels, Jesus addresses the disciples' debate about which of them was the greatest in the same way, setting up a child as the paradigm for kingdom greatness. Mark, however, conflates what are two different stories in Matthew. The latter saves Jesus's paradoxical teaching on kingdom discipleship (i.e., whoever wants to be "first/great" must be "last/servant") for his third and final passion prediction (see Mt 20:26-28).

¹ At that time the disciples came to Jesus and asked, "So who is greatest in the kingdom of heaven?" ² He called a child and had him stand among them. ³ "Truly I tell you," he said, "unless you turn and become like children, you will never enter the kingdom of heaven. ⁴ Therefore, whoever humbles himself like this child — this one is the greatest in the kingdom of heaven. ⁵ And whoever welcomes one child like this in my name welcomes me."

³³ They came to Capernaum. When he was in the house, he asked them, "What were you arguing about on the way?" ³⁴ But they were silent, because on the way they had been arguing with one another about who was the greatest. ³⁵ Sitting down, he called the Twelve and said to them, "If anyone wants to be first, he must be last and servant of all." ³⁶ He took a child, had him stand among them, and taking him in his arms, he said to them, ³⁷ "Whoever welcomes one little child such as this in my name welcomes me. And whoever welcomes me does not welcome me, but him who sent me."

⁴⁶ An argument started among them about who was the greatest of them. ⁴⁷ But Jesus, knowing their inner thoughts, took a little child and had him stand next to him. ⁴⁸ He told them, "Whoever welcomes this little child in my name welcomes me. And whoever welcomes me welcomes him who sent me. For whoever is least among you — this one is great."

JESUS ALLOWS OTHERS TO EXORCISE DEMONS IN HIS NAME

MK 9:38-41   LK 9:49-50

Mark and Luke include this brief account of someone manifesting some of the same healing powers as Jesus's disciples. It is best to see this as another demonstration of rivalry among Jesus's closest followers (see "The Argument about Being Greatest" above), as well as an indication of the ultimate expansion of the kingdom of God through, yet beyond, the immediate twelve disciples.

³⁸ John said to him, "Teacher, we saw someone driving out demons in your name, and we tried to stop him because he wasn't following us."

³⁹ "Don't stop him," said Jesus, "because there is no one who will perform a miracle in my name who can soon afterward speak evil of me. ⁴⁰ For whoever is not against us is for us. ⁴¹ And whoever gives you a cup of water to drink in my name, because you belong to Christ — truly I tell you, he will never lose his reward."

⁴⁹ John responded, "Master, we saw someone driving out demons in your name, and we tried to stop him because he does not follow us."

⁵⁰ "Don't stop him," Jesus told him, "because whoever is not against you is for you."

In Matthew this piercing admonition flows from the focus on "little ones" who were previously upheld as the paradigm for kingdom greatness. The reference to the "cutting off a hand" or "gouging out an eye" uses the same hyperbolic reasoning that appears in one of the earlier antitheses (cp. Mt 5:29-30). Yet, the metaphor is now generalized to include offences to oneself or others that cause irreparable spiritual damage. Mark conveys the same message with a bit more penetrating language. Interestingly, he adds a saying about "salt" that is closely paralleled in Matthew's Sermon on the Mount (cp. 5:13). Yet, such a saying was likely spoken by Jesus on a number of occasions.

6 "But whoever causes one of these little ones who believe in me to fall away — it would be better for him if a heavy millstone were hung around his neck and he were drowned in the depths of the sea. **7** Woe to the world because of offenses. For offenses will inevitably come, but woe to that person by whom the offense comes. **8** If your hand or your foot causes you to fall away, cut it off and throw it away. It is better for you to enter life maimed or lame than to have two hands or two feet and be thrown into the eternal fire. **9** And if your eye causes you to fall away, gouge it out and throw it away. It is better for you to enter life with one eye than to have two eyes and be thrown into hellfire.

10 "See to it that you don't despise one of these little ones, because I tell you that in heaven their angels continually view the face of my Father in heaven."

42 "But whoever causes one of these little ones who believe in me to fall away — it would be better for him if a heavy millstone were hung around his neck and he were thrown into the sea.

43 "And if your hand causes you to fall away, cut it off. It is better for you to enter life maimed than to have two hands and go to hell, the unquenchable fire. **45** And if your foot causes you to fall away, cut it off. It is better for you to enter life lame than to have two feet and be thrown into hell. **47** And if your eye causes you to fall away, gouge it out. It is better for you to enter the kingdom of God with one eye than to have two eyes and be thrown into hell, **48** where **their worm does not die, and the fire is not quenched.** **49** For everyone will be salted with fire. **50** Salt is good, but if the salt should lose its flavor, how can you season it? Have salt among yourselves, and be at peace with one another."

THE PARABLE OF THE LOST SHEEP

12 "What do you think? If someone has a hundred sheep, and one of them goes astray, won't he leave the ninety-nine on the hillside and go and search for the stray? **13** And if he finds it, truly I tell you, he rejoices over that sheep more than over the ninety-nine that did not go astray. **14** In the same way, it is not the will of your Father in heaven that one of these little ones perish."

JESUS SPEAKS ABOUT RESTORING A BROTHER

15 "If your brother sins against you, go and rebuke him in private. If he listens to you, you have won your brother. **16** But if he won't listen, take one or two others with you, so that **by the testimony of two or three witnesses every fact may be established.** **17** If he doesn't pay attention to them, tell the church. If he doesn't pay attention even to the church, let him be like a Gentile and a tax collector to you. **18** Truly I tell you, whatever you bind on earth will have been bound in heaven, and whatever you loose on earth will have been loosed in heaven. **19** Again, truly I tell you, if two of you on earth agree about any matter that you pray for, it will be done for you by my Father in heaven. **20** For where two or three are gathered together in my name, I am there among them."

THE PARABLE OF THE UNFORGIVING SERVANT

21 Then Peter approached him and asked, "Lord, how many times shall I forgive my brother or sister who sins against me? As many as seven times?"

22 "I tell you, not as many as seven," Jesus replied, "but seventy times seven.

MATTHEW   MARK   LUKE   JOHN

23 "For this reason, the kingdom of heaven can be compared to a king who wanted to settle accounts with his servants. **24** When he began to settle accounts, one who owed ten thousand talents was brought before him. **25** Since he did not have the money to pay it back, his master commanded that he, his wife, his children, and everything he had be sold to pay the debt.

26 "At this, the servant fell facedown before him and said, 'Be patient with me, and I will pay you everything.' **27** Then the master of that servant had compassion, released him, and forgave him the loan.

28 "That servant went out and found one of his fellow servants who owed him a hundred denarii. He grabbed him, started choking him, and said, 'Pay what you owe!'

29 "At this, his fellow servant fell down and began begging him, 'Be patient with me, and I will pay you back.' **30** But he wasn't willing. Instead, he went and threw him into prison until he could pay what was owed. **31** When the other servants saw what had taken place, they were deeply distressed and went and reported to their master everything that had happened. **32** Then, after he had summoned him, his master said to him, 'You wicked servant! I forgave you all that debt because you begged me. **33** Shouldn't you also have had mercy on your fellow servant, as I had mercy on you?' **34** And because he was angry, his master handed him over to the jailers to be tortured until he could pay everything that was owed. **35** So also my heavenly Father will do to you unless every one of you forgives his brother or sister from your heart."

JESUS AND HIS BROTHERS JN 7:1-9

1 After this, Jesus traveled in Galilee, since he did not want to travel in Judea because the Jews were trying to kill him. **2** The Jewish Festival of Shelters was near. **3** So his brothers said to him, "Leave here and go to Judea so your disciples can see your works that you are doing. **4** For no one does anything in secret while he's seeking public recognition. If you do these things, show yourself to the world." **5** (For not even his brothers believed in him.)

6 Jesus told them, "My time has not yet arrived, but your time is always at hand. **7** The world cannot hate you, but it does hate me because I testify about it — that its works are evil. **8** Go up to the festival yourselves. I'm not going up to this festival, because my time has not yet fully come." **9** After he had said these things, he stayed in Galilee.

JESUS TURNS HIS FOCUS TOWARD JUDEA

JESUS TRAVELS SOUTH TOWARD JERUSALEM   MT 19:1-2   MK 10:1   LK 9:51   JN 7:10

All four Gospel writers record a significant shift in Jesus's ministry where he sets his sights on Jerusalem. However, each author presents that moment with a different level of significance in relation to its role in his narrative. Matthew and Mark draw less attention to Jerusalem as the objective; yet, for both, these transitional verses mark a section that is characterized by sustained conflict between Jesus and the religious officials that builds toward the passion. Luke is the most overt in giving the reason for Jesus's move toward Jerusalem—namely, because the time had come for him to be "taken up." This narrative cue alerts the reader to the significance of the following events. John associates the shift more narrowly with a feast and states that he went up alone. There need not be any conflict with the Synoptic accounts since John is likely drawing significance from a different moment of Jesus's journey to Jerusalem.

1 When Jesus had finished saying these things, he departed from Galilee and went to the region of Judea across the Jordan. 2 Large crowds followed him, and he healed them there.

1 He set out from there and went to the region of Judea and across the Jordan. Then crowds converged on him again, and as was his custom he taught them again.

51 When the days were coming to a close for him to be taken up, he determined to journey to Jerusalem.

10 After his brothers had gone up to the festival, then he also went up, not openly but secretly.

JESUS IS REJECTED IN A SAMARITAN VILLAGE   LK 9:52-56

52 He sent messengers ahead of himself, and on the way they entered a village of the Samaritans to make preparations for him. 53 But they did not welcome him, because he determined to journey to Jerusalem. 54 When the disciples James and John saw this, they said, "Lord, do you want us to call down fire from heaven to consume them?"
55 But he turned and rebuked them, 56 and they went to another village.

THE CONSEQUENCES OF FOLLOWING JESUS   MT 8:18-22   LK 9:57-62

Matthew and Luke both record a brief encounter between Jesus and what appears to be a number of vacillating followers. The focus is on the cost of discipleship, and the few differences between the two accounts could be explained by the fact the Jesus likely spoke on discipleship in this way on a number of occasions during his ministry.

18 When Jesus saw a large crowd around him, he gave the order to go to the other side of the sea. 19 A scribe approached him and said, "Teacher, I will follow you wherever you go."
20 Jesus told him, "Foxes have dens, and birds of the sky have nests, but the Son of Man has no place to lay his head."
21 "Lord," another of his disciples said, "first let me go bury my father."
22 But Jesus told him, "Follow me, and let the dead bury their own dead."

57 As they were traveling on the road someone said to him, "I will follow you wherever you go."
58 Jesus told him, "Foxes have dens, and birds of the sky have nests, but the Son of Man has no place to lay his head." 59 Then he said to another, "Follow me."
"Lord," he said, "first let me go bury my father."
60 But he told him, "Let the dead bury their own dead, but you go and spread the news of the kingdom of God."

⁶¹ Another said, "I will follow you, Lord, but first let me go and say good-bye to those at my house."

⁶² But Jesus said to him, "No one who puts his hand to the plow and looks back is fit for the kingdom of God."

JESUS IN JERUSALEM AT THE FESTIVAL OF SHELTERS

JN 7:11-24

¹¹ The Jews were looking for him at the festival and saying, "Where is he?" ¹² And there was a lot of murmuring about him among the crowds. Some were saying, "He's a good man." Others were saying, "No, on the contrary, he's deceiving the people." ¹³ Still, nobody was talking publicly about him for fear of the Jews.

¹⁴ When the festival was already half over, Jesus went up into the temple and began to teach. ¹⁵ Then the Jews were amazed and said, "How is this man so learned, since he hasn't been trained?"

¹⁶ Jesus answered them, "My teaching isn't mine but is from the one who sent me. ¹⁷ If anyone wants to do his will, he will know whether the teaching is from God or whether I am speaking on my own. ¹⁸ The one who speaks on his own seeks his own glory; but he who seeks the glory of the one who sent him is true, and there is no unrighteousness in him. ¹⁹ Didn't Moses give you the law? Yet none of you keeps the law. Why are you trying to kill me?"

²⁰ "You have a demon!" the crowd responded. "Who is trying to kill you?"

²¹ "I performed one work, and you are all amazed," Jesus answered. ²² "This is why Moses has given you circumcision — not that it comes from Moses but from the fathers — and you circumcise a man on the Sabbath. ²³ If a man receives circumcision on the Sabbath so that the law of Moses won't be broken, are you angry at me because I made a man entirely well on the Sabbath? ²⁴ Stop judging according to outward appearances; rather judge according to righteous judgment."

ARGUMENTS OVER JESUS'S MESSIANIC CLAIMS

JN 7:25-53

²⁵ Some of the people of Jerusalem were saying, "Isn't this the man they are trying to kill? ²⁶ Yet, look, he's speaking publicly and they're saying nothing to him. Can it be true that the authorities know he is the Messiah? ²⁷ But we know where this man is from. When the Messiah comes, nobody will know where he is from."

²⁸ As he was teaching in the temple, Jesus cried out, "You know me and you know where I am from. Yet I have not come on my own, but the one who sent me is true. You don't know him; ²⁹ I know him because I am from him, and he sent me."

³⁰ Then they tried to seize him. Yet no one laid a hand on him because his hour had not yet come. ³¹ However, many from the crowd believed in him and said, "When the Messiah comes, he won't perform more signs than this man has done, will he?" ³² The Pharisees heard the crowd murmuring these things about him, and so the chief priests and the Pharisees sent servants to arrest him.

³³ Then Jesus said, "I am only with you for a short time. Then I'm going to the one who sent me. ³⁴ You will look for me, but you will not find me; and where I am, you cannot come."

³⁵ Then the Jews said to one another, "Where does he intend to go so we won't find him? He doesn't intend to go to the Jewish people dispersed among the Greeks and teach the Greeks,

does he? **36** What is this remark he made: 'You will look for me, and you will not find me; and where I am, you cannot come'?"

37 On the last and most important day of the festival, Jesus stood up and cried out, "If anyone is thirsty, let him come to me and drink. **38** The one who believes in me, as the Scripture has said, will have streams of living water flow from deep within him." **39** He said this about the Spirit. Those who believed in Jesus were going to receive the Spirit, for the Spirit had not yet been given because Jesus had not yet been glorified.

40 When some from the crowd heard these words, they said, "This truly is the Prophet." **41** Others said, "This is the Messiah." But some said, "Surely the Messiah doesn't come from Galilee, does he? **42** Doesn't the Scripture say that the Messiah comes from David's offspring and from the town of Bethlehem, where David lived?" **43** So the crowd was divided because of him. **44** Some of them wanted to seize him, but no one laid hands on him.

45 Then the servants came to the chief priests and Pharisees, who asked them, "Why didn't you bring him?"

46 The servants answered, "No man ever spoke like this!"

47 Then the Pharisees responded to them: "Are you fooled too? **48** Have any of the rulers or Pharisees believed in him? **49** But this crowd, which doesn't know the law, is accursed."

50 Nicodemus — the one who came to him previously and who was one of them — said to them, **51** "Our law doesn't judge a man before it hears from him and knows what he's doing, does it?"

52 "You aren't from Galilee too, are you?" they replied. "Investigate and you will see that no prophet arises from Galilee."

53 Then each one went to his house.

JESUS FORGIVES AN ADULTERESS   JN 8:1-11

---

1 But Jesus went to the Mount of Olives.

2 At dawn he went to the temple again, and all the people were coming to him. He sat down and began to teach them.

3 Then the scribes and the Pharisees brought a woman caught in adultery, making her stand in the center. **4** "Teacher," they said to him, "this woman was caught in the act of committing adultery. **5** In the law Moses commanded us to stone such women. So what do you say?" **6** They asked this to trap him, in order that they might have evidence to accuse him.

Jesus stooped down and started writing on the ground with his finger. **7** When they persisted in questioning him, he stood up and said to them, "The one without sin among you should be the first to throw a stone at her." **8** Then he stooped down again and continued writing on the ground. **9** When they heard this, they left one by one, starting with the older men. Only he was left, with the woman in the center. **10** When Jesus stood up, he said to her, "Woman, where are they? Has no one condemned you?"

11 "No one, Lord," she answered.

"Neither do I condemn you," said Jesus. "Go, and from now on do not sin anymore."

JESUS CLAIMS TO BE THE LIGHT OF THE WORLD   JN 8:12-20

---

12 Jesus spoke to them again: "I am the light of the world. Anyone who follows me will never walk in the darkness but will have the light of life."

---

¹³ So the Pharisees said to him, "You are testifying about yourself. Your testimony is not valid."

¹⁴ "Even if I testify about myself," Jesus replied, "My testimony is true, because I know where I came from and where I'm going. But you don't know where I come from or where I'm going. ¹⁵ You judge by human standards. I judge no one. ¹⁶ And if I do judge, my judgment is true, because it is not I alone who judge, but I and the Father who sent me. ¹⁷ Even in your law it is written that the testimony of two witnesses is true. ¹⁸ I am the one who testifies about myself, and the Father who sent me testifies about me."

¹⁹ Then they asked him, "Where is your Father?"

"You know neither me nor my Father," Jesus answered. "If you knew me, you would also know my Father." ²⁰ He spoke these words by the treasury, while teaching in the temple. But no one seized him, because his hour had not yet come.

JESUS PREDICTS HIS DEPARTURE

JN 8:21-29

²¹ Then he said to them again, "I'm going away; you will look for me, and you will die in your sin. Where I'm going, you cannot come."

²² So the Jews said again, "He won't kill himself, will he, since he says, 'Where I'm going, you cannot come'?"

²³ "You are from below," he told them, "I am from above. You are of this world; I am not of this world. ²⁴ Therefore I told you that you will die in your sins. For if you do not believe that I am he, you will die in your sins."

²⁵ "Who are you?" they questioned.

"Exactly what I've been telling you from the very beginning," Jesus told them. ²⁶ "I have many things to say and to judge about you, but the one who sent me is true, and what I have heard from him — these things I tell the world."

²⁷ They did not know he was speaking to them about the Father. ²⁸ So Jesus said to them, "When you lift up the Son of Man, then you will know that I am he, and that I do nothing on my own. But just as the Father taught me, I say these things. ²⁹ The one who sent me is with me. He has not left me alone, because I always do what pleases him."

CHILDREN OF ABRAHAM AND CHILDREN OF GOD

JN 8:30-59

³⁰ As he was saying these things, many believed in him.

³¹ Then Jesus said to the Jews who had believed him, "If you continue in my word, you really are my disciples. ³² You will know the truth, and the truth will set you free."

³³ "We are descendants of Abraham," they answered him, "and we have never been enslaved to anyone. How can you say, 'You will become free'?"

³⁴ Jesus responded, "Truly I tell you, everyone who commits sin is a slave of sin. ³⁵ A slave does not remain in the household forever, but a son does remain forever. ³⁶ So if the Son sets you free, you really will be free. ³⁷ I know you are descendants of Abraham, but you are trying to kill me because my word has no place among you. ³⁸ I speak what I have seen in the presence of the Father; so then, you do what you have heard from your father."

³⁹ "Our father is Abraham," they replied.

"If you were Abraham's children," Jesus told them, "you would do what Abraham did. ⁴⁰ But now you are trying to kill me, a man who has told you the truth that I heard from God. Abraham did not do this. ⁴¹ You're doing what your father does."

"We weren't born of sexual immorality," they said. "We have one Father — God."

⁴² Jesus said to them, "If God were your Father, you would love me, because I came from God and I am here. For I didn't come on my own, but he sent me. ⁴³ Why don't you understand what I say? Because you cannot listen to my word. ⁴⁴ You are of your father the devil, and you want to carry out your father's desires. He was a murderer from the beginning and does not stand in the truth, because there is no truth in him. When he tells a lie, he speaks from his own nature, because he is a liar and the father of lies. ⁴⁵ Yet because I tell the truth, you do not believe me. ⁴⁶ Who among you can convict me of sin? If I am telling the truth, why don't you believe me? ⁴⁷ The one who is from God listens to God's words. This is why you don't listen, because you are not from God."

⁴⁸ The Jews responded to him, "Aren't we right in saying that you're a Samaritan and have a demon?"

⁴⁹ "I do not have a demon," Jesus answered. "On the contrary, I honor my Father and you dishonor me. ⁵⁰ I do not seek my own glory; there is one who seeks it and judges. ⁵¹ Truly I tell you, if anyone keeps my word, he will never see death."

⁵² Then the Jews said, "Now we know you have a demon. Abraham died and so did the prophets. You say, 'If anyone keeps my word, he will never taste death.' ⁵³ Are you greater than our father Abraham who died? And the prophets died. Who do you claim to be?"

⁵⁴ "If I glorify myself," Jesus answered, "my glory is nothing. My Father — about whom you say, 'He is our God' — he is the one who glorifies me. ⁵⁵ You do not know him, but I know him. If I were to say I don't know him, I would be a liar like you. But I do know him, and I keep his word. ⁵⁶ Your father Abraham rejoiced to see my day; he saw it and was glad."

⁵⁷ The Jews replied, "You aren't fifty years old yet, and you've seen Abraham?"

⁵⁸ Jesus said to them, "Truly I tell you, before Abraham was, I am."

⁵⁹ So they picked up stones to throw at him. But Jesus was hidden and went out of the temple.

JESUS HEALS A MAN WHO WAS BORN BLIND   JN 9:1-12

---

¹ As he was passing by, he saw a man blind from birth. ² His disciples asked him: "Rabbi, who sinned, this man or his parents, that he was born blind?"

³ "Neither this man nor his parents sinned," Jesus answered. "This came about so that God's works might be displayed in him. ⁴ We must do the works of him who sent me while it is day. Night is coming when no one can work. ⁵ As long as I am in the world, I am the light of the world."

⁶ After he said these things he spit on the ground, made some mud from the saliva, and spread the mud on his eyes. ⁷ "Go," he told him, "wash in the pool of Siloam" (which means "Sent"). So he left, washed, and came back seeing.

⁸ His neighbors and those who had seen him before as a beggar said, "Isn't this the one who used to sit begging?" ⁹ Some said, "He's the one." Others were saying, "No, but he looks like him."

He kept saying, "I'm the one."

¹⁰ So they asked him, "Then how were your eyes opened?"

¹¹ He answered, "The man called Jesus made mud, spread it on my eyes, and told me, 'Go to Siloam and wash.' So when I went and washed I received my sight."

¹² "Where is he?" they asked.

"I don't know," he said.

¹³ They brought the man who used to be blind to the Pharisees. ¹⁴ The day that Jesus made the mud and opened his eyes was a Sabbath. ¹⁵ Then the Pharisees asked him again how he received his sight.

"He put mud on my eyes," he told them. "I washed and I can see."

¹⁶ Some of the Pharisees said, "This man is not from God, because he doesn't keep the Sabbath." But others were saying, "How can a sinful man perform such signs?" And there was a division among them.

¹⁷ Again they asked the blind man, "What do you say about him, since he opened your eyes?"

"He's a prophet," he said.

¹⁸ The Jews did not believe this about him — that he was blind and received sight — until they summoned the parents of the one who had received his sight. ¹⁹ They asked them, "Is this your son, the one you say was born blind? How then does he now see?"

²⁰ "We know this is our son and that he was born blind," his parents answered. ²¹ "But we don't know how he now sees, and we don't know who opened his eyes. Ask him; he's of age. He will speak for himself." ²² His parents said these things because they were afraid of the Jews, since the Jews had already agreed that if anyone confessed him as the Messiah, he would be banned from the synagogue. ²³ This is why his parents said, "He's of age; ask him."

²⁴ So a second time they summoned the man who had been blind and told him, "Give glory to God. We know that this man is a sinner."

²⁵ He answered, "Whether or not he's a sinner, I don't know. One thing I do know: I was blind, and now I can see!"

²⁶ Then they asked him, "What did he do to you? How did he open your eyes?"

²⁷ "I already told you," he said, "and you didn't listen. Why do you want to hear it again? You don't want to become his disciples too, do you?"

²⁸ They ridiculed him: "You're that man's disciple, but we're Moses's disciples. ²⁹ We know that God has spoken to Moses. But this man — we don't know where he's from."

³⁰ "This is an amazing thing!" the man told them. "You don't know where he is from, and yet he opened my eyes. ³¹ We know that God doesn't listen to sinners, but if anyone is God-fearing and does his will, he listens to him. ³² Throughout history no one has ever heard of someone opening the eyes of a person born blind. ³³ If this man were not from God, he wouldn't be able to do anything."

³⁴ "You were born entirely in sin," they replied, "and are you trying to teach us?" Then they threw him out.

THE BLIND MAN'S SIGHT AND THE PHARISEES' BLINDNESS

³⁵ Jesus heard that they had thrown the man out, and when he found him, he asked, "Do you believe in the Son of Man?"

³⁶ "Who is he, Sir, that I may believe in him?" he asked.

³⁷ Jesus answered, "You have seen him; in fact, he is the one speaking with you."

³⁸ "I believe, Lord!" he said, and he worshiped him.

³⁹ Jesus said, "I came into this world for judgment, in order that those who do not see will see and those who do see will become blind."

40 Some of the Pharisees who were with him heard these things and asked him, "We aren't blind too, are we?"

41 "If you were blind," Jesus told them, "you wouldn't have sin. But now that you say, 'We see,' your sin remains."

JESUS IS THE GOOD SHEPHERD   JN 10:1-21

---

1 "Truly I tell you, anyone who doesn't enter the sheep pen by the gate but climbs in some other way is a thief and a robber. **2** The one who enters by the gate is the shepherd of the sheep. **3** The gatekeeper opens it for him, and the sheep hear his voice. He calls his own sheep by name and leads them out. **4** When he has brought all his own outside, he goes ahead of them. The sheep follow him because they know his voice. **5** They will never follow a stranger; instead they will run away from him, because they don't know the voice of strangers." **6** Jesus gave them this figure of speech, but they did not understand what he was telling them.

7 Jesus said again, "Truly I tell you, I am the gate for the sheep. **8** All who came before me are thieves and robbers, but the sheep didn't listen to them. **9** I am the gate. If anyone enters by me, he will be saved and will come in and go out and find pasture. **10** A thief comes only to steal and kill and destroy. I have come so that they may have life and have it in abundance.

11 "I am the good shepherd. The good shepherd lays down his life for the sheep. **12** The hired hand, since he is not the shepherd and doesn't own the sheep, leaves them and runs away when he sees a wolf coming. The wolf then snatches and scatters them. **13** This happens because he is a hired hand and doesn't care about the sheep.

14 "I am the good shepherd. I know my own, and my own know me, **15** just as the Father knows me, and I know the Father. I lay down my life for the sheep. **16** But I have other sheep that are not from this sheep pen; I must bring them also, and they will listen to my voice. Then there will be one flock, one shepherd. **17** This is why the Father loves me, because I lay down my life so that I may take it up again. **18** No one takes it from me, but I lay it down on my own. I have the right to lay it down, and I have the right to take it up again. I have received this command from my Father."

19 Again the Jews were divided because of these words. **20** Many of them were saying, "He has a demon and he's crazy. Why do you listen to him?" **21** Others were saying, "These aren't the words of someone who is demon-possessed. Can a demon open the eyes of the blind?"

THE SENDING OUT AND RETURN OF SEVENTY-TWO MESSENGERS   LK 10:1-24

---

1 After this, the Lord appointed seventy-two others, and he sent them ahead of him in pairs to every town and place where he himself was about to go. **2** He told them, "The harvest is abundant, but the workers are few. Therefore, pray to the Lord of the harvest to send out workers into his harvest. **3** Now go; I'm sending you out like lambs among wolves. **4** Don't carry a money-bag, traveling bag, or sandals; don't greet anyone along the road. **5** Whatever house you enter, first say, 'Peace to this household.' **6** If a person of peace is there, your peace will rest on him; but if not, it will return to you. **7** Remain in the same house, eating and drinking what they offer, for the worker is worthy of his wages. Don't move from house to house. **8** When you enter any town, and they welcome you, eat the things set before you. **9** Heal the sick who are there, and tell them, 'The kingdom of God has come near you.' **10** When you enter any town, and they don't welcome you, go out into its streets and say, **11** 'We are wiping off even the dust of your

---

town that clings to our feet as a witness against you. Know this for certain: The kingdom of God has come near.' [12] I tell you, on that day it will be more tolerable for Sodom than for that town.

[13] "Woe to you, Chorazin! Woe to you, Bethsaida! For if the miracles that were done in you had been done in Tyre and Sidon, they would have repented long ago, sitting in sackcloth and ashes. [14] But it will be more tolerable for Tyre and Sidon at the judgment than for you. [15] And you, Capernaum, will you be exalted to heaven? No, you will go down to Hades. [16] Whoever listens to you listens to me. Whoever rejects you rejects me. And whoever rejects me rejects the one who sent me."

[17] The seventy-two returned with joy, saying, "Lord, even the demons submit to us in your name."

[18] He said to them, "I watched Satan fall from heaven like lightning. [19] Look, I have given you the authority to trample on snakes and scorpions and over all the power of the enemy; nothing at all will harm you. [20] However, don't rejoice that the spirits submit to you, but rejoice that your names are written in heaven."

[21] At that time he rejoiced in the Holy Spirit and said, "I praise you, Father, Lord of heaven and earth, because you have hidden these things from the wise and intelligent and revealed them to infants. Yes, Father, because this was your good pleasure. [22] All things have been entrusted to me by my Father. No one knows who the Son is except the Father, and who the Father is except the Son, and anyone to whom the Son desires to reveal him."

[23] Then turning to his disciples he said privately, "Blessed are the eyes that see the things you see! [24] For I tell you that many prophets and kings wanted to see the things you see but didn't see them; to hear the things you hear but didn't hear them."

THE PARABLE OF THE GOOD SAMARITAN

LK 10:25-37

[25] Then an expert in the law stood up to test him, saying, "Teacher, what must I do to inherit eternal life?"

[26] "What is written in the law?" he asked him. "How do you read it?"

[27] He answered, **"Love the Lord your God with all your heart, with all your soul, with all your strength, and with all your mind;"** and **"your neighbor as yourself."**

[28] "You've answered correctly," he told him. "Do this and you will live."

[29] But wanting to justify himself, he asked Jesus, "And who is my neighbor?"

[30] Jesus took up the question and said: "A man was going down from Jerusalem to Jericho and fell into the hands of robbers. They stripped him, beat him up, and fled, leaving him half dead. [31] A priest happened to be going down that road. When he saw him, he passed by on the other side. [32] In the same way, a Levite, when he arrived at the place and saw him, passed by on the other side. [33] But a Samaritan on his journey came up to him, and when he saw the man, he had compassion. [34] He went over to him and bandaged his wounds, pouring on olive oil and wine. Then he put him on his own animal, brought him to an inn, and took care of him. [35] The next day he took out two denarii, gave them to the innkeeper, and said, 'Take care of him. When I come back I'll reimburse you for whatever extra you spend.'

[36] "Which of these three do you think proved to be a neighbor to the man who fell into the hands of the robbers?"

[37] "The one who showed mercy to him," he said.

Then Jesus told him, "Go and do the same."

[38] While they were traveling, he entered a village, and a woman named Martha welcomed him into her home. [39] She had a sister named Mary, who also sat at the Lord's feet and was listening to what he said. [40] But Martha was distracted by her many tasks, and she came up and asked, "Lord, don't you care that my sister has left me to serve alone? So tell her to give me a hand."

[41] The Lord answered her, "Martha, Martha, you are worried and upset about many things, [42] but one thing is necessary. Mary has made the right choice, and it will not be taken away from her."

JESUS TEACHES ABOUT PRAYER

[1] He was praying in a certain place, and when he finished, one of his disciples said to him, "Lord, teach us to pray, just as John also taught his disciples."

[2] He said to them, "Whenever you pray, say,

Father,
your name be honored as holy.
Your kingdom come.
[3]   Give us each day our daily bread.
[4]   And forgive us our sins,
for we ourselves also forgive everyone
in debt to us.
And do not bring us into temptation."

[5] He also said to them: "Suppose one of you has a friend and goes to him at midnight and says to him, 'Friend, lend me three loaves of bread, [6] because a friend of mine on a journey has come to me, and I don't have anything to offer him.' [7] Then he will answer from inside and say, 'Don't bother me! The door is already locked, and my children and I have gone to bed. I can't get up to give you anything.' [8] I tell you, even though he won't get up and give him anything because he is his friend, yet because of his friend's shameless boldness, he will get up and give him as much as he needs.

[9] "So I say to you, ask, and it will be given to you. Seek, and you will find. Knock, and the door will be opened to you. [10] For everyone who asks receives, and the one who seeks finds, and to the one who knocks, the door will be opened. [11] What father among you, if his son asks for a fish, will give him a snake instead of a fish? [12] Or if he asks for an egg, will give him a scorpion? [13] If you then, who are evil, know how to give good gifts to your children, how much more will the heavenly Father give the Holy Spirit to those who ask him?"

JESUS TEACHES ABOUT THE LIGHT OF THE BODY

[33] "No one lights a lamp and puts it in the cellar or under a basket, but on a lampstand, so that those who come in may see its light. [34] Your eye is the lamp of the body. When your eye is healthy, your whole body is also full of light. But when it is bad, your body is also full of darkness. [35] Take care, then, that the light in you is not darkness. [36] If, therefore, your whole body is full of light, with no part of it in darkness, it will be entirely illuminated, as when a lamp shines its light on you."

[37] As he was speaking, a Pharisee asked him to dine with him. So he went in and reclined at the table. [38] When the Pharisee saw this, he was amazed that he did not first perform the ritual washing before dinner. [39] But the Lord said to him, "Now you Pharisees clean the outside of the cup and dish, but inside you are full of greed and evil. [40] Fools! Didn't he who made the outside make the inside too? [41] But give from what is within to the poor, and then everything is clean for you.

[42] "But woe to you Pharisees! You give a tenth of mint, rue, and every kind of herb, and you bypass justice and love for God. These things you should have done without neglecting the others.

[43] "Woe to you Pharisees! You love the front seat in the synagogues and greetings in the marketplaces.

[44] "Woe to you! You are like unmarked graves; the people who walk over them don't know it."

[45] One of the experts in the law answered him, "Teacher, when you say these things you insult us too."

[46] Then he said: "Woe also to you experts in the law! You load people with burdens that are hard to carry, and yet you yourselves don't touch these burdens with one of your fingers.

[47] "Woe to you! You build tombs for the prophets, and your fathers killed them. [48] Therefore, you are witnesses that you approve the deeds of your fathers, for they killed them, and you build their monuments. [49] Because of this, the wisdom of God said, 'I will send them prophets and apostles, and some of them they will kill and persecute,' [50] so that this generation may be held responsible for the blood of all the prophets shed since the foundation of the world — [51] from the blood of Abel to the blood of Zechariah, who perished between the altar and the sanctuary.

"Yes, I tell you, this generation will be held responsible.

[52] "Woe to you experts in the law! You have taken away the key to knowledge. You didn't go in yourselves, and you hindered those who were trying to go in."

[53] When he left there, the scribes and the Pharisees began to oppose him fiercely and to cross-examine him about many things; [54] they were lying in wait for him to trap him in something he said.

JESUS DENOUNCES HYPOCRISY AND ENCOURAGES FEARLESSNESS

[1] Meanwhile, a crowd of many thousands came together, so that they were trampling on one another. He began to say to his disciples first, "Be on your guard against the leaven of the Pharisees, which is hypocrisy. [2] There is nothing covered that won't be uncovered, nothing hidden that won't be made known. [3] Therefore, whatever you have said in the dark will be heard in the light, and what you have whispered in an ear in private rooms will be proclaimed on the housetops.

[4] "I say to you, my friends, don't fear those who kill the body, and after that can do nothing more. [5] But I will show you the one to fear: Fear him who has authority to throw people into hell after death. Yes, I say to you, this is the one to fear! [6] Aren't five sparrows sold for two pennies? Yet not one of them is forgotten in God's sight. [7] Indeed, the hairs of your head are all counted. Don't be afraid; you are worth more than many sparrows.

[8] "And I say to you, anyone who acknowledges me before others, the Son of Man will also acknowledge him before the angels of God, [9] but whoever denies me before others will be denied

before the angels of God. [10] Anyone who speaks a word against the Son of Man will be forgiven, but the one who blasphemes against the Holy Spirit will not be forgiven. [11] Whenever they bring you before synagogues and rulers and authorities, don't worry about how you should defend yourselves or what you should say. [12] For the Holy Spirit will teach you at that very hour what must be said."

THE PARABLE OF THE RICH FOOL

[13] Someone from the crowd said to him, "Teacher, tell my brother to divide the inheritance with me."

[14] "Friend," he said to him, "who appointed me a judge or arbitrator over you?" [15] He then told them, "Watch out and be on guard against all greed, because one's life is not in the abundance of his possessions."

[16] Then he told them a parable: "A rich man's land was very productive. [17] He thought to himself, 'What should I do, since I don't have anywhere to store my crops? [18] I will do this,' he said. 'I'll tear down my barns and build bigger ones and store all my grain and my goods there. [19] Then I'll say to myself, "You have many goods stored up for many years. Take it easy; eat, drink, and enjoy yourself."'

[20] "But God said to him, 'You fool! This very night your life is demanded of you. And the things you have prepared—whose will they be?'

[21] "That's how it is with the one who stores up treasure for himself and is not rich toward God."

JESUS WARNS ABOUT WORRY AND FUTURE DIFFICULTIES
LK 12:22-59

[22] Then he said to his disciples: "Therefore I tell you, don't worry about your life, what you will eat; or about the body, what you will wear. [23] For life is more than food and the body more than clothing. [24] Consider the ravens: They don't sow or reap; they don't have a storeroom or a barn; yet God feeds them. Aren't you worth much more than the birds? [25] Can any of you add one moment to his life-span by worrying? [26] If then you're not able to do even a little thing, why worry about the rest?

[27] "Consider how the wildflowers grow: They don't labor or spin thread. Yet I tell you, not even Solomon in all his splendor was adorned like one of these. [28] If that's how God clothes the grass, which is in the field today and is thrown into the furnace tomorrow, how much more will he do for you—you of little faith? [29] Don't strive for what you should eat and what you should drink, and don't be anxious. [30] For the Gentile world eagerly seeks all these things, and your Father knows that you need them.

[31] "But seek his kingdom, and these things will be provided for you. [32] Don't be afraid, little flock, because your Father delights to give you the kingdom. [33] Sell your possessions and give to the poor. Make money-bags for yourselves that won't grow old, an inexhaustible treasure in heaven, where no thief comes near and no moth destroys. [34] For where your treasure is, there your heart will be also.

[35] "Be ready for service and have your lamps lit. [36] You are to be like people waiting for their master to return from the wedding banquet so that when he comes and knocks, they can open the door for him at once. [37] Blessed will be those servants the master finds alert when he comes. Truly I tell you, he will get ready, have them recline at the table, then come and serve

80   JESUS TURNS HIS FOCUS TOWARD JUDEA   MATTHEW   MARK   LUKE   JOHN

them. ³⁸ If he comes in the middle of the night, or even near dawn, and finds them alert, blessed are those servants. ³⁹ But know this: If the homeowner had known at what hour the thief was coming, he would not have let his house be broken into. ⁴⁰ You also be ready, because the Son of Man is coming at an hour you do not expect."

⁴¹ "Lord," Peter asked, "are you telling this parable to us or to everyone?"

⁴² The Lord said: "Who then is the faithful and sensible manager his master will put in charge of his household servants to give them their allotted food at the proper time? ⁴³ Blessed is that servant whom the master finds doing his job when he comes. ⁴⁴ Truly I tell you, he will put him in charge of all his possessions. ⁴⁵ But if that servant says in his heart, 'My master is delaying his coming,' and starts to beat the male and female servants, and to eat and drink and get drunk, ⁴⁶ that servant's master will come on a day he does not expect him and at an hour he does not know. He will cut him to pieces and assign him a place with the unfaithful. ⁴⁷ And that servant who knew his master's will and didn't prepare himself or do it will be severely beaten. ⁴⁸ But the one who did not know and did what deserved punishment will receive a light beating. From everyone who has been given much, much will be required; and from the one who has been entrusted with much, even more will be expected.

⁴⁹ "I came to bring fire on the earth, and how I wish it were already set ablaze! ⁵⁰ But I have a baptism to undergo, and how it consumes me until it is finished! ⁵¹ Do you think that I came here to bring peace on the earth? No, I tell you, but rather division. ⁵² From now on, five in one household will be divided: three against two, and two against three.

⁵³ They will be divided, father against son,
son against father,
mother against daughter,
daughter against mother,
mother-in-law against her daughter-in-law,
and daughter-in-law against mother-in-law."

⁵⁴ He also said to the crowds: "When you see a cloud rising in the west, right away you say, 'A storm is coming,' and so it does. ⁵⁵ And when the south wind is blowing, you say, 'It's going to be hot,' and it is. ⁵⁶ Hypocrites! You know how to interpret the appearance of the earth and the sky, but why don't you know how to interpret this present time?

⁵⁷ "Why don't you judge for yourselves what is right? ⁵⁸ As you are going with your adversary to the ruler, make an effort to settle with him on the way. Then he won't drag you before the judge, the judge hand you over to the bailiff, and the bailiff throw you into prison. ⁵⁹ I tell you, you will never get out of there until you have paid the last cent."

JESUS TEACHES ABOUT THE NEED FOR REPENTANCE   LK 13:1-9

¹ At that time, some people came and reported to him about the Galileans whose blood Pilate had mixed with their sacrifices. ² And he responded to them, "Do you think that these Galileans were more sinful than all the other Galileans because they suffered these things? ³ No, I tell you; but unless you repent, you will all perish as well. ⁴ Or those eighteen that the tower in Siloam fell on and killed — do you think they were more sinful than all the other people who live in Jerusalem? ⁵ No, I tell you; but unless you repent, you will all perish as well."

⁶ And he told this parable: "A man had a fig tree that was planted in his vineyard. He came looking for fruit on it and found none. ⁷ He told the vineyard worker, 'Listen, for three years I

have come looking for fruit on this fig tree and haven't found any. Cut it down! Why should it even waste the soil?'

⁸ "But he replied to him, 'Sir, leave it this year also, until I dig around it and fertilize it. ⁹ Perhaps it will produce fruit next year, but if not, you can cut it down.'"

JESUS HEALS THE CRIPPLED WOMAN

LK 13:10-17

¹⁰ As he was teaching in one of the synagogues on the Sabbath, ¹¹ a woman was there who had been disabled by a spirit for over eighteen years. She was bent over and could not straighten up at all. ¹² When Jesus saw her, he called out to her, "Woman, you are free of your disability." ¹³ Then he laid his hands on her, and instantly she was restored and began to glorify God.

¹⁴ But the leader of the synagogue, indignant because Jesus had healed on the Sabbath, responded by telling the crowd, "There are six days when work should be done; therefore come on those days and be healed and not on the Sabbath day."

¹⁵ But the Lord answered him and said, "Hypocrites! Doesn't each one of you untie his ox or donkey from the feeding trough on the Sabbath and lead it to water? ¹⁶ Satan has bound this woman, a daughter of Abraham, for eighteen years — shouldn't she be untied from this bondage on the Sabbath day?"

¹⁷ When he had said these things, all his adversaries were humiliated, but the whole crowd was rejoicing over all the glorious things he was doing.

JESUS IN THE TEMPLE AT THE FESTIVAL OF DEDICATION

JN 10:22-42

²² Then the Festival of Dedication took place in Jerusalem, and it was winter. ²³ Jesus was walking in the temple in Solomon's Colonnade. ²⁴ The Jews surrounded him and asked, "How long are you going to keep us in suspense? If you are the Messiah, tell us plainly."

²⁵ "I did tell you and you don't believe," Jesus answered them. "The works that I do in my Father's name testify about me. ²⁶ But you don't believe because you are not of my sheep. ²⁷ My sheep hear my voice, I know them, and they follow me. ²⁸ I give them eternal life, and they will never perish. No one will snatch them out of my hand. ²⁹ My Father, who has given them to me, is greater than all. No one is able to snatch them out of the Father's hand. ³⁰ I and the Father are one."

³¹ Again the Jews picked up rocks to stone him.

³² Jesus replied, "I have shown you many good works from the Father. For which of these works are you stoning me?"

³³ "We aren't stoning you for a good work," the Jews answered, "but for blasphemy, because you — being a man — make yourself God."

³⁴ Jesus answered them, "Isn't it written in your law, **I said, you are gods**? ³⁵ If he called those whom the word of God came to 'gods' — and the Scripture cannot be broken — ³⁶ do you say, 'You are blaspheming' to the one the Father set apart and sent into the world, because I said: I am the Son of God? ³⁷ If I am not doing my Father's works, don't believe me. ³⁸ But if I am doing them and you don't believe me, believe the works. This way you will know and understand that the Father is in me and I in the Father." ³⁹ Then they were trying again to seize him, but he eluded their grasp.

⁴⁰ So he departed again across the Jordan to the place where John had been baptizing earlier, and he remained there. ⁴¹ Many came to him and said, "John never did a sign, but everything John said about this man was true." ⁴² And many believed in him there.

[22] He went through one town and village after another, teaching and making his way to Jerusalem. [23] "Lord," someone asked him, "are only a few people going to be saved?"

He said to them, [24] "Make every effort to enter through the narrow door, because I tell you, many will try to enter and won't be able [25] once the homeowner gets up and shuts the door. Then you will stand outside and knock on the door, saying, 'Lord, open up for us!' He will answer you, 'I don't know you or where you're from.' [26] Then you will say, 'We ate and drank in your presence, and you taught in our streets.' [27] But he will say, 'I tell you, I don't know you or where you're from. Get away from me, all you evildoers!' [28] There will be weeping and gnashing of teeth in that place, when you see Abraham, Isaac, Jacob, and all the prophets in the kingdom of God, but yourselves thrown out. [29] They will come from east and west, from north and south, to share the banquet in the kingdom of God. [30] Note this: Some who are last will be first, and some who are first will be last."

JESUS GRIEVES OVER JERUSALEM   MT 23:37-39   LK 13:31-35

Both Matthew and Luke record Jesus's lament over Jerusalem, and the wording of the lament is quite similar in both. In addition, the lament comes at approximately the same time in each Gospel. However, Matthew does not include the warning from the Pharisees about Herod's plan to kill Jesus. Given Jesus's scathing rebuke against the Pharisees in the preceding woes (23:1-36), Matthew, it seems, is not interested in deflecting culpability from the religious officials at this point in his narrative. Luke's "woes," however, come later in his Gospel. Yet both authors have strategically placed them for literary and theological purposes, and the lament is a fitting addition to both contexts.

[37] "Jerusalem, Jerusalem, who kills the prophets and stones those who are sent to her. How often I wanted to gather your children together, as a hen gathers her chicks under her wings, but you were not willing! [38] See, your house is left to you desolate. [39] For I tell you, you will not see me again until you say, 'Blessed is he who comes in the name of the Lord'!"

[31] At that time some Pharisees came and told him, "Go, get out of here. Herod wants to kill you." [32] He said to them, "Go tell that fox, 'Look, I'm driving out demons and performing healings today and tomorrow, and on the third day I will complete my work.' [33] Yet it is necessary that I travel today, tomorrow, and the next day, because it is not possible for a prophet to perish outside of Jerusalem.

[34] "Jerusalem, Jerusalem, who kills the prophets and stones those who are sent to her. How often I wanted to gather your children together, as a hen gathers her chicks under her wings, but you were not willing! [35] See, your house is abandoned to you. I tell you, you will not see me until the time comes when you say, 'Blessed is he who comes in the name of the Lord'!"

JESUS HEALS A MAN WHOSE BODY WAS SWOLLEN WITH FLUID   LK 14:1-6

[1] One Sabbath, when he went in to eat at the house of one of the leading Pharisees, they were watching him closely. [2] There in front of him was a man whose body was swollen with fluid. [3] In response, Jesus asked the law experts and the Pharisees, "Is it lawful to heal on the Sabbath or not?" [4] But they kept silent. He took the man, healed him, and sent him away. [5] And to them, he said, "Which of you whose son or ox falls into a well, will not immediately pull him out on the Sabbath day?" [6] They could find no answer to these things.

⁷ He told a parable to those who were invited, when he noticed how they would choose the best places for themselves: ⁸ "When you are invited by someone to a wedding banquet, don't recline at the best place, because a more distinguished person than you may have been invited by your host. ⁹ The one who invited both of you may come and say to you, 'Give your place to this man,' and then in humiliation, you will proceed to take the lowest place.

¹⁰ "But when you are invited, go and recline in the lowest place, so that when the one who invited you comes, he will say to you, 'Friend, move up higher.' You will then be honored in the presence of all the other guests. ¹¹ For everyone who exalts himself will be humbled, and the one who humbles himself will be exalted."

¹² He also said to the one who had invited him, "When you give a lunch or a dinner, don't invite your friends, your brothers or sisters, your relatives, or your rich neighbors, because they might invite you back, and you would be repaid. ¹³ On the contrary, when you host a banquet, invite those who are poor, maimed, lame, or blind. ¹⁴ And you will be blessed, because they cannot repay you; for you will be repaid at the resurrection of the righteous."

¹⁵ When one of those who reclined at the table with him heard these things, he said to him, "Blessed is the one who will eat bread in the kingdom of God!"

¹⁶ Then he told him: "A man was giving a large banquet and invited many. ¹⁷ At the time of the banquet, he sent his servant to tell those who were invited, 'Come, because everything is now ready.'

¹⁸ "But without exception they all began to make excuses. The first one said to him, 'I have bought a field, and I must go out and see it. I ask you to excuse me.'

¹⁹ "Another said, 'I have bought five yoke of oxen, and I'm going to try them out. I ask you to excuse me.'

²⁰ "And another said, 'I just got married, and therefore I'm unable to come.'

²¹ "So the servant came back and reported these things to his master. Then in anger, the master of the house told his servant, 'Go out quickly into the streets and alleys of the city, and bring in here the poor, maimed, blind, and lame.'

²² " 'Master,' the servant said, 'what you ordered has been done, and there's still room.'

²³ "Then the master told the servant, 'Go out into the highways and hedges and make them come in, so that my house may be filled. ²⁴ For I tell you, not one of those people who were invited will enjoy my banquet.' "

²⁵ Now great crowds were traveling with him. So he turned and said to them: ²⁶ "If anyone comes to me and does not hate his own father and mother, wife and children, brothers and sisters — yes, and even his own life — he cannot be my disciple. ²⁷ Whoever does not bear his own cross and come after me cannot be my disciple.

²⁸ "For which of you, wanting to build a tower, doesn't first sit down and calculate the cost to see if he has enough to complete it? ²⁹ Otherwise, after he has laid the foundation and cannot

finish it, all the onlookers will begin to ridicule him, [30] saying, 'This man started to build and wasn't able to finish.'

[31] "Or what king, going to war against another king, will not first sit down and decide if he is able with ten thousand to oppose the one who comes against him with twenty thousand? [32] If not, while the other is still far off, he sends a delegation and asks for terms of peace. [33] In the same way, therefore, every one of you who does not renounce all his possessions cannot be my disciple.

[34] "Now, salt is good, but if salt should lose its taste, how will it be made salty? [35] It isn't fit for the soil or for the manure pile; they throw it out. Let anyone who has ears to hear listen."

THE PARABLES OF THE LOST SHEEP AND THE LOST COIN — LK 15:1-10

[1] All the tax collectors and sinners were approaching to listen to him. [2] And the Pharisees and scribes were complaining, "This man welcomes sinners and eats with them."

[3] So he told them this parable: [4] "What man among you, who has a hundred sheep and loses one of them, does not leave the ninety-nine in the open field and go after the lost one until he finds it? [5] When he has found it, he joyfully puts it on his shoulders, [6] and coming home, he calls his friends and neighbors together, saying to them, 'Rejoice with me, because I have found my lost sheep!' [7] I tell you, in the same way, there will be more joy in heaven over one sinner who repents than over ninety-nine righteous people who don't need repentance.

[8] "Or what woman who has ten silver coins, if she loses one coin, does not light a lamp, sweep the house, and search carefully until she finds it? [9] When she finds it, she calls her friends and neighbors together, saying, 'Rejoice with me, because I have found the silver coin I lost!' [10] I tell you, in the same way, there is joy in the presence of God's angels over one sinner who repents."

THE PARABLE OF THE LOST SON — LK 15:11-32

[11] He also said: "A man had two sons. [12] The younger of them said to his father, 'Father, give me the share of the estate I have coming to me.' So he distributed the assets to them. [13] Not many days later, the younger son gathered together all he had and traveled to a distant country, where he squandered his estate in foolish living. [14] After he had spent everything, a severe famine struck that country, and he had nothing. [15] Then he went to work for one of the citizens of that country, who sent him into his fields to feed pigs. [16] He longed to eat his fill from the pods that the pigs were eating, but no one would give him anything. [17] When he came to his senses, he said, 'How many of my father's hired workers have more than enough food, and here I am dying of hunger! [18] I'll get up, go to my father, and say to him, "Father, I have sinned against heaven and in your sight. [19] I'm no longer worthy to be called your son. Make me like one of your hired workers."' [20] So he got up and went to his father. But while the son was still a long way off, his father saw him and was filled with compassion. He ran, threw his arms around his neck, and kissed him. [21] The son said to him, 'Father, I have sinned against heaven and in your sight. I'm no longer worthy to be called your son.'

[22] "But the father told his servants, 'Quick! Bring out the best robe and put it on him; put a ring on his finger and sandals on his feet. [23] Then bring the fattened calf and slaughter it, and let's celebrate with a feast, [24] because this son of mine was dead and is alive again; he was lost and is found!' So they began to celebrate.

[25] "Now his older son was in the field; as he came near the house, he heard music and dancing. [26] So he summoned one of the servants, questioning what these things meant. [27] 'Your brother is here,' he told him, 'and your father has slaughtered the fattened calf because he has him back safe and sound.'

[28] "Then he became angry and didn't want to go in. So his father came out and pleaded with him. [29] But he replied to his father, 'Look, I have been slaving many years for you, and I have never disobeyed your orders, yet you never gave me a goat so that I could celebrate with my friends. [30] But when this son of yours came, who has devoured your assets with prostitutes, you slaughtered the fattened calf for him.'

[31] " 'Son,' he said to him, 'you are always with me, and everything I have is yours. [32] But we had to celebrate and rejoice, because this brother of yours was dead and is alive again; he was lost and is found.' "

THE PARABLE OF THE DISHONEST MANAGER

LK 16:1-18

[1] Now he said to the disciples: "There was a rich man who received an accusation that his manager was squandering his possessions. [2] So he called the manager in and asked, 'What is this I hear about you? Give an account of your management, because you can no longer be my manager.'

[3] "Then the manager said to himself, 'What will I do since my master is taking the management away from me? I'm not strong enough to dig; I'm ashamed to beg. [4] I know what I'll do so that when I'm removed from management, people will welcome me into their homes.'

[5] "So he summoned each one of his master's debtors. 'How much do you owe my master?' he asked the first one.

[6] " 'A hundred measures of olive oil,' he said.

" 'Take your invoice,' he told him, 'sit down quickly, and write fifty.'

[7] "Next he asked another, 'How much do you owe?'

" 'A hundred measures of wheat,' he said.

" 'Take your invoice,' he told him, 'and write eighty.'

[8] "The master praised the unrighteous manager because he had acted shrewdly. For the children of this age are more shrewd than the children of light in dealing with their own people. [9] And I tell you, make friends for yourselves by means of worldly wealth so that when it fails, they may welcome you into eternal dwellings. [10] Whoever is faithful in very little is also faithful in much, and whoever is unrighteous in very little is also unrighteous in much. [11] So if you have not been faithful with worldly wealth, who will trust you with what is genuine? [12] And if you have not been faithful with what belongs to someone else, who will give you what is your own? [13] No servant can serve two masters, since either he will hate one and love the other, or he will be devoted to one and despise the other. You cannot serve both God and money."

[14] The Pharisees, who were lovers of money, were listening to all these things and scoffing at him. [15] And he told them, "You are the ones who justify yourselves in the sight of others, but God knows your hearts. For what is highly admired by people is revolting in God's sight.

[16] "The Law and the Prophets were until John; since then, the good news of the kingdom of God has been proclaimed, and everyone is urgently invited to enter it. [17] But it is easier for heaven and earth to pass away than for one stroke of a letter in the law to drop out.

[18] "Everyone who divorces his wife and marries another woman commits adultery, and everyone who marries a woman divorced from her husband commits adultery."

[19] "There was a rich man who would dress in purple and fine linen, feasting lavishly every day. [20] But a poor man named Lazarus, covered with sores, was lying at his gate. [21] He longed to be filled with what fell from the rich man's table, but instead the dogs would come and lick his sores. [22] One day the poor man died and was carried away by the angels to Abraham's side. The rich man also died and was buried. [23] And being in torment in Hades, he looked up and saw Abraham a long way off, with Lazarus at his side. [24] 'Father Abraham!' he called out, 'Have mercy on me and send Lazarus to dip the tip of his finger in water and cool my tongue, because I am in agony in this flame!'

[25] " 'Son,' Abraham said, 'remember that during your life you received your good things, just as Lazarus received bad things, but now he is comforted here, while you are in agony. [26] Besides all this, a great chasm has·been fixed between us and you, so that those who want to pass over from here to you cannot; neither can those from there cross over to us.'

[27] " 'Father,' he said, 'then I beg you to send him to my father's house — [28] because I have five brothers — to warn them, so they won't also come to this place of torment.'

[29] "But Abraham said, 'They have Moses and the prophets; they should listen to them.'

[30] " 'No, father Abraham,' he said. 'But if someone from the dead goes to them, they will repent.'

[31] "But he told him, 'If they don't listen to Moses and the prophets, they will not be persuaded if someone rises from the dead.' "

JESUS TEACHES ABOUT RESPONSIBILITY OF DOWNFALL, FAITH, AND DUTY

[1] He said to his disciples, "Offenses will certainly come, but woe to the one through whom they come! [2] It would be better for him if a millstone were hung around his neck and he were thrown into the sea than for him to cause one of these little ones to stumble. [3] Be on your guard. If your brother sins, rebuke him, and if he repents, forgive him. [4] And if he sins against you seven times in a day, and comes back to you seven times, saying, 'I repent,' you must forgive him."

[5] The apostles said to the Lord, "Increase our faith."

[6] "If you have faith the size of a mustard seed," the Lord said, "you can say to this mulberry tree, 'Be uprooted and planted in the sea,' and it will obey you.

[7] "Which one of you having a servant tending sheep or plowing will say to him when he comes in from the field, 'Come at once and sit down to eat'? [8] Instead, will he not tell him, 'Prepare something for me to eat, get ready, and serve me while I eat and drink; later you can eat and drink'? [9] Does he thank that servant because he did what was commanded? [10] In the same way, when you have done all that you were commanded, you should say, 'We are worthless servants; we've only done our duty.' "

LAZARUS DIES AND JESUS CALLS HIM BACK TO LIFE

[1] Now a man was sick, Lazarus from Bethany, the village of Mary and her sister Martha. [2] Mary was the one who anointed the Lord with perfume and wiped his feet with her hair, and it was her brother Lazarus who was sick. [3] So the sisters sent a message to him: "Lord, the one you love is sick."

[4] When Jesus heard it, he said, "This sickness will not end in death but is for the glory of God, so that the Son of God may be glorified through it." [5] Now Jesus loved Martha, her sister, and

Lazarus. ⁶ So when he heard that he was sick, he stayed two more days in the place where he was. ⁷ Then after that, he said to the disciples, "Let's go to Judea again."

⁸ "Rabbi," the disciples told him, "just now the Jews tried to stone you, and you're going there again?"

⁹ "Aren't there twelve hours in a day?" Jesus answered. "If anyone walks during the day, he doesn't stumble, because he sees the light of this world. ¹⁰ But if anyone walks during the night, he does stumble, because the light is not in him."

¹¹ He said this, and then he told them, "Our friend Lazarus has fallen asleep, but I'm on my way to wake him up."

¹² Then the disciples said to him, "Lord, if he has fallen asleep, he will get well."

¹³ Jesus, however, was speaking about his death, but they thought he was speaking about natural sleep. ¹⁴ So Jesus then told them plainly, "Lazarus has died. ¹⁵ I'm glad for you that I wasn't there so that you may believe. But let's go to him."

¹⁶ Then Thomas (called "Twin") said to his fellow disciples, "Let's go too so that we may die with him."

¹⁷ When Jesus arrived, he found that Lazarus had already been in the tomb four days. ¹⁸ Bethany was near Jerusalem (less than two miles away). ¹⁹ Many of the Jews had come to Martha and Mary to comfort them about their brother.

²⁰ As soon as Martha heard that Jesus was coming, she went to meet him, but Mary remained seated in the house. ²¹ Then Martha said to Jesus, "Lord, if you had been here, my brother wouldn't have died. ²² Yet even now I know that whatever you ask from God, God will give you."

²³ "Your brother will rise again," Jesus told her.

²⁴ Martha said to him, "I know that he will rise again in the resurrection at the last day."

²⁵ Jesus said to her, "I am the resurrection and the life. The one who believes in me, even if he dies, will live. ²⁶ Everyone who lives and believes in me will never die. Do you believe this?"

²⁷ "Yes, Lord," she told him, "I believe you are the Messiah, the Son of God, who comes into the world."

²⁸ Having said this, she went back and called her sister Mary, saying in private, "The Teacher is here and is calling for you."

²⁹ As soon as Mary heard this, she got up quickly and went to him. ³⁰ Jesus had not yet come into the village but was still in the place where Martha had met him. ³¹ The Jews who were with her in the house consoling her saw that Mary got up quickly and went out. They followed her, supposing that she was going to the tomb to cry there.

³² As soon as Mary came to where Jesus was and saw him, she fell at his feet and told him, "Lord, if you had been here, my brother would not have died!"

³³ When Jesus saw her crying, and the Jews who had come with her crying, he was deeply moved in his spirit and troubled. ³⁴ "Where have you put him?" he asked.

"Lord," they told him, "come and see."

³⁵ Jesus wept.

³⁶ So the Jews said, "See how he loved him!" ³⁷ But some of them said, "Couldn't he who opened the blind man's eyes also have kept this man from dying?"

³⁸ Then Jesus, deeply moved again, came to the tomb. It was a cave, and a stone was lying against it. ³⁹ "Remove the stone," Jesus said.

Martha, the dead man's sister, told him, "Lord, there is already a stench because he has been dead four days."

⁴⁰ Jesus said to her, "Didn't I tell you that if you believed you would see the glory of God?"

[41] So they removed the stone. Then Jesus raised his eyes and said, "Father, I thank you that you heard me. [42] I know that you always hear me, but because of the crowd standing here I said this, so that they may believe you sent me." [43] After he said this, he shouted with a loud voice, "Lazarus, come out!" [44] The dead man came out bound hand and foot with linen strips and with his face wrapped in a cloth. Jesus said to them, "Unwrap him and let him go."

THE JEWISH LEADERS DECIDE TO KILL JESUS

JN 11:45-57

[45] Therefore, many of the Jews who came to Mary and saw what he did believed in him. [46] But some of them went to the Pharisees and told them what Jesus had done.

[47] So the chief priests and the Pharisees convened the Sanhedrin and were saying, "What are we going to do since this man is doing many signs? [48] If we let him go on like this, everyone will believe in him, and the Romans will come and take away both our place and our nation."

[49] One of them, Caiaphas, who was high priest that year, said to them, "You know nothing at all! [50] You're not considering that it is to your advantage that one man should die for the people rather than the whole nation perish." [51] He did not say this on his own, but being high priest that year he prophesied that Jesus was going to die for the nation, [52] and not for the nation only, but also to unite the scattered children of God. [53] So from that day on they plotted to kill him.

[54] Jesus therefore no longer walked openly among the Jews but departed from there to the countryside near the wilderness, to a town called Ephraim, and he stayed there with the disciples.

[55] Now the Jewish Passover was near, and many went up to Jerusalem from the country to purify themselves before the Passover. [56] They were looking for Jesus and asking one another as they stood in the temple: "What do you think? He won't come to the festival, will he?" [57] The chief priests and the Pharisees had given orders that if anyone knew where he was, he should report it so that they could arrest him.

JESUS HEALS TEN LEPROUS MEN

LK 17:11-19

[11] While traveling to Jerusalem, he passed between Samaria and Galilee. [12] As he entered a village, ten men with leprosy met him. They stood at a distance [13] and raised their voices, saying, "Jesus, Master, have mercy on us!"

[14] When he saw them, he told them, "Go and show yourselves to the priests." And while they were going, they were cleansed.

[15] But one of them, seeing that he was healed, returned and, with a loud voice, gave glory to God. [16] He fell facedown at his feet, thanking him. And he was a Samaritan.

[17] Then Jesus said, "Were not ten cleansed? Where are the nine? [18] Didn't any return to give glory to God except this foreigner?" [19] And he told him, "Get up and go on your way. Your faith has saved you."

JESUS TEACHES ABOUT THE COMING OF THE KINGDOM

LK 17:20-37

[20] Being asked by the Pharisees when the kingdom of God would come, he answered them, "The kingdom of God is not coming with something observable; [21] no one will say, 'See here!' or 'There!' For you see, the kingdom of God is in your midst."

[22] Then he told the disciples: "The days are coming when you will long to see one of the days of the Son of Man, but you won't see it. [23] They will say to you, 'See there!' or 'See here!' Don't

follow or run after them. [24] For as the lightning flashes from horizon to horizon and lights up the sky, so the Son of Man will be in his day. [25] But first it is necessary that he suffer many things and be rejected by this generation.

[26] "Just as it was in the days of Noah, so it will be in the days of the Son of Man: [27] People went on eating, drinking, marrying and giving in marriage until the day Noah boarded the ark, and the flood came and destroyed them all. [28] It will be the same as it was in the days of Lot: People went on eating, drinking, buying, selling, planting, building. [29] But on the day Lot left Sodom, fire and sulfur rained from heaven and destroyed them all. [30] It will be like that on the day the Son of Man is revealed. [31] On that day, a man on the housetop, whose belongings are in the house, must not come down to get them. Likewise the man who is in the field must not turn back. [32] Remember Lot's wife! [33] Whoever tries to make his life secure will lose it, and whoever loses his life will preserve it. [34] I tell you, on that night two will be in one bed; one will be taken and the other will be left. [35] Two women will be grinding grain together; one will be taken and the other left."

[37] "Where, Lord?" they asked him.

He said to them, "Where the corpse is, there also the vultures will be gathered."

THE PARABLE OF THE PERSISTENT WIDOW
LK 18:1-8

[1] Now he told them a parable on the need for them to pray always and not give up. [2] "There was a judge in a certain town who didn't fear God or respect people. [3] And a widow in that town kept coming to him, saying, 'Give me justice against my adversary.'

[4] "For a while he was unwilling, but later he said to himself, 'Even though I don't fear God or respect people, [5] yet because this widow keeps pestering me, I will give her justice, so that she doesn't wear me out by her persistent coming.'"

[6] Then the Lord said, "Listen to what the unjust judge says. [7] Will not God grant justice to his elect who cry out to him day and night? Will he delay helping them? [8] I tell you that he will swiftly grant them justice. Nevertheless, when the Son of Man comes, will he find faith on earth?"

THE PARABLE OF THE PHARISEE AND THE TAX COLLECTOR
LK 18:9-14

[9] He also told this parable to some who trusted in themselves that they were righteous and looked down on everyone else: [10] "Two men went up to the temple to pray, one a Pharisee and the other a tax collector. [11] The Pharisee was standing and praying like this about himself: 'God, I thank you that I'm not like other people — greedy, unrighteous, adulterers, or even like this tax collector. [12] I fast twice a week; I give a tenth of everything I get.'

[13] "But the tax collector, standing far off, would not even raise his eyes to heaven but kept striking his chest and saying, 'God, have mercy on me, a sinner!' [14] I tell you, this one went down to his house justified rather than the other; because everyone who exalts himself will be humbled, but the one who humbles himself will be exalted."

JESUS TEACHES ABOUT DIVORCE
MT 19:3-12   MK 10:2-12

In both Matthew and Mark, Jesus's teaching on divorce appears within a controversy between Jesus and the Pharisees. However, in both cases (more so in Matthew), the dialogue shifts toward a teaching moment between Jesus and his disciples. For both authors, this story functions, first, to describe

---

the escalation of the conflict between Jesus and the religious officials and, second, to emphasize the radical ideals of kingdom discipleship. Matthew's

inclusion of the "eunuch" saying reinforces this purpose and expands upon Jesus's teaching in 5:32.

[3] Some Pharisees approached him to test him. They asked, "Is it lawful for a man to divorce his wife on any grounds?"

[4] "Haven't you read," he replied, "that he who created them in the beginning **made them male and female**," [5] and he also said, "**For this reason a man will leave his father and mother and be joined to his wife, and the two will become one flesh**? [6] So they are no longer two, but one flesh. Therefore, what God has joined together, let no one separate."

[7] "Why then," they asked him, "did Moses command us to give divorce papers and to send her away?"

[8] He told them, "Moses permitted you to divorce your wives because of the hardness of your hearts, but it was not like that from the beginning. [9] I tell you, whoever divorces his wife, except for sexual immorality, and marries another commits adultery."

[10] His disciples said to him, "If the relationship of a man with his wife is like this, it's better not to marry."

[11] He responded, "Not everyone can accept this saying, but only those to whom it has been given. [12] For there are eunuchs who were born that way from their mother's womb, there are eunuchs who were made by men, and there are eunuchs who have made themselves that way because of the kingdom of heaven. The one who is able to accept it should accept it."

[2] Some Pharisees came to test him, asking, "Is it lawful for a man to divorce his wife?"

[3] He replied to them, "What did Moses command you?"

[4] They said, "Moses permitted us to write divorce papers and send her away."

[5] But Jesus told them, "He wrote this command for you because of the hardness of your hearts. [6] But from the beginning of creation God **made them male and female.** [7] **For this reason a man will leave his father and mother** [8] **and the two will become one flesh.** So they are no longer two, but one flesh. [9] Therefore what God has joined together, let no one separate."

[10] When they were in the house again, the disciples questioned him about this matter. [11] He said to them, "Whoever divorces his wife and marries another commits adultery against her. [12] Also, if she divorces her husband and marries another, she commits adultery."

JESUS BLESSES THE CHILDREN

MT 19:13-15   MK 10:13-16   LK 18:15-17

The Synoptic Gospels reflect Jesus's special interest in children. Yet the way in which children serve as a paradigm for kingdom discipleship should also not be lost on the reader. That the disciples are slow to learn this lesson is clear from the fact that this is now the second time in the Synoptic tradition that Jesus has appealed to children as the model for discipleship (see "The Argument about Being Greatest" on p. 67). There are some minor variations between the Synoptic accounts here, yet Jesus surely had a number of such interchanges with children in the various towns and villages he visited on his journey to Jerusalem.

[13] Then children were brought to Jesus for him to place his hands on them and pray, but the disciples rebuked them. [14] Jesus said, "Leave the children alone, and don't try to keep them from coming to me, because the kingdom of heaven belongs to such as these." [15] After placing his hands on them, he went on from there.

[13] People were bringing little children to him in order that he might touch them, but the disciples rebuked them. [14] When Jesus saw it, he was indignant and said to them, "Let the little children come to me. Don't stop them, because the kingdom of God belongs to such as these. [15] Truly I tell you, whoever does not receive the kingdom of God like a little child will never enter it." [16] After taking them in his arms, he laid his hands on them and blessed them.

[15] People were bringing infants to him so he might touch them, but when the disciples saw it, they rebuked them. [16] Jesus, however, invited them: "Let the little children come to me, and don't stop them, because the kingdom of God belongs to such as these. [17] Truly I tell you, whoever does not receive the kingdom of God like a little child will never enter it."

The Synoptic accounts of Jesus's interaction with the rich young man/ruler is consistent across all three Gospels. The occasional omission of various details from one Gospel to the next can be explained by the impulse toward brevity or selectivity based on a given author's literary and theological purposes. There is, however, one significant variation among the list of commandments that deserves some comment. Matthew alone, for example, includes in his list the second greatest commandment (i.e., "love your neighbor"), a well-known axiom from Leviticus 19:18 that is, nevertheless, not part of the Ten Commandments. That this adage was omitted from Mark and Luke shows their preference for the five latter commandments that encompass the conventional Jewish view of "good" behavior. The addition of Leviticus 19:18 by Matthew, however, shows his interest in what most consider an apt summary of the entire Ten Commandments. And it is a fitting addition given his recurring use of this Jewish axiom at strategic points in his Gospel (cp. 5:43 and 22:39).

16 Just then someone came up and asked him, "Teacher, what good must I do to have eternal life?"

17 "Why do you ask me about what is good?" he said to him. "There is only one who is good. If you want to enter into life, keep the commandments."

18 "Which ones?" he asked him.

Jesus answered: **Do not murder; do not commit adultery; do not steal; do not bear false witness;** 19 **honor your father and your mother; and love your neighbor as yourself.**

20 "I have kept all these," the young man told him. "What do I still lack?"

21 "If you want to be perfect," Jesus said to him, "go, sell your belongings and give to the poor, and you will have treasure in heaven. Then come, follow me."

22 When the young man heard that, he went away grieving, because he had many possessions.

23 Jesus said to his disciples, "Truly I tell you, it will be hard for a rich person to enter the kingdom of heaven. 24 Again I tell you, it is easier for a camel to go through the eye of a needle than for a rich person to enter the kingdom of God."

25 When the disciples heard this, they were utterly astonished and asked, "Then who can be saved?"

26 Jesus looked at them and said, "With man this is impossible, but with God all things are possible."

27 Then Peter responded to him, "See, we have left everything and followed you. So what will there be for us?"

17 As he was setting out on a journey, a man ran up, knelt down before him, and asked him, "Good teacher, what must I do to inherit eternal life?"

18 "Why do you call me good?" Jesus asked him. "No one is good except God alone. 19 You know the commandments: **Do not murder; do not commit adultery; do not steal; do not bear false witness; do not defraud; honor your father and mother.**"

20 He said to him, "Teacher, I have kept all these from my youth."

21 Looking at him, Jesus loved him and said to him, "You lack one thing: Go, sell all you have and give to the poor, and you will have treasure in heaven. Then come, follow me."

22 But he was dismayed by this demand, and he went away grieving, because he had many possessions.

23 Jesus looked around and said to his disciples, "How hard it is for those who have wealth to enter the kingdom of God!"

24 The disciples were astonished at his words. Again Jesus said to them, "Children, how hard it is to enter the kingdom of God! 25 It is easier for a camel to go through the eye of a needle than for a rich person to enter the kingdom of God."

26 They were even more astonished, saying to one another, "Then who can be saved?"

27 Looking at them, Jesus said, "With man it is impossible, but not with God, because all things are possible with God."

28 Peter began to tell him, "Look, we have left everything and followed you."

18 A ruler asked him, "Good teacher, what must I do to inherit eternal life?"

19 "Why do you call me good?" Jesus asked him. "No one is good except God alone. 20 You know the commandments: **Do not commit adultery; do not murder; do not steal; do not bear false witness; honor your father and mother.**"

21 "I have kept all these from my youth," he said.

22 When Jesus heard this, he told him, "You still lack one thing: Sell all you have and distribute it to the poor, and you will have treasure in heaven. Then come, follow me."

23 After he heard this, he became extremely sad, because he was very rich.

24 Seeing that he became sad, Jesus said, "How hard it is for those who have wealth to enter the kingdom of God! 25 For it is easier for a camel to go through the eye of a needle than for a rich person to enter the kingdom of God."

26 Those who heard this asked, "Then who can be saved?"

27 He replied, "What is impossible with man is possible with God."

28 Then Peter said, "Look, we have left what we had and followed you."

29 So he said to them, "Truly I tell you, there is no one who has left a house, wife or brothers or sisters, parents or children because of the kingdom of God, 30 who will not receive many times more at this time, and eternal life in the age to come."

28 Jesus said to them, "Truly I tell you, in the renewal of all things, when the Son of Man sits on his glorious throne, you who have followed me will also sit on twelve thrones, judging the twelve tribes of Israel. 29 And everyone who has left houses or brothers or sisters or father or mother or children or fields because of my name will receive a hundred times more and will inherit eternal life. 30 But many who are first will be last, and the last first."

29 "Truly I tell you," Jesus said, "there is no one who has left house or brothers or sisters or mother or father or children or fields for my sake and for the sake of the gospel, 30 who will not receive a hundred times more, now at this time — houses, brothers and sisters, mothers and children, and fields, with persecutions — and eternal life in the age to come. 31 But many who are first will be last, and the last first."

THE PARABLE OF THE VINEYARD WORKERS
MT 20:1-16

1 "For the kingdom of heaven is like a landowner who went out early in the morning to hire workers for his vineyard. 2 After agreeing with the workers on one denarius, he sent them into his vineyard for the day. 3 When he went out about nine in the morning, he saw others standing in the marketplace doing nothing. 4 He said to them, 'You also go into my vineyard, and I'll give you whatever is right.' So off they went. 5 About noon and about three, he went out again and did the same thing. 6 Then about five he went and found others standing around and said to them, 'Why have you been standing here all day doing nothing?'

7 " 'Because no one hired us,' they said to him.

" 'You also go into my vineyard,' he told them. 8 When evening came, the owner of the vineyard told his foreman, 'Call the workers and give them their pay, starting with the last and ending with the first.'

9 "When those who were hired about five came, they each received one denarius. 10 So when the first ones came, they assumed they would get more, but they also received a denarius each. 11 When they received it, they began to complain to the landowner: 12 'These last men put in one hour, and you made them equal to us who bore the burden of the day's work and the burning heat.'

13 "He replied to one of them, 'Friend, I'm doing you no wrong. Didn't you agree with me on a denarius? 14 Take what's yours and go. I want to give this last man the same as I gave you. 15 Don't I have the right to do what I want with what is mine? Are you jealous because I'm generous?'

16 "So the last will be first, and the first last."

JESUS'S THIRD PREDICTION OF HIS DEATH
MT 20:17-19   MK 10:32-34   LK 18:31-34

In this third, and final, prediction of Jesus's death, all three Synoptics focus on the passion of Jesus, toward which the three have been moving. They are quite similar, but only Luke connects this final prediction to the OT prophetic tradition, by which he more clearly links the passion to salvation history.

17 While going up to Jerusalem, Jesus took the twelve disciples aside privately and said to them on the way, 18 "See, we are going up to Jerusalem. The Son of Man will be handed over to the chief priests and scribes, and they will condemn him to death. 19 They

32 They were on the road, going up to Jerusalem, and Jesus was walking ahead of them. The disciples were astonished, but those who followed him were afraid. Taking the Twelve aside again, he began to tell them the things that would happen to him. 33 "See, we are going up to Jerusalem. The Son of Man will be handed over to the chief priests and the scribes, and they will condemn him to death. Then they will hand him over to the Gentiles, 34 and they will mock him, spit on him, flog him, and kill him, and he will rise after three days."

31 Then he took the Twelve aside and told them, "See, we are going up to Jerusalem. Everything that is written through the prophets about the Son of Man will be accomplished. 32 For he will be handed over to the Gentiles, and he will be mocked, insulted, spit

will hand him over to the Gentiles to be mocked, flogged, and crucified, and on the third day he will be raised."

on; [33] and after they flog him, they will kill him, and he will rise on the third day."

[34] They understood none of these things. The meaning of the saying was hidden from them, and they did not grasp what was said.

JESUS TEACHES ABOUT SUFFERING AND SERVICE

MT 20:20-28   MK 10:35-45

Matthew and Mark are quite similar in their accounts of this exchange between Jesus and the "sons of Zebedee," except that according to Matthew the request originated from their mother, while Mark has the request come from James and John. But in both accounts Jesus's reply is directed at the disciples. This implies that, regardless of who vocalized the request, it was instigated by James and John. Mark's account, then, more succinctly reflects the disciples' role by omitting the reference to the mother, while Matthew includes the mother perhaps to draw attention to another unlikely follower of Jesus who will have significance later in the story (cp. 27:56). More important is the role this narrative plays in conjunction with the account of Jesus's healing of the two blind men. These accounts serve as the culmination of a section centered on the disciples and their understanding of Jesus's mission and its implications for kingdom discipleship.

[20] Then the mother of Zebedee's sons approached him with her sons. She knelt down to ask him for something. [21] "What do you want?" he asked her.

"Promise," she said to him, "that these two sons of mine may sit, one on your right and the other on your left, in your kingdom."

[22] Jesus answered, "You don't know what you're asking. Are you able to drink the cup that I am about to drink?"

"We are able," they said to him.

[23] He told them, "You will indeed drink my cup, but to sit at my right and left is not mine to give; instead, it is for those for whom it has been prepared by my Father."

[24] When the ten disciples heard this, they became indignant with the two brothers. [25] Jesus called them over and said, "You know that the rulers of the Gentiles lord it over them, and those in high positions act as tyrants over them. [26] It must not be like that among you. On the contrary, whoever wants to become great among you must be your servant, [27] and whoever wants to be first among you must be your slave; [28] just as the Son of Man did not come to be served, but to serve, and to give his life as a ransom for many."

[35] James and John, the sons of Zebedee, approached him and said, "Teacher, we want you to do whatever we ask you."

[36] "What do you want me to do for you?" he asked them.

[37] They answered him, "Allow us to sit at your right and at your left in your glory."

[38] Jesus said to them, "You don't know what you're asking. Are you able to drink the cup I drink or to be baptized with the baptism I am baptized with?"

[39] "We are able," they told him.

Jesus said to them, "You will drink the cup I drink, and you will be baptized with the baptism I am baptized with. [40] But to sit at my right or left is not mine to give; instead, it is for those for whom it has been prepared."

[41] When the ten disciples heard this, they began to be indignant with James and John. [42] Jesus called them over and said to them, "You know that those who are regarded as rulers of the Gentiles lord it over them, and those in high positions act as tyrants over them. [43] But it is not so among you. On the contrary, whoever wants to become great among you will be your servant, [44] and whoever wants to be first among you will be a slave to all. [45] For even the Son of Man did not come to be served, but to serve, and to give his life as a ransom for many."

JESUS HEALS TWO BLIND MEN

MT 20:29-34   MK 10:46-52   LK 18:35-43

The significance of this healing of the two blind men is more manifest in Matthew and Mark, given its proximity to the previous account, which clearly demonstrated the enduring dullness of the disciples. With this in mind, Jesus's query ("What do you want me to do for you?") and the blind man/men's response ("open our eyes"/"I want to see") clearly connect the disciples' lack of spiritual insight with the beggars' blindness. The same call for spiritual insight is evident in Luke as well, even if a bit more implicit. Brief comment, however, needs to be made about the discrepancy between Matthew, who has two blind men, and Mark and Luke, who have only one. Matthew, as has been noted, has a penchant for doublets (see "Jesus Sends Demons into Pigs" on p. 49).

Furthermore, Mark and Luke may have been interested in drawing attention to only one character, even though two were present. After all, if there were two blind men, there was at least one. This may not resolve the issue for everyone, but neither does this variation qualify as a contradiction.

³⁹ As they were leaving Jericho, a large crowd followed him. ³⁰ There were two blind men sitting by the road. When they heard that Jesus was passing by, they cried out, "Lord, have mercy on us, Son of David!" ³¹ The crowd demanded that they keep quiet, but they cried out all the more, "Lord, have mercy on us, Son of David!"

³² Jesus stopped, called them, and said, "What do you want me to do for you?"

³³ "Lord," they said to him, "open our eyes." ³⁴ Moved with compassion, Jesus touched their eyes. Immediately they could see, and they followed him.

⁴⁶ They came to Jericho. And as he was leaving Jericho with his disciples and a large crowd, Bartimaeus (the son of Timaeus), a blind beggar, was sitting by the road. ⁴⁷ When he heard that it was Jesus of Nazareth, he began to cry out, "Jesus, Son of David, have mercy on me!" ⁴⁸ Many warned him to keep quiet, but he was crying out all the more, "Have mercy on me, Son of David!"

⁴⁹ Jesus stopped and said, "Call him."

So they called the blind man and said to him, "Have courage! Get up; he's calling for you." ⁵⁰ He threw off his coat, jumped up, and came to Jesus.

⁵¹ Then Jesus answered him, "What do you want me to do for you?"

"*Rabboni,*" the blind man said to him, "I want to see."

⁵² Jesus said to him, "Go, your faith has saved you." Immediately he could see and began to follow Jesus on the road.

³⁵ As he approached Jericho, a blind man was sitting by the road begging. ³⁶ Hearing a crowd passing by, he inquired what was happening. ³⁷ "Jesus of Nazareth is passing by," they told him.

³⁸ So he called out, "Jesus, Son of David, have mercy on me!" ³⁹ Then those in front told him to keep quiet, but he kept crying out all the more, "Son of David, have mercy on me!"

⁴⁰ Jesus stopped and commanded that he be brought to him. When he came closer, he asked him, ⁴¹ "What do you want me to do for you?"

"Lord," he said, "I want to see."

⁴² "Receive your sight." Jesus told him. "Your faith has saved you." ⁴³ Instantly he could see, and he began to follow him, glorifying God. All the people, when they saw it, gave praise to God.

JESUS VISITS ZACCHAEUS
LK 19:1-10

¹ He entered Jericho and was passing through. ² There was a man named Zacchaeus who was a chief tax collector, and he was rich. ³ He was trying to see who Jesus was, but he was not able because of the crowd, since he was a short man. ⁴ So running ahead, he climbed up a sycamore tree to see Jesus, since he was about to pass that way. ⁵ When Jesus came to the place, he looked up and said to him, "Zacchaeus, hurry and come down because today it is necessary for me to stay at your house."

⁶ So he quickly came down and welcomed him joyfully. ⁷ All who saw it began to complain, "He's gone to stay with a sinful man."

⁸ But Zacchaeus stood there and said to the Lord, "Look, I'll give half of my possessions to the poor, Lord. And if I have extorted anything from anyone, I'll pay back four times as much."

⁹ "Today salvation has come to this house," Jesus told him, "because he too is a son of Abraham. ¹⁰ For the Son of Man has come to seek and to save the lost."

THE PARABLE OF THE KING'S TEN SERVANTS
LK 19:11-27

¹¹ As they were listening to this, he went on to tell a parable because he was near Jerusalem, and they thought the kingdom of God was going to appear right away.

¹² Therefore he said: "A nobleman traveled to a far country to receive for himself authority to be king and then to return. ¹³ He called ten of his servants, gave them ten minas, and told them, 'Engage in business until I come back.'

¹⁴ "But his subjects hated him and sent a delegation after him, saying, 'We don't want this man to rule over us.'

¹⁵ "At his return, having received the authority to be king, he summoned those servants he had given the money to, so that he could find out how much they had made in business. ¹⁶ The first came forward and said, 'Master, your mina has earned ten more minas.'

¹⁷ " 'Well done, good servant!' he told him. 'Because you have been faithful in a very small matter, have authority over ten towns.'

¹⁸ "The second came and said, 'Master, your mina has made five minas.'

¹⁹ "So he said to him, 'You will be over five towns.'

²⁰ "And another came and said, 'Master, here is your mina. I have kept it safe in a cloth ²¹ because I was afraid of you since you're a harsh man: you collect what you didn't deposit and reap what you didn't sow.'

²² "He told him, 'I will condemn you by what you have said, you evil servant! If you knew I was a harsh man, collecting what I didn't deposit and reaping what I didn't sow, ²³ why, then, didn't you put my money in the bank? And when I returned, I would have collected it with interest.' ²⁴ So he said to those standing there, 'Take the mina away from him and give it to the one who has ten minas.'

²⁵ "But they said to him, 'Master, he has ten minas.'

²⁶ " 'I tell you, that to everyone who has, more will be given; and from the one who does not have, even what he does have will be taken away. ²⁷ But bring here these enemies of mine, who did not want me to rule over them, and slaughter them in my presence.' "

THE ANOINTING OF JESUS AT BETHANY

MT 26:6-13   MK 14:3-9   JN 12:1-11

There is little variation between Matthew and Mark on the account of Jesus's anointing. John, however, fills in a number of details that are left unstated in the Synoptics. John, for example, highlights the role of Lazarus, Mary, and Martha, three key characters in his Gospel. A harmony of the three accounts would seem to indicate that Jesus, his disciples, Lazarus, Mary, and Martha were all present at the home of Simon, a man presumably healed of leprosy by Jesus. John singles out Judas Iscariot's indignation, whereas Matthew and Mark refer more generally to all the disciples. This shows the underlying contrast John is seeking to make between Mary's devotion and Judas's impending betrayal.

⁶ While Jesus was in Bethany at the house of Simon the leper, ⁷ a woman approached him with an alabaster jar of very expensive perfume. She poured it on his head as he was reclining at the table. ⁸ When the disciples saw it, they were indignant. "Why this waste?" they asked. ⁹ "This might have been sold for a great deal and given to the poor."

¹⁰ Aware of this, Jesus said to them, "Why are you bothering this woman? She has done a noble thing for me. ¹¹ You always have the poor with you, but you do not always have me. ¹² By pouring this perfume on my body, she has prepared me for burial. ¹³ Truly I tell you, wherever this gospel is proclaimed in

³ While he was in Bethany at the house of Simon the leper, as he was reclining at the table, a woman came with an alabaster jar of very expensive perfume of pure nard. She broke the jar and poured it on his head. ⁴ But some were expressing indignation to one another: "Why has this perfume been wasted? ⁵ For this perfume might have been sold for more than three hundred denarii and given to the poor." And they began to scold her.

⁶ Jesus replied, "Leave her alone. Why are you bothering her? She has done a noble thing for me. ⁷ You always have the poor with you, and you can do what is good for them whenever you want, but you do not always have me.

¹ Six days before the Passover, Jesus came to Bethany where Lazarus was, the one Jesus had raised from the dead. ² So they gave a dinner for him there; Martha was serving them, and Lazarus was one of those reclining at the table with him. ³ Then Mary took a pound of perfume, pure and expensive nard, anointed Jesus's feet, and wiped his feet with her hair. So the house was filled with the fragrance of the perfume.

⁴ Then one of his disciples, Judas Iscariot (who was about to betray him), said, ⁵ "Why wasn't this perfume sold for three hundred denarii and given to the poor?" ⁶ He didn't say this because he cared about the poor but

---

MATTHEW   MARK   LUKE   JOHN

the whole world, what she has done will also be told in memory of her."

⁸ She has done what she could; she has anointed my body in advance for burial. ⁹ Truly I tell you, wherever the gospel is proclaimed in the whole world, what she has done will also be told in memory of her."

because he was a thief. He was in charge of the money-bag and would steal part of what was put in it.

⁷ Jesus answered, "Leave her alone; she has kept it for the day of my burial. ⁸ For you always have the poor with you, but you do not always have me."

⁹ Then a large crowd of the Jews learned he was there. They came not only because of Jesus but also to see Lazarus, the one he had raised from the dead. ¹⁰ But the chief priests had decided to kill Lazarus also, ¹¹ because he was the reason many of the Jews were deserting them and believing in Jesus.

THE LAST WEEK IN JERUSALEM

JESUS RIDES INTO JERUSALEM ON A DONKEY   MT 21:1-11   MK 11:1-11   LK 19:28-40   JN 12:12-19

All four Gospel writers recount Jesus's entrance into Jerusalem on a donkey, the first of three key symbolic actions in his move toward the cross. The variation in detail among the Gospel writers illuminates each author's unique theological purposes. Matthew and John are interested in connecting this event to OT fulfillment. For John, this link with the Hebrew Scriptures, along with the presence of certain key characters, "bears witness" to the veracity of the event. Mark, as is his pattern, gives a bit more graphic detail. Matthew makes sure his readers are aware that the donkey was accompanied by a colt. The other three writers do not include this detail, but such an omission does not mean the colt was not there. By now, readers ought to be well accustomed to Matthew's "doubles." In all, the accounts are quite cohesive, giving the reader slightly different angles of the same event.

MATTHEW

[1] When they approached Jerusalem and came to Bethphage at the Mount of Olives, Jesus then sent two disciples, [2] telling them, "Go into the village ahead of you. At once you will find a donkey tied there with her foal. Untie them and bring them to me. [3] If anyone says anything to you, say that the Lord needs them, and he will send them at once."

[4] This took place so that what was spoken through the prophet might be fulfilled:

[5]   Tell Daughter Zion,
    "See, your King is coming
        to you,
    gentle, and mounted
        on a donkey,
    and on a colt,
    the foal of a donkey."

[6] The disciples went and did just as Jesus directed them. [7] They brought the donkey and its foal; then they laid their clothes on them, and he sat on them. [8] A very large crowd spread their clothes on the road; others were cutting branches from the trees

MARK

[1] When they approached Jerusalem, at Bethphage and Bethany near the Mount of Olives, he sent two of his disciples [2] and told them, "Go into the village ahead of you. As soon as you enter it, you will find a colt tied there, on which no one has ever sat. Untie it and bring it. [3] If anyone says to you, 'Why are you doing this?' say, 'The Lord needs it and will send it back here right away.'"

[4] So they went and found a colt outside in the street, tied by a door. They untied it, [5] and some of those standing there said to them, "What are you doing, untying the colt?" [6] They answered them just as Jesus had said; so they let them go. [7] They brought the donkey to Jesus and threw their clothes on it, and he sat on it. [8] Many people spread their clothes on the road, and others spread leafy branches cut from the fields. [9] Those who went ahead and those who followed shouted:

    Hosanna!
    Blessed is he who comes
    in the name of the Lord!

LUKE

[28] When he had said these things, he went on ahead, going up to Jerusalem. [29] As he approached Bethphage and Bethany, at the place called the Mount of Olives, he sent two of the disciples [30] and said, "Go into the village ahead of you. As you enter it, you will find a young donkey tied there, on which no one has ever sat. Untie it and bring it. [31] If anyone asks you, 'Why are you untying it?' say this: 'The Lord needs it.'"

[32] So those who were sent left and found it just as he had told them. [33] As they were untying the young donkey, its owners said to them, "Why are you untying the donkey?" [34] "The Lord needs it," they said. [35] Then they brought it to Jesus, and after throwing their clothes on the donkey, they helped Jesus get on it. [36] As he was going along, they were spreading their clothes on the road. [37] Now he came near the path down the Mount of Olives, and the whole crowd of the disciples began to praise God joyfully with a loud

JOHN

[12] The next day, when the large crowd that had come to the festival heard that Jesus was coming to Jerusalem, [13] they took palm branches and went out to meet him. They kept shouting:

    "Hosanna!
    Blessed is he who comes
        in the name of the Lord
    —the King of Israel!"
[14] Jesus found a young donkey and sat on it, just as it is written:
[15]   Do not be afraid,
    Daughter Zion. Look, your
        King is coming,
    sitting on a donkey's colt.
[16] His disciples did not understand these things at first. However, when Jesus was glorified, then they remembered that these things had been written about him and that they had done these things to him.

[17] Meanwhile, the crowd, which had been with him when he called Lazarus out of the tomb and raised him from the dead, continued to testify. [18] This is also why the crowd met him, because they heard he had done this sign.

and spreading them on the road. ⁹ Then the crowds who went ahead of him and those who followed shouted:

Hosanna to the Son of David! **Blessed is he who comes in the name of the Lord!** Hosanna

in the highest heaven!

¹⁰ When he entered Jerusalem, the whole city was in an uproar, saying, "Who is this?" ¹¹ The crowds were saying, "This is the prophet Jesus from Nazareth in Galilee."

¹⁰ Blessed is the coming kingdom of our father David! Hosanna

in the highest heaven!

¹¹ He went into Jerusalem and into the temple. After looking around at everything, since it was already late, he went out to Bethany with the Twelve.

voice for all the miracles they had seen:

³⁸ **Blessed is the King who comes in the name of the Lord.** Peace in heaven and glory

in the highest heaven!

³⁹ Some of the Pharisees from the crowd told him, "Teacher, rebuke your disciples."

⁴⁰ He answered, "I tell you, if they were to keep silent, the stones would cry out."

¹⁹ Then the Pharisees said to one another, "You see? You've accomplished nothing. Look, the world has gone after him!"

JESUS GRIEVES OVER JERUSALEM AGAIN

LK 19:41-44

⁴¹ As he approached and saw the city, he wept for it, ⁴² saying, "If you knew this day what would bring peace—but now it is hidden from your eyes. ⁴³ For the days will come on you when your enemies will build a barricade around you, surround you, and hem you in on every side. ⁴⁴ They will crush you and your children among you to the ground, and they will not leave one stone on another in your midst, because you did not recognize the time when God visited you."

THE SECOND CLEANSING OF THE TEMPLE

MT 21:12-17   MK 11:15-19   LK 19:45-48

If Jesus's epic entry into Jerusalem was not shocking enough, his cleansing of the temple would mark a definitive point of no return—as is evident by the response of the Pharisees. In this second of three symbolic actions (see "Jesus Rides into Jerusalem on a Donkey" on p. 98), Jesus shows explicitly the implications of his mission for the temple. Mark alone includes a brief reference to the temple being a house of prayer "for all nations," which points to his interest in the Gentiles. Since reforming the temple was not Jesus's ultimate aim, the omission of this in Matthew and Luke is more theologically significant, implying that in the "new" community, Jesus is the new temple.

¹² Jesus went into the temple and threw out all those buying and selling. He overturned the tables of the money changers and the chairs of those selling doves. ¹³ He said to them, "It is written, **my house will be called a house of prayer,** but you are making it **a den of thieves!**"

¹⁴ The blind and the lame came to him in the temple, and he healed them. ¹⁵ When the chief priests and the scribes saw the wonders that he did and the children shouting in the temple, "Hosanna to the Son of David!" they

¹⁵ They came to Jerusalem, and he went into the temple and began to throw out those buying and selling. He overturned the tables of the money changers and the chairs of those selling doves, ¹⁶ and would not permit anyone to carry goods through the temple. ¹⁷ He was teaching them: "Is it not written, **My house will be called a house of prayer for all nations**? But you have made it **a den of thieves!**"

¹⁸ The chief priests and the scribes heard it and started looking for a way to kill him. For

⁴⁵ He went into the temple and began to throw out those who were selling, ⁴⁶ and he said, "It is written, **my house will be a house of prayer,** but you have made it **a den of thieves!**"

⁴⁷ Every day he was teaching in the temple. The chief priests, the scribes, and the leaders of the people were looking for a way to kill him, ⁴⁸ but they could not find a way to do it, because all the people were captivated by what they heard.

---

were indignant [16] and said to him, "Do you hear what these children are saying?"

Jesus replied, "Yes, have you never read:

You have prepared praise
from the mouths of infants and nursing babies?"

[17] Then he left them, went out of the city to Bethany, and spent the night there.

they were afraid of him, because the whole crowd was astonished by his teaching.

[19] Whenever evening came, they would go out of the city.

JESUS EXPLAINS WHY HE MUST DIE AND SUMMARIZES HIS MESSAGES

JN 12:20-50

[20] Now some Greeks were among those who went up to worship at the festival. [21] So they came to Philip, who was from Bethsaida in Galilee, and requested of him, "Sir, we want to see Jesus." [22] Philip went and told Andrew; then Andrew and Philip went and told Jesus.

[23] Jesus replied to them, "The hour has come for the Son of Man to be glorified. [24] Truly I tell you, unless a grain of wheat falls to the ground and dies, it remains by itself. But if it dies, it produces much fruit. [25] The one who loves his life will lose it, and the one who hates his life in this world will keep it for eternal life. [26] If anyone serves me, he must follow me. Where I am, there my servant also will be. If anyone serves me, the Father will honor him.

[27] "Now my soul is troubled. What should I say — Father, save me from this hour? But that is why I came to this hour. [28] Father, glorify your name."

Then a voice came from heaven: "I have glorified it, and I will glorify it again."

[29] The crowd standing there heard it and said it was thunder. Others said, "An angel has spoken to him."

[30] Jesus responded, "This voice came, not for me, but for you. [31] Now is the judgment of this world. Now the ruler of this world will be cast out. [32] As for me, if I am lifted up from the earth I will draw all people to myself." [33] He said this to indicate what kind of death he was about to die.

[34] Then the crowd replied to him, "We have heard from the law that the Messiah will remain forever. So how can you say, 'The Son of Man must be lifted up'? Who is this Son of Man?"

[35] Jesus answered, "The light will be with you only a little longer. Walk while you have the light so that darkness doesn't overtake you. The one who walks in darkness doesn't know where he's going. [36] While you have the light, believe in the light so that you may become children of light." Jesus said this, then went away and hid from them.

[37] Even though he had performed so many signs in their presence, they did not believe in him. [38] This was to fulfill the word of Isaiah the prophet, who said:

Lord, who has believed our message?
And to whom has the arm of the Lord
been revealed?

[39] This is why they were unable to believe, because Isaiah also said:

[40] **He has blinded their eyes**
and hardened their hearts,
so that they would not see with their eyes
or understand with their hearts,
and turn,
and I would heal them.

[41] Isaiah said these things because he saw his glory and spoke about him.

⁴²Nevertheless, many did believe in him even among the rulers, but because of the Pharisees they did not confess him, so that they would not be banned from the synagogue. ⁴³For they loved human praise more than praise from God.

⁴⁴Jesus cried out, "The one who believes in me believes not in me, but in him who sent me. ⁴⁵And the one who sees me sees him who sent me. ⁴⁶I have come as light into the world, so that everyone who believes in me would not remain in darkness. ⁴⁷If anyone hears my words and doesn't keep them, I do not judge him; for I did not come to judge the world but to save the world. ⁴⁸The one who rejects me and doesn't receive my sayings has this as his judge: The word I have spoken will judge him on the last day. ⁴⁹For I have not spoken on my own, but the Father himself who sent me has given me a command to say everything I have said. ⁵⁰I know that his command is eternal life. So the things that I speak, I speak just as the Father has told me."

JESUS CURSES A FIG TREE

MT 21:18-19   MK 11:12-14

Matthew and Mark record Jesus's third symbolic act (see "Jesus Rides into Jerusalem on a Donkey" and "The Second Cleansing of the Temple" on pp. 98 and 99) as the narrative moves with increasing momentum toward the cross. That the fig tree was often used as a metaphor for the nation of Israel in the OT suggests that such an act by Jesus symbolized judgment upon Israel for failure to bear fruit. Much has been made of Mark's reference to Jesus cursing a tree whose fruit was out of season. Yet one should not press every detail of an event. The best explanation is that Jesus's hunger, and subsequent expectation of fruit, is secondary to his symbolic cursing.

¹⁸Early in the morning, as he was returning to the city, he was hungry. ¹⁹Seeing a lone fig tree by the road, he went up to it and found nothing on it except leaves. And he said to it, "May no fruit ever come from you again!" At once the fig tree withered.

¹²The next day when they went out from Bethany, he was hungry. ¹³Seeing in the distance a fig tree with leaves, he went to find out if there was anything on it. When he came to it, he found nothing but leaves; for it was not the season for figs. ¹⁴He said to it, "May no one ever eat fruit from you again!" And his disciples heard it.

JESUS USES THE CURSED TREE TO TEACH THE DISCIPLES

MT 21:20-22   MK 11:20-26

Jesus's teaching focuses mainly on the divine power, through prayer, to enact the curse as opposed to the implied meaning of the curse itself (see previous account). Both Matthew and Mark seek to accomplish a number of things with this event related to Jesus's identity and the nature of discipleship. As such, it is through the "new" Israel that even greater things than cursing will occur, namely forgiveness of sins.

²⁰When the disciples saw it, they were amazed and said, "How did the fig tree wither so quickly?"
²¹Jesus answered them, "Truly I tell you, if you have faith and do not doubt, you will not only do what was done to the fig tree, but even if you tell this mountain, 'Be lifted up and thrown into the sea,' it will be done. ²²And if you believe, you will receive whatever you ask for in prayer."

²⁰Early in the morning, as they were passing by, they saw the fig tree withered from the roots up. ²¹Then Peter remembered and said to him, "Rabbi, look! The fig tree that you cursed has withered."
²²Jesus replied to them, "Have faith in God. ²³Truly I tell you, if anyone says to this mountain, 'Be lifted up and thrown into the sea,' and does not doubt in his heart, but believes that what he says will happen, it will be done for him. ²⁴Therefore I tell you, everything you pray and ask for—believe that you have received it and it will be yours. ²⁵And whenever you stand praying, if you have anything against anyone, forgive him, so that your Father in heaven will also forgive you your wrongdoing."

The next six entries leading up to the plot to kill Jesus represent the culmination of the mounting tension between Jesus and the religious officials. The question here about Jesus's authority follows his provocative cleansing of the temple. All three Synoptic authors recount, almost verbatim, how Jesus turned the tables on his interrogators with a question on the origin of John the Baptist's authority. Since the religious leaders failed to take a position on John, Jesus likewise refused to defend himself with an answer. Of course, for the reader, the answer to both questions is obvious.

23 When he entered the temple, the chief priests and the elders of the people came to him as he was teaching and said, "By what authority are you doing these things? Who gave you this authority?"

24 Jesus answered them, "I will also ask you one question, and if you answer it for me, then I will tell you by what authority I do these things. **25** Did John's baptism come from heaven, or was it of human origin?"

They discussed it among themselves, "If we say, 'From heaven,' he will say to us, 'Then why didn't you believe him?' **26** But if we say, 'Of human origin,' we're afraid of the crowd, because everyone considers John to be a prophet." **27** So they answered Jesus, "We don't know."

And he said to them, "Neither will I tell you by what authority I do these things."

27 They came again to Jerusalem. As he was walking in the temple, the chief priests, the scribes, and the elders came **28** and asked him, "By what authority are you doing these things? Who gave you this authority to do these things?"

29 Jesus said to them, "I will ask you one question; then answer me, and I will tell you by what authority I do these things. **30** Was John's baptism from heaven or of human origin? Answer me."

31 They discussed it among themselves: "If we say, 'From heaven,' he will say, 'Then why didn't you believe him?' **32** But if we say, 'Of human origin'"—they were afraid of the crowd, because everyone thought that John was truly a prophet. **33** So they answered Jesus, "We don't know."

And Jesus said to them, "Neither will I tell you by what authority I do these things."

1 One day as he was teaching the people in the temple and proclaiming the good news, the chief priests and the scribes, with the elders, came **2** and said to him: "Tell us, by what authority are you doing these things? Who is it who gave you this authority?"

3 He answered them, "I will also ask you a question. Tell me, **4** was the baptism of John from heaven or of human origin?"

5 They discussed it among themselves: "If we say, 'From heaven,' he will say, 'Why didn't you believe him?' **6** But if we say, 'Of human origin,' all the people will stone us, because they are convinced that John was a prophet." **7** So they answered that they did not know its origin.

8 And Jesus said to them, "Neither will I tell you by what authority I do these things."

THE PARABLE OF THE TWO SONS　　　　　　　　　　　　　　　　　　　　　MT 21:28-32

28 "What do you think? A man had two sons. He went to the first and said, 'My son, go work in the vineyard today.'

29 "He answered, 'I don't want to,' but later he changed his mind and went. **30** Then the man went to the other and said the same thing. 'I will, sir,' he answered, but he didn't go. **31** Which of the two did his father's will?"

They said, "The first."

Jesus said to them, "Truly I tell you, tax collectors and prostitutes are entering the kingdom of God before you. **32** For John came to you in the way of righteousness, and you didn't believe him. Tax collectors and prostitutes did believe him; but you, when you saw it, didn't even change your minds then and believe him.

THE PARABLE OF THE VINEYARD OWNER　　　　　　　　　MT 21:33-46　　　MK 12:1-12　　　**LK 20:9-19**

All three Synoptic Gospels include the core of this scathing parable directed against the religious officials. As in other parables, the few minor variations are likely due to different versions of the same essential story told at different times. They are acceptable variations within a heavily oral culture. There is some variation between Matthew, Mark, and Luke with regard to the quote from Psalm 118:22-23, but Jesus's quotation of the OT text is not in question. One could explore the differences in each as a means of identifying each author's unique theological purposes. More notable, however, is Matthew's reference to the kingdom of God being given to a "people" that bears fruit. Such a statement reveals Matthew's burden to show how Jesus's suffering will bring about, not just new leadership, but a new people of God.

---

33 "Listen to another parable: There was a landowner, who planted a vineyard, put a fence around it, dug a winepress in it, and built a watchtower. He leased it to tenant farmers and went away. **34** When the time came to harvest fruit, he sent his servants to the farmers to collect his fruit. **35** The farmers took his servants, beat one, killed another, and stoned a third. **36** Again, he sent other servants, more than the first group, and they did the same to them. **37** Finally, he sent his son to them. 'They will respect my son,' he said.

38 "But when the tenant farmers saw the son, they said to each other, 'This is the heir. Come, let's kill him and take his inheritance.' **39** So they seized him, threw him out of the vineyard, and killed him. **40** Therefore, when the owner of the vineyard comes, what will he do to those farmers?"

41 "He will completely destroy those terrible men," they told him, "and lease his vineyard to other farmers who will give him his fruit at the harvest."

42 Jesus said to them, "Have you never read in the Scriptures:

The stone that the builders rejected
has become the cornerstone.
This is what the Lord has done
and it is wonderful in our eyes?

43 Therefore I tell you, the kingdom of God will be taken away from you and given to a people producing its fruit. **44** Whoever falls on this stone will be broken to pieces; but on whomever it falls, it will shatter him."

45 When the chief priests and the Pharisees heard his parables, they knew he was speaking about them. **46** Although they were looking for a way to arrest him, they feared the crowds, because the people regarded him as a prophet.

1 He began to speak to them in parables: "A man planted a vineyard, put a fence around it, dug out a pit for a winepress, and built a watchtower. Then he leased it to tenant farmers and went away. **2** At harvest time he sent a servant to the farmers to collect some of the fruit of the vineyard from them. **3** But they took him, beat him, and sent him away empty-handed. **4** Again he sent another servant to them, and they hit him on the head and treated him shamefully. **5** Then he sent another, and they killed that one. He also sent many others; some they beat, and others they killed. **6** He still had one to send, a beloved son. Finally he sent him to them, saying, 'They will respect my son.' **7** But those tenant farmers said to one another, 'This is the heir. Come, let's kill him, and the inheritance will be ours.' **8** So they seized him, killed him, and threw him out of the vineyard. **9** What then will the owner of the vineyard do? He will come and kill the farmers and give the vineyard to others. **10** Haven't you read this Scripture:

The stone that the builders rejected
has become the cornerstone.
11 This came about from the Lord
and is wonderful in our eyes?"

12 They were looking for a way to arrest him but feared the crowd because they knew he had spoken this parable against them. So they left him and went away.

9 Now he began to tell the people this parable: "A man planted a vineyard, leased it to tenant farmers, and went away for a long time. **10** At harvest time he sent a servant to the farmers so that they might give him some fruit from the vineyard. But the farmers beat him and sent him away empty-handed. **11** He sent yet another servant, but they beat that one too, treated him shamefully, and sent him away empty-handed. **12** And he sent yet a third, but they wounded this one too and threw him out.

13 "Then the owner of the vineyard said, 'What should I do? I will send my beloved son. Perhaps they will respect him.'

14 "But when the tenant farmers saw him, they discussed it among themselves and said, 'This is the heir. Let's kill him, so that the inheritance will be ours.' **15** So they threw him out of the vineyard and killed him.

"What then will the owner of the vineyard do to them? **16** He will come and kill those farmers and give the vineyard to others."

But when they heard this they said, "That must never happen!"

17 But he looked at them and said, "Then what is the meaning of this Scripture:

The stone that the builders rejected
has become the cornerstone?
18 Everyone who falls on that stone will be broken to pieces, but on whomever it falls, it will shatter him."

19 Then the scribes and the chief priests looked for a way to get their hands on him that very hour, because they knew he had told this parable against them, but they feared the people.

¹ Once more Jesus spoke to them in parables: ² "The kingdom of heaven is like a king who gave a wedding banquet for his son. ³ He sent his servants to summon those invited to the banquet, but they didn't want to come. ⁴ Again, he sent out other servants and said, 'Tell those who are invited: See, I've prepared my dinner; my oxen and fattened cattle have been slaughtered, and everything is ready. Come to the wedding banquet.'

⁵ "But they paid no attention and went away, one to his own farm, another to his business, ⁶ while the rest seized his servants, mistreated them, and killed them. ⁷ The king was enraged, and he sent out his troops, killed those murderers, and burned down their city.

⁸ "Then he told his servants, 'The banquet is ready, but those who were invited were not worthy. ⁹ Go then to where the roads exit the city and invite everyone you find to the banquet.' ¹⁰ So those servants went out on the roads and gathered everyone they found, both evil and good. The wedding banquet was filled with guests. ¹¹ When the king came in to see the guests, he saw a man there who was not dressed for a wedding. ¹² So he said to him, 'Friend, how did you get in here without wedding clothes?' The man was speechless.

¹³ "Then the king told the attendants, 'Tie him up hand and foot, and throw him into the outer darkness, where there will be weeping and gnashing of teeth.'

¹⁴ "For many are invited, but few are chosen."

QUESTIONS ABOUT TAXES AND THE RESURRECTION   MT 22:15-33   MK 12:13-27   LK 20:20-40

All three Synoptic authors frame the questions by the religious officials as attempts to test Jesus. Similar attempts earlier in each Gospel were made by none other than Satan himself. The implicit message is that the earlier antagonistic role of Satan gives way to a more sustained conflict between Jesus and the religious officials who test Jesus in the same way as Satan.

The accounts are similar, although Luke alone appeals to the OT to show how God is the God of the living. In addition, Jesus's answer in Luke marks the end of the attempts to test him. As he did with Satan, Jesus silences his detractors with an unparalleled appeal to Scripture.

¹⁵ Then the Pharisees went and plotted how to trap him by what he said. ¹⁶ So they sent their disciples to him, along with the Herodians. "Teacher," they said, "we know that you are truthful and teach truthfully the way of God. You don't care what anyone thinks nor do you show partiality. ¹⁷ Tell us, then, what you think. Is it lawful to pay taxes to Caesar or not?"

¹⁸ Perceiving their malicious intent, Jesus said, "Why are you testing me, hypocrites? ¹⁹ Show me the coin used for the tax." They brought him a denarius. ²⁰ "Whose image and inscription is this?" he asked them.

²¹ "Caesar's," they said to him.

Then he said to them, "Give, then, to Caesar the things that are Caesar's, and to God the

¹³ Then they sent some of the Pharisees and the Herodians to Jesus to trap him in his words. ¹⁴ When they came, they said to him, "Teacher, we know you are truthful and don't care what anyone thinks, nor do you show partiality but teach the way of God truthfully. Is it lawful to pay taxes to Caesar or not? Should we pay or shouldn't we?"

¹⁵ But knowing their hypocrisy, he said to them, "Why are you testing me? Bring me a denarius to look at." ¹⁶ They brought a coin. "Whose image and inscription is this?" he asked them.

"Caesar's," they replied.

¹⁷ Jesus told them, "Give to Caesar the things that are Caesar's, and to God the things that are God's." And they were utterly amazed at him.

²⁰ They watched closely and sent spies who pretended to be righteous, so that they could catch him in what he said, to hand him over to the governor's rule and authority. ²¹ They questioned him, "Teacher, we know that you speak and teach correctly, and you don't show partiality but teach truthfully the way of God. ²² Is it lawful for us to pay taxes to Caesar or not?"

²³ But detecting their craftiness, he said to them, ²⁴ "Show me a denarius. Whose image and inscription does it have?"

"Caesar's," they said.

²⁵ "Well then," he told them, "give to Caesar the things that are Caesar's, and to God the things that are God's."

things that are God's." **22** When they heard this, they were amazed. So they left him and went away.

23 That same day some Sadducees, who say there is no resurrection, came up to him and questioned him: **24** "Teacher, Moses said, **if a man dies, having no children, his brother is to marry his wife and raise up offspring for his brother. 25** Now there were seven brothers among us. The first got married and died. Having no offspring, he left his wife to his brother. **26** The same thing happened to the second also, and the third, and so on to all seven. **27** Last of all, the woman died. **28** In the resurrection, then, whose wife will she be of the seven? For they all had married her."

29 Jesus answered them, "You are mistaken, because you don't know the Scriptures or the power of God. **30** For in the resurrection they neither marry nor are given in marriage but are like angels in heaven. **31** Now concerning the resurrection of the dead, haven't you read what was spoken to you by God: **32 I am the God of Abraham and the God of Isaac and the God of Jacob**? He is not the God of the dead, but of the living."

33 And when the crowds heard this, they were astonished at his teaching.

---

18 Sadducees, who say there is no resurrection, came to him and questioned him: **19** "Teacher, Moses wrote for us that **if a man's brother dies**, leaving a wife behind but **no child, that man should take the wife and raise up offspring for his brother. 20** There were seven brothers. The first married a woman, and dying, left no offspring. **21** The second also took her, and he died, leaving no offspring. And the third likewise. **22** None of the seven left offspring. Last of all, the woman died too. **23** In the resurrection, when they rise, whose wife will she be, since the seven had married her?"

24 Jesus spoke to them, "Isn't this the reason why you're mistaken: you don't know the Scriptures or the power of God? **25** For when they rise from the dead, they neither marry nor are given in marriage but are like angels in heaven. **26** And as for the dead being raised —haven't you read in the book of Moses, in the passage about the burning bush, how God said to him: **I am the God of Abraham and the God of Isaac and the God of Jacob**? **27** He is not the God of the dead but of the living. You are badly mistaken."

---

26 They were not able to catch him in what he said in public, and being amazed at his answer, they became silent.

27 Some of the Sadducees, who say there is no resurrection, came up and questioned him: **28** "Teacher, Moses wrote for us that **if a man's brother** has a wife, and **dies childless, his brother should take the wife and produce offspring for his brother. 29** Now there were seven brothers. The first took a wife and died without children. **30** Also the second **31** and the third took her. In the same way, all seven died and left no children. **32** Finally, the woman died too. **33** In the resurrection, therefore, whose wife will the woman be? For all seven had married her."

34 Jesus told them, "The children of this age marry and are given in marriage. **35** But those who are counted worthy to take part in that age and in the resurrection from the dead neither marry nor are given in marriage. **36** For they can no longer die, because they are like angels and are children of God, since they are children of the resurrection. **37** Moses even indicated in the passage about the burning bush that the dead are raised, where he calls the Lord **the God of Abraham and the God of Isaac and the God of Jacob. 38** He is not the God of the dead but of the living, because all are living to him."

39 Some of the scribes answered, "Teacher, you have spoken well." **40** And they no longer dared to ask him anything.

QUESTIONS ABOUT THE GREATEST COMMAND MT 22:34-40   MK 12:28-34

The Pharisees' question to Jesus about the "greatest commandment" is only recorded by Matthew and Mark. As noted above, for Luke, Jesus's answer to the question about the resurrection of the dead is the last time anyone asked him a question. Matthew and Mark frame this last question a bit differently. For Matthew, the query is another attempt to test him. In Mark, the inquisitor is presented in a slightly better light as one who was "not far from the kingdom of heaven." The accounts, however, remain quite compatible since Matthew will silence his opponents, not with an answer to one of their questions, but by asking a question they apparently are unable to answer (see "Jesus Exposes and Warns against Hypocrisy" on p. 106).

34 When the Pharisees heard that he had silenced the Sadducees, they came together. **35** And one of them, an expert in the law, asked a question to test him: **36** "Teacher, which command in the law is the greatest?"

28 One of the scribes approached. When he heard them debating and saw that Jesus answered them well, he asked him, "Which command is the most important of all?"

³⁷ He said to him, "**Love the Lord your God with all your heart, with all your soul, and with all your mind.** ³⁸ This is the greatest and most important command. ³⁹ The second is like it: **Love your neighbor as yourself.** ⁴⁰ All the Law and the Prophets depend on these two commands."

²⁹ Jesus answered, "The most important is **Listen, O Israel! The Lord our God, the Lord is one.** ³⁰ **Love the Lord your God with all your heart, with all your soul, with all your mind, and with all your strength.** ³¹ The second is, **Love your neighbor as yourself.** There is no other command greater than these."

³² Then the scribe said to him, "You are right, teacher. You have correctly said that he is one, and there is no one else except him. ³³ And to love him with all your heart, with all your understanding, and with all your strength, and to love your neighbor as yourself, is far more important than all the burnt offerings and sacrifices."

³⁴ When Jesus saw that he answered wisely, he said to him, "You are not far from the kingdom of God." And no one dared to question him any longer.

JESUS EXPOSES AND WARNS AGAINST HYPOCRISY MT 22:41—23:12 MK 12:35-40 **LK 20:41-47**

Mark and Luke record very similar versions of this scathing speech by Jesus. Matthew, though, expands with a fuller account. This interchange with the religious officials marks the introduction to Matthew's fifth and final major discourse. He includes a series of "woes" in 23:13-36 that are absent at this point in the narrative in Mark and Luke, although Luke includes a version of the woes earlier in his Gospel.

⁴¹ While the Pharisees were together, Jesus questioned them, ⁴² "What do you think about the Messiah? Whose son is he?"

They replied, "David's."

⁴³ He asked them, "How is it then that David, inspired by the Spirit, calls him 'Lord':

⁴⁴   The Lord declared to my Lord,
    'Sit at my right hand
    until I put your enemies
        under your feet'?

⁴⁵ "If David calls him 'Lord,' how then can he be his son?" ⁴⁶ No one was able to answer him at all, and from that day no one dared to question him anymore.

¹ Then Jesus spoke to the crowds and to his disciples: ² "The scribes and the Pharisees are seated in the chair of Moses. ³ Therefore do whatever they tell you, and observe it. But don't do what they do, because they don't practice what they teach. ⁴ They tie up heavy loads that are hard to carry and put them on people's shoulders, but they themselves aren't willing to lift a finger to move them. ⁵ They do everything to be seen by others: They enlarge their phylacteries and lengthen their tassels. ⁶ They love the place of honor at banquets, the front seats in the synagogues, ⁷ greetings in the marketplaces, and to be called 'Rabbi' by people.

⁸ "But you are not to be called 'Rabbi,' because you have one Teacher, and you are all brothers and sisters. ⁹ Do not call anyone on earth your father, because you have one Father, who is in heaven. ¹⁰ You are not to be called instructors either, because you have one Instructor, the Messiah. ¹¹ The greatest among you will be your servant. ¹² Whoever exalts himself will be humbled, and whoever humbles himself will be exalted."

³⁵ While Jesus was teaching in the temple, he asked, "How can the scribes say that the Messiah is the son of David? ³⁶ David himself says by the Holy Spirit:

    The Lord declared to my Lord,
    'Sit at my right hand
    until I put your enemies
        under your feet.'

³⁷ David himself calls him 'Lord'; how then can he be his son?" And the large crowd was listening to him with delight.

³⁸ He also said in his teaching, "Beware of the scribes, who want to go around in long robes and who want greetings in the marketplaces, ³⁹ the best seats in the synagogues, and the places of honor at banquets. ⁴⁰ They devour widows' houses and say long prayers just for show. These will receive harsher judgment."

⁴¹ Then he said to them, "How can they say that the Christ is the son of David? ⁴² For David himself says in the Book of Psalms:

    The Lord declared to my Lord,
    'Sit at my right hand
⁴³   until I make your enemies
        your footstool.'

⁴⁴ David calls him 'Lord' how then can the Christ be his son?"

⁴⁵ While all the people were listening, he said to his disciples, ⁴⁶ "Beware of the scribes, who want to go around in long robes and who love greetings in the marketplaces, the best seats in the synagogues, and the places of honor at banquets. ⁴⁷ They devour widows' houses and say long prayers just for show. These will receive harsher judgment."

13 "Woe to you, scribes and Pharisees, hypocrites! You shut the door of the kingdom of heaven in people's faces. For you don't go in, and you don't allow those entering to go in.

15 "Woe to you, scribes and Pharisees, hypocrites! You travel over land and sea to make one convert, and when he becomes one, you make him twice as fit for hell as you are!

16 "Woe to you, blind guides, who say, 'Whoever takes an oath by the temple, it means nothing. But whoever takes an oath by the gold of the temple is bound by his oath.' **17** Blind fools! For which is greater, the gold or the temple that sanctified the gold? **18** Also, 'Whoever takes an oath by the altar, it means nothing; but whoever takes an oath by the gift that is on it is bound by his oath.' **19** Blind people! For which is greater, the gift or the altar that sanctifies the gift? **20** Therefore, the one who takes an oath by the altar takes an oath by it and by everything on it. **21** The one who takes an oath by the temple takes an oath by it and by him who dwells in it. **22** And the one who takes an oath by heaven takes an oath by God's throne and by him who sits on it.

23 "Woe to you, scribes and Pharisees, hypocrites! You pay a tenth of mint, dill, and cumin, and yet you have neglected the more important matters of the law — justice, mercy, and faithfulness. These things should have been done without neglecting the others. **24** Blind guides! You strain out a gnat, but gulp down a camel!

25 "Woe to you, scribes and Pharisees, hypocrites! You clean the outside of the cup and dish, but inside they are full of greed and self-indulgence. **26** Blind Pharisee! First clean the inside of the cup, so that the outside of it may also become clean.

27 "Woe to you, scribes and Pharisees, hypocrites! You are like whitewashed tombs, which appear beautiful on the outside, but inside are full of the bones of the dead and every kind of impurity. **28** In the same way, on the outside you seem righteous to people, but inside you are full of hypocrisy and lawlessness.

29 "Woe to you, scribes and Pharisees, hypocrites! You build the tombs of the prophets and decorate the graves of the righteous, **30** and you say, 'If we had lived in the days of our ancestors, we wouldn't have taken part with them in shedding the prophets' blood.' **31** So you testify against yourselves that you are descendants of those who murdered the prophets. **32** Fill up, then, the measure of your ancestors' sins!

33 "Snakes! Brood of vipers! How can you escape being condemned to hell? **34** This is why I am sending you prophets, sages, and scribes. Some of them you will kill and crucify, and some of them you will flog in your synagogues and pursue from town to town. **35** So all the righteous blood shed on the earth will be charged to you, from the blood of righteous Abel to the blood of Zechariah, son of Berechiah, whom you murdered between the sanctuary and the altar. **36** Truly I tell you, all these things will come on this generation."

THE POOR GENEROUS WIDOW   MK 12:41-44   LK 21:1-4

Mark and Luke record the account of the poor widow putting all she owned in the treasury box. The event is a fitting counterexample to the hypocrisy of the religious officials just exposed by Jesus.

41 Sitting across from the temple treasury, he watched how the crowd dropped money into the treasury. Many rich people were putting in large sums. **42** Then a poor widow came and dropped in two tiny coins

1 He looked up and saw the rich dropping their offerings into the temple treasury. **2** He also saw a poor widow dropping in two tiny coins. **3** "Truly I tell you," he said. "This poor widow has put in more than all

worth very little. [43] Summoning his disciples, he said to them, "Truly I tell you, this poor widow has put more into the treasury than all the others. [44] For they all gave out of their surplus, but she out of her poverty has put in everything she had — all she had to live on."

of them. [4] For all these people have put in gifts out of their surplus, but she out of her poverty has put in all she had to live on."

As stated above, this is the last of Matthew's five lengthy discourses around which his narrative is structured, but this is the only one of those five that is given the same space in Mark and Luke. What's more, all three authors retain essentially the same structure of the discourse. Of course, there are a number of variations but one could envision Jesus giving this speech on a number of occasions throughout his ministry. With that said, each author has retained components of the discourse that, when carefully examined, reveals his own literary and theological agenda.

[1] As Jesus left and was going out of the temple, his disciples came up and called his attention to its buildings. [2] He replied to them, "Do you see all these things? Truly I tell you, not one stone will be left here on another that will not be thrown down."

[3] While he was sitting on the Mount of Olives, the disciples approached him privately and said, "Tell us, when will these things happen? And what is the sign of your coming and of the end of the age?"

[4] Jesus replied to them: "Watch out that no one deceives you. [5] For many will come in my name, saying, 'I am the Messiah,' and they will deceive many. [6] You are going to hear of wars and rumors of wars. See that you are not alarmed, because these things must take place, but the end is not yet. [7] For nation will rise up against nation, and kingdom against kingdom. There will be famines and earthquakes in various places. [8] All these events are the beginning of labor pains.

[9] "Then they will hand you over to be persecuted, and they will kill you. You will be hated by all nations because of my name. [10] Then many will fall away, betray one another, and hate one another. [11] Many false prophets will rise up and deceive many. [12] Because lawlessness will multiply, the love of many will grow cold. [13] But the one who endures to the end will be saved. [14] This good news of the kingdom will be proclaimed in all the world as a testimony to all nations, and then the end will come.

[1] As he was going out of the temple, one of his disciples said to him, "Teacher, look! What massive stones! What impressive buildings!"

[2] Jesus said to him, "Do you see these great buildings? Not one stone will be left upon another — all will be thrown down."

[3] While he was sitting on the Mount of Olives across from the temple, Peter, James, John, and Andrew asked him privately, [4] "Tell us, when will these things happen? And what will be the sign when all these things are about to be accomplished?"

[5] Jesus told them, "Watch out that no one deceives you. [6] Many will come in my name, saying, 'I am he,' and they will deceive many. [7] When you hear of wars and rumors of wars, don't be alarmed; these things must take place, but it is not yet the end. [8] For nation will rise up against nation, and kingdom against kingdom. There will be earthquakes in various places, and famines. These are the beginning of birth pains.

[9] "But you, be on your guard! They will hand you over to local courts, and you will be flogged in the synagogues. You will stand before governors and kings because of me, as a witness to them. [10] And it is necessary that the gospel be preached to all nations. [11] So when they arrest you and hand you over, don't worry beforehand what you will say, but say whatever is given to you at that time, for it isn't you speaking, but the Holy Spirit.

[12] "Brother will betray brother to death, and a father his child. Children will rise up

[5] As some were talking about the temple, how it was adorned with beautiful stones and gifts dedicated to God, he said, [6] "These things that you see — the days will come when not one stone will be left on another that will not be thrown down."

[7] "Teacher," they asked him, "so when will these things happen? And what will be the sign when these things are about to take place?"

[8] Then he said, "Watch out that you are not deceived. For many will come in my name, saying, 'I am he,' and, 'The time is near.' Don't follow them. [9] When you hear of wars and rebellions, don't be alarmed. Indeed, it is necessary that these things take place first, but the end won't come right away."

[10] Then he told them: "Nation will be raised up against nation, and kingdom against kingdom. [11] There will be violent earthquakes, and famines and plagues in various places, and there will be terrifying sights and great signs from heaven. [12] But before all these things, they will lay their hands on you and persecute you. They will hand you over to the synagogues and prisons, and you will be brought before kings and governors because of my name. [13] This will give you an opportunity to bear witness. [14] Therefore make up your minds not to prepare your defense ahead of time, [15] for I will give you such words and a wisdom that none of your adversaries will be able to resist or contradict. [16] You will even be

¹⁵ "So when you see **the abomination of desolation**, spoken of by the prophet Daniel, standing in the holy place" (let the reader understand), ¹⁶ "then those in Judea must flee to the mountains. ¹⁷ A man on the housetop must not come down to get things out of his house, ¹⁸ and a man in the field must not go back to get his coat. ¹⁹ Woe to pregnant women and nursing mothers in those days! ²⁰ Pray that your escape may not be in winter or on a Sabbath. ²¹ For at that time there will be great distress, the kind that hasn't taken place from the beginning of the world until now and never will again. ²² Unless those days were cut short, no one would be saved. But those days will be cut short because of the elect.

²³ "If anyone tells you then, 'See, here is the Messiah!' or, 'Over here!' do not believe it. ²⁴ For false messiahs and false prophets will arise and perform great signs and wonders to lead astray, if possible, even the elect. ²⁵ Take note: I have told you in advance. ²⁶ So if they tell you, 'See, he's in the wilderness!' don't go out; or, 'See, he's in the storerooms!' do not believe it. ²⁷ For as the lightning comes from the east and flashes as far as the west, so will be the coming of the Son of Man. ²⁸ Wherever the carcass is, there the vultures will gather.

²⁹ "Immediately after the distress of those days, the sun will be darkened, and the moon will not shed its light; the stars will fall from the sky, and the powers of the heavens will be shaken. ³⁰ Then the sign of the Son of Man will appear in the sky, and then all the peoples of the earth will mourn; and they will see the Son of Man coming on the clouds of heaven with power and great glory. ³¹ He will send out his angels with a loud trumpet, and they will gather his elect from the four winds, from one end of the sky to the other.

³² "Learn this lesson from the fig tree: As soon as its branch becomes tender and sprouts leaves, you know that summer is near. ³³ In the same way, when you see all these things, recognize that he is near — at the door.

against parents and have them put to death. ¹³ You will be hated by everyone because of my name, but the one who endures to the end will be saved.

¹⁴ "When you see **the abomination of desolation** standing where it should not be" (let the reader understand), "then those in Judea must flee to the mountains. ¹⁵ A man on the housetop must not come down or go in to get anything out of his house, ¹⁶ and a man in the field must not go back to get his coat. ¹⁷ Woe to pregnant women and nursing mothers in those days!

¹⁸ "Pray it won't happen in winter. ¹⁹ For those will be days of tribulation, the kind that hasn't been from the beginning of creation until now and never will be again. ²⁰ If the Lord had not cut those days short, no one would be saved. But he cut those days short for the sake of the elect, whom he chose.

²¹ "Then if anyone tells you, 'See, here is the Messiah! See, there!' do not believe it. ²² For false messiahs and false prophets will arise and will perform signs and wonders to lead astray, if possible, the elect. ²³ And you must watch! I have told you everything in advance.

²⁴ "But in those days, after that tribulation: The sun will be darkened, and the moon will not shed its light; ²⁵ the stars will be falling from the sky, and the powers in the heavens will be shaken. ²⁶ Then they will see the Son of Man coming in clouds with great power and glory. ²⁷ He will send out the angels and gather his elect from the four winds, from the ends of the earth to the ends of heaven.

²⁸ "Learn this lesson from the fig tree: As soon as its branch becomes tender and sprouts leaves, you know that summer is near. ²⁹ In the same way, when you see these things happening, recognize that he is near — at the door.

³⁰ "Truly I tell you, this generation will certainly not pass away until all these things take place. ³¹ Heaven and earth will pass away, but my words will never pass away.

betrayed by parents, brothers, relatives, and friends. They will kill some of you. ¹⁷ You will be hated by everyone because of my name, ¹⁸ but not a hair of your head will be lost. ¹⁹ By your endurance, gain your lives.

²⁰ "When you see Jerusalem surrounded by armies, then recognize that its desolation has come near. ²¹ Then those in Judea must flee to the mountains. Those inside the city must leave it, and those who are in the country must not enter it, ²² because these are days of vengeance to fulfill all the things that are written. ²³ Woe to pregnant women and nursing mothers in those days, for there will be great distress in the land and wrath against this people. ²⁴ They will be killed by the sword and be led captive into all the nations, and Jerusalem will be trampled by the Gentiles until the times of the Gentiles are fulfilled.

²⁵ "Then there will be signs in the sun, moon, and stars; and there will be anguish on the earth among nations bewildered by the roaring of the sea and the waves. ²⁶ People will faint from fear and expectation of the things that are coming on the world, because the powers of the heavens will be shaken. ²⁷ Then they will see the Son of Man coming in a cloud with power and great glory. ²⁸ But when these things begin to take place, stand up and lift up your heads, because your redemption is near."

²⁹ Then he told them a parable: "Look at the fig tree, and all the trees. ³⁰ As soon as they put out leaves you can see for yourselves and recognize that summer is already near. ³¹ In the same way, when you see these things happening, recognize that the kingdom of God is near. ³² Truly I tell you, this generation will certainly not pass away until all things take place. ³³ Heaven and earth will pass away, but my words will never pass away.

³⁴ "Be on your guard, so that your minds are not dulled from carousing, drunkenness, and worries of life, or that day will come on you unexpectedly ³⁵ like a trap. For it will come on all who live on the face of the whole earth. ³⁶ But be alert at all times, praying that you

⁴⁴ Truly I tell you, this generation will certainly not pass away until all these things take place. ³⁵ Heaven and earth will pass away, but my words will never pass away.

³⁶ "Now concerning that day and hour no one knows — neither the angels of heaven nor the Son — except the Father alone. ³⁷ As the days of Noah were, so the coming of the Son of Man will be. ³⁸ For in those days before the flood they were eating and drinking, marrying and giving in marriage, until the day Noah boarded the ark. ³⁹ They didn't know until the flood came and swept them all away. This is the way the coming of the Son of Man will be. ⁴⁰ Then two men will be in the field; one will be taken and one left. ⁴¹ Two women will be grinding grain with a hand mill; one will be taken and one left. ⁴² Therefore be alert, since you don't know what day your Lord is coming.

³² "Now concerning that day or hour no one knows — neither the angels in heaven nor the Son — but only the Father.

³³ "Watch! Be alert! For you don't know when the time is coming.

³⁴ "It is like a man on a journey, who left his house, gave authority to his servants, gave each one his work, and commanded the door-keeper to be alert. ³⁵ Therefore be alert, since you don't know when the master of the house is coming — whether in the evening or at midnight or at the crowing of the rooster or early in the morning. ³⁶ Otherwise, when he comes suddenly he might find you sleeping. ³⁷ And what I say to you, I say to everyone: Be alert!"

may have strength to escape all these things that are going to take place and to stand before the Son of Man."

³⁷ During the day, he was teaching in the temple, but in the evening he would go out and spend the night on what is called the Mount of Olives. ³⁸ Then all the people would come early in the morning to hear him in the temple.

⁴³ But know this: If the homeowner had known what time the thief was coming, he would have stayed alert and not let his house be broken into. ⁴⁴ This is why you are also to be ready, because the Son of Man is coming at an hour you do not expect.

⁴⁵ "Who then is a faithful and wise servant, whom his master has put in charge of his household, to give them food at the proper time? ⁴⁶ Blessed is that servant whom the master finds doing his job when he comes. ⁴⁷ Truly I tell you, he will put him in charge of all his possessions. ⁴⁸ But if that wicked servant says in his heart, 'My master is delayed,' ⁴⁹ and starts to beat his fellow servants, and eats and drinks with drunkards, ⁵⁰ that servant's master will come on a day he does not expect him and at an hour he does not know. ⁵¹ He will cut him to pieces and assign him a place with the hypocrites, where there will be weeping and gnashing of teeth."

THE PARABLE OF THE TEN VIRGINS

MT 25:1-13

¹ "At that time the kingdom of heaven will be like ten virgins who took their lamps and went out to meet the groom. ² Five of them were foolish and five were wise. ³ When the foolish took their lamps, they didn't take oil with them; ⁴ but the wise ones took oil in their flasks with their lamps. ⁵ When the groom was delayed, they all became drowsy and fell asleep.

⁶ "In the middle of the night there was a shout: 'Here's the groom! Come out to meet him.'

⁷ "Then all the virgins got up and trimmed their lamps. ⁸ The foolish ones said to the wise ones, 'Give us some of your oil, because our lamps are going out.'

⁹ "The wise ones answered, 'No, there won't be enough for us and for you. Go instead to those who sell oil, and buy some for yourselves.'

¹⁰ "When they had gone to buy some, the groom arrived, and those who were ready went in with him to the wedding banquet, and the door was shut. ¹¹ Later the rest of the virgins also came and said, 'Master, master, open up for us!'

¹² "He replied, 'Truly I tell you, I don't know you!'

¹³ "Therefore be alert, because you don't know either the day or the hour."

14 "For it is just like a man about to go on a journey. He called his own servants and entrusted his possessions to them. **15** To one he gave five talents, to another two talents, and to another one talent, depending on each one's ability. Then he went on a journey. Immediately **16** the man who had received five talents went, put them to work, and earned five more. **17** In the same way the man with two earned two more. **18** But the man who had received one talent went off, dug a hole in the ground, and hid his master's money.

19 "After a long time the master of those servants came and settled accounts with them. **20** The man who had received five talents approached, presented five more talents, and said, 'Master, you gave me five talents. See, I've earned five more talents.'

21 "His master said to him, 'Well done, good and faithful servant! You were faithful over a few things; I will put you in charge of many things. Share your master's joy.'

22 "The man with two talents also approached. He said, 'Master, you gave me two talents. See, I've earned two more talents.'

23 "His master said to him, 'Well done, good and faithful servant! You were faithful over a few things; I will put you in charge of many things. Share your master's joy.'

24 "The man who had received one talent also approached and said, 'Master, I know you. You're a harsh man, reaping where you haven't sown and gathering where you haven't scattered seed. **25** So I was afraid and went off and hid your talent in the ground. See, you have what is yours.'

26 "His master replied to him, 'You evil, lazy servant! If you knew that I reap where I haven't sown and gather where I haven't scattered, **27** then you should have deposited my money with the bankers, and I would have received my money back with interest when I returned.

28 " 'So take the talent from him and give it to the one who has ten talents. **29** For to everyone who has, more will be given, and he will have more than enough. But from the one who does not have, even what he has will be taken away from him. **30** And throw this good-for-nothing servant into the outer darkness, where there will be weeping and gnashing of teeth.' "

JESUS TEACHES ABOUT THE FINAL JUDGMENT

31 "When the Son of Man comes in his glory, and all the angels with him, then he will sit on his glorious throne. **32** All the nations will be gathered before him, and he will separate them one from another, just as a shepherd separates the sheep from the goats. **33** He will put the sheep on his right and the goats on the left. **34** Then the King will say to those on his right, 'Come, you who are blessed by my Father; inherit the kingdom prepared for you from the foundation of the world.

35 " 'For I was hungry and you gave me something to eat; I was thirsty and you gave me something to drink; I was a stranger and you took me in; **36** I was naked and you clothed me; I was sick and you took care of me; I was in prison and you visited me.'

37 "Then the righteous will answer him, 'Lord, when did we see you hungry and feed you, or thirsty and give you something to drink? **38** When did we see you a stranger and take you in, or without clothes and clothe you? **39** When did we see you sick, or in prison, and visit you?'

40 "And the King will answer them, 'Truly I tell you, whatever you did for one of the least of these brothers and sisters of mine, you did for me.'

41 "Then he will also say to those on the left, 'Depart from me, you who are cursed, into the eternal fire prepared for the devil and his angels! **42** For I was hungry and you gave me nothing to eat; I was thirsty and you gave me nothing to drink; [43] I was a stranger and you didn't take me in; I was naked and you didn't clothe me, sick and in prison and you didn't take care of me.'

[44] "Then they too will answer, 'Lord, when did we see you hungry, or thirsty, or a stranger, or without clothes, or sick, or in prison, and not help you?'

[45] "Then he will answer them, 'Truly I tell you, whatever you did not do for one of the least of these, you did not do for me.'

[46] "And they will go away into eternal punishment, but the righteous into eternal life."

THE JEWISH LEADERS PLOT TO KILL JESUS

MT 26:1-5   MK 14:1-2   LK 22:1-2

The Synoptic tradition is unified on the general time frame of the final plot by the religious officials to destroy Jesus—that is, a few days prior to the Passover feast. Matthew alone couples this plot with yet another prediction by Jesus of his death. This functions to set the unfolding events squarely within the sovereign plan of God. This short account also sets up the following account of Judas's betrayal.

[1] When Jesus had finished saying all these things, he told his disciples, [2] "You know that the Passover takes place after two days, and the Son of Man will be handed over to be crucified."

[3] Then the chief priests and the elders of the people assembled in the courtyard of the high priest, who was named Caiaphas, [4] and they conspired to arrest Jesus in a treacherous way and kill him. [5] "Not during the festival," they said, "so there won't be rioting among the people."

[1] It was two days before the Passover and the Festival of Unleavened Bread. The chief priests and the scribes were looking for a cunning way to arrest Jesus and kill him. [2] "Not during the festival," they said, "so that there won't be a riot among the people."

[1] The Festival of Unleavened Bread, which is called Passover, was approaching. [2] The chief priests and the scribes were looking for a way to put him to death, because they were afraid of the people.

JUDAS AGREES TO BETRAY JESUS

MT 26:14-16   MK 14:10-11   LK 22:3-6

All three Synoptic Gospels record Judas as plotting to betray Jesus for a sum of money. Matthew offers further details regarding the amount of money exchanged. Luke mentions the involvement of Satan in Judas's treachery.

[14] Then one of the Twelve, the man called Judas Iscariot, went to the chief priests [15] and said, "What are you willing to give me if I hand him over to you?" So they weighed out thirty pieces of silver for him. [16] And from that time he started looking for a good opportunity to betray him.

[10] Then Judas Iscariot, one of the Twelve, went to the chief priests to betray Jesus to them. [11] And when they heard this, they were glad and promised to give him money. So he started looking for a good opportunity to betray him.

[3] Then Satan entered Judas, called Iscariot, who was numbered among the Twelve. [4] He went away and discussed with the chief priests and temple police how he could hand him over to them. [5] They were glad and agreed to give him silver. [6] So he accepted the offer and started looking for a good opportunity to betray him to them when the crowd was not present.

THE PASSION OF JESUS

As one moves into the account of Jesus's passion, the variations among the accounts become a bit more historically challenging given that such events only occurred once. It becomes all the more necessary, then, to hold in tension the Gospel authors' historical, literary, and theological purposes.

Regarding the preparation for the Passover meal, the core details of this event are retained by all three Synoptic authors, but there is increasing detail as one moves from Matthew, to Mark, to Luke. For example, Matthew refers to the disciples as a group, Mark records two disciples actually fulfilling the mission, and Luke further explains that those two disciples were Peter and John. The detail provided by both Mark and Luke demonstrates their interest in the unfolding of Jesus's predictions.

[17] On the first day of Unleavened Bread the disciples came to Jesus and asked, "Where do you want us to make preparations for you to eat the Passover?"

[18] "Go into the city to a certain man," he said, "and tell him, 'The Teacher says: My time is near; I am celebrating the Passover at your place with my disciples.'" [19] So the disciples did as Jesus had directed them and prepared the Passover.

[12] On the first day of Unleavened Bread, when they sacrifice the Passover lamb, his disciples asked him, "Where do you want us to go and prepare the Passover so that you may eat it?"

[13] So he sent two of his disciples and told them, "Go into the city, and a man carrying a jar of water will meet you. Follow him. [14] Wherever he enters, tell the owner of the house, 'The Teacher says, "Where is my guest room where I may eat the Passover with my disciples?"' [15] He will show you a large room upstairs, furnished and ready. Make the preparations for us there." [16] So the disciples went out, entered the city, and found it just as he had told them, and they prepared the Passover.

[7] Then the Day of Unleavened Bread came when the Passover lamb had to be sacrificed. [8] Jesus sent Peter and John, saying, "Go and make preparations for us to eat the Passover."

[9] "Where do you want us to prepare it?" they asked him.

[10] "Listen," he said to them, "when you've entered the city, a man carrying a water jug will meet you. Follow him into the house he enters. [11] Tell the owner of the house, 'The Teacher asks you, "Where is the guest room where I can eat the Passover with my disciples?"' [12] Then he will show you a large, furnished room upstairs. Make the preparations there."

[13] So they went and found it just as he had told them, and they prepared the Passover.

[1] Before the Passover Festival, Jesus knew that his hour had come to depart from this world to the Father. Having loved his own who were in the world, he loved them to the end.

[2] Now when it was time for supper, the devil had already put it into the heart of Judas, Simon Iscariot's son, to betray him. [3] Jesus knew that the Father had given everything into his hands, that he had come from God, and that he was going back to God. [4] So he got up from supper, laid aside his outer clothing, took a towel, and tied it around himself. [5] Next, he poured water into a basin and began to wash his disciples' feet and to dry them with the towel tied around him.

[6] He came to Simon Peter, who asked him, "Lord, are you going to wash my feet?"

[7] Jesus answered him, "What I'm doing you don't realize now, but afterward you will understand."

8 "You will never wash my feet," Peter said.

Jesus replied, "If I don't wash you, you have no part with me."

9 Simon Peter said to him, "Lord, not only my feet, but also my hands and my head."

10 "One who has bathed," Jesus told him, "doesn't need to wash anything except his feet, but he is completely clean. You are clean, but not all of you." 11 For he knew who would betray him. This is why he said, "Not all of you are clean."

12 When Jesus had washed their feet and put on his outer clothing, he reclined again and said to them, "Do you know what I have done for you? 13 You call me Teacher and Lord — and you are speaking rightly, since that is what I am. 14 So if I, your Lord and Teacher, have washed your feet, you also ought to wash one another's feet. 15 For I have given you an example, that you also should do just as I have done for you.

16 "Truly I tell you, a servant is not greater than his master, and a messenger is not greater than the one who sent him. 17 If you know these things, you are blessed if you do them.

18 "I'm not speaking about all of you; I know those I have chosen. But the Scripture must be fulfilled: **The one who eats my bread has raised his heel against me.** 19 I am telling you now before it happens, so that when it does happen you will believe that I am he. 20 Truly I tell you, whoever receives anyone I send receives me, and the one who receives me receives him who sent me."

THE FIRST LORD'S SUPPER   MT 26:20-30   MK 14:17-26   LK 22:14-30   JN 13:21-30

To be sure, all four Gospel writers retain the essence of the Lord's Supper, although the order varies. At the heart of this event is the announcement of Jesus's impending betrayal and Jesus's commentary on the symbolic meaning of the meal. Regarding the latter, only the Synoptic authors include the important reference to the "new covenant." John omits this and much of the actual account of the meal. Instead, in the preceding account of Jesus washing the disciples' feet, John focuses on the symbolic character of the foot washing.

The differences between John and the Synoptics with regard to the announcement of Jesus's betrayer are a bit more challenging. Yet before one levies an accusation of discrepancy, we should observe that, in all four accounts, the identification of the betrayer remains ultimately unclear. For the Synoptics, with everyone dipping in a common bowl (as was customary), Jesus's statement about the one who dips with him stops short of a clear disclosure. Even Jesus's response directly to Judas in Matthew remains cryptic. For John, the more specific identification notwithstanding, in the end the disciples remain unclear of his intent, as is evident from John's explanation. Ultimately, one does not want to miss the broader literary and theological intent of the author, namely to show how the imminent suffering of Jesus will occur according to the declared will of God, yet without denying the pivotal role of free and responsible humans.

20 When evening came, he was reclining at the table with the Twelve. 21 While they were eating, he said, "Truly I tell you, one of you will betray me."

22 Deeply distressed, each one began to say to him, "Surely not I, Lord?"

23 He replied, "The one who dipped his hand with me in the bowl — he will betray me. 24 The Son of Man will go just as it is written about him, but woe to that man by whom the Son of

17 When evening came, he arrived with the Twelve. 18 While they were reclining and eating, Jesus said, "Truly I tell you, one of you will betray me — one who is eating with me."

19 They began to be distressed and to say to him one by one, "Surely not I?"

20 He said to them, "It is one of the Twelve — the one who is dipping bread in the bowl with me. 21 For the Son of Man will go just as it is written about him, but

14 When the hour came, he reclined at the table, and the apostles with him. 15 Then he said to them, "I have fervently desired to eat this Passover with you before I suffer. 16 For I tell you, I will not eat it again until it is fulfilled in the kingdom of God." 17 Then he took a cup, and after giving thanks, he said, "Take this and share it among yourselves. 18 For I tell you, from now on I will not drink of the fruit of the vine until the kingdom of God comes."

21 When Jesus had said this, he was troubled in his spirit and testified, "Truly I tell you, one of you will betray me."

22 The disciples started looking at one another — uncertain which one he was speaking about. 23 One of his disciples, the one Jesus loved, was reclining close beside Jesus. 24 Simon Peter motioned to him to find out who it was he was talking about. 25 So he leaned back against Jesus and asked him, "Lord, who is it?"

Man is betrayed! It would have been better for him if he had not been born."

²⁵ Judas, his betrayer, replied, "Surely not I, Rabbi?"

"You have said it," he told him.

²⁶ As they were eating, Jesus took bread, blessed and broke it, gave it to the disciples, and said, "Take and eat it; this is my body." ²⁷ Then he took a cup, and after giving thanks, he gave it to them and said, "Drink from it, all of you. ²⁸ For this is my blood of the covenant, which is poured out for many for the forgiveness of sins. ²⁹ But I tell you, I will not drink from this fruit of the vine from now on until that day when I drink it new with you in my Father's kingdom." ³⁰ After singing a hymn, they went out to the Mount of Olives.

woe to that man by whom the Son of Man is betrayed! It would have been better for him if he had not been born."

²² As they were eating, he took bread, blessed and broke it, gave it to them, and said, "Take it; this is my body." ²³ Then he took a cup, and after giving thanks, he gave it to them, and they all drank from it. ²⁴ He said to them, "This is my blood of the covenant, which is poured out for many. ²⁵ Truly I tell you, I will no longer drink of the fruit of the vine until that day when I drink it new in the kingdom of God."

²⁶ After singing a hymn, they went out to the Mount of Olives.

¹⁹ And he took bread, gave thanks, broke it, gave it to them, and said, "This is my body, which is given for you. Do this in remembrance of me."

²⁰ In the same way he also took the cup after supper and said, "This cup is the new covenant in my blood, which is poured out for you. ²¹ But look, the hand of the one betraying me is at the table with me. ²² For the Son of Man will go away as it has been determined, but woe to that man by whom he is betrayed!"

²³ So they began to argue among themselves which of them it could be who was going to do it.

²⁴ Then a dispute also arose among them about who should be considered the greatest. ²⁵ But he said to them, "The kings of the Gentiles lord it over them, and those who have authority over them have themselves called 'Benefactors.' ²⁶ It is not to be like that among you. On the contrary, whoever is greatest among you should become like the youngest, and whoever leads, like the one serving. ²⁷ For who is greater, the one at the table or the one serving? Isn't it the one at the table? But I am among you as the one who serves. ²⁸ You are those who stood by me in my trials. ²⁹ I bestow on you a kingdom, just as my Father bestowed one on me, ³⁰ so that you may eat and drink at my table in my kingdom. And you will sit on thrones judging the twelve tribes of Israel."

²⁶ Jesus replied, "He's the one I give the piece of bread to after I have dipped it." When he had dipped the bread, he gave it to Judas, Simon Iscariot's son. ²⁷ After Judas ate the piece of bread, Satan entered him. So Jesus told him, "What you're doing, do quickly."

²⁸ None of those reclining at the table knew why he said this to him. ²⁹ Since Judas kept the money-bag, some thought that Jesus was telling him, "Buy what we need for the festival," or that he should give something to the poor. ³⁰ After receiving the piece of bread, he immediately left. And it was night.

THE NEW COMMAND

JN 13:31-35

³¹ When he had left, Jesus said, "Now the Son of Man is glorified, and God is glorified in him. ³² If God is glorified in him, God will also glorify him in himself and will glorify him at once. ³³ Children, I am with you a little while longer. You will look for me, and just as I told the Jews, so now I tell you: 'Where I am going, you cannot come.'

³⁴ "I give you a new command: Love one another. Just as I have loved you, you are also to love one another. ³⁵ By this everyone will know that you are my disciples, if you love one another."

All four Gospel writers recount Jesus's prediction of Peter's denial. Matthew and Mark are almost verbatim in their account and are distinct from Luke and John in two ways. First, both appeal to Zechariah 13:7 as a means of showing yet again how the unfolding events fulfill Scripture. Second, the prediction is applied to all the disciples, although Peter ultimately becomes the center of attention. Luke and John, on the other hand, zero in on Peter from the beginning. Taken together, the reader can piece together a more expansive discussion that included a warning from Jesus that applied to all the disciples but narrowed in on Peter.

³¹ Then Jesus said to them, "Tonight all of you will fall away because of me, for it is written:

I will strike the shepherd,
and the sheep of the flock
will be scattered.

³² But after I have risen, I will go ahead of you to Galilee."

³³ Peter told him, "Even if everyone falls away because of you, I will never fall away."

³⁴ "Truly I tell you," Jesus said to him, "tonight, before the rooster crows, you will deny me three times."

³⁵ "Even if I have to die with you," Peter told him, "I will never deny you," and all the disciples said the same thing.

²⁷ Then Jesus said to them, "All of you will fall away, because it is written:

I will strike the shepherd,
and the sheep
will be scattered.

²⁸ But after I have risen, I will go ahead of you to Galilee."

²⁹ Peter told him, "Even if everyone falls away, I will not."

³⁰ "Truly I tell you," Jesus said to him, "today, this very night, before the rooster crows twice, you will deny me three times."

³¹ But he kept insisting, "If I have to die with you, I will never deny you." And they all said the same thing.

³¹ "Simon, Simon, look out. Satan has asked to sift you like wheat. ³² But I have prayed for you that your faith may not fail. And you, when you have turned back, strengthen your brothers."

³³ "Lord," he told him, "I'm ready to go with you both to prison and to death."

³⁴ "I tell you, Peter," he said, "the rooster will not crow today until you deny three times that you know me."

³⁶ "Lord," Simon Peter said to him, "where are you going?"

Jesus answered, "Where I am going you cannot follow me now, but you will follow later."

³⁷ "Lord," Peter asked, "why can't I follow you now? I will lay down my life for you."

³⁸ Jesus replied, "Will you lay down your life for me? Truly I tell you, a rooster will not crow until you have denied me three times.

JESUS WARNS HIS DISCIPLES TO BE PREPARED   LK 22:35-38

³⁵ He also said to them, "When I sent you out without money-bag, traveling bag, or sandals, did you lack anything?"

"Not a thing," they said.

³⁶ Then he said to them, "But now, whoever has a money-bag should take it, and also a traveling bag. And whoever doesn't have a sword should sell his robe and buy one. ³⁷ For I tell you, what is written must be fulfilled in me: **And he was counted among the lawless.** Yes, what is written about me is coming to its fulfillment."

³⁸ "Lord," they said, "look, here are two swords."

"That is enough!" he told them.

JESUS SAYS THAT HE IS THE WAY TO THE FATHER   JN 14:1-14

¹ "Don't let your heart be troubled. Believe in God; believe also in me. ² In my Father's house are many rooms; if not, I would have told you. I am going away to prepare a place for you. ³ If I go away and prepare a place for you, I will come again and take you to myself, so that where I am you may be also. ⁴ You know the way to where I am going."

⁵ "Lord," Thomas said, "we don't know where you're going. How can we know the way?"

⁶ Jesus told him, "I am the way, the truth, and the life. No one comes to the Father except through me. ⁷ If you know me, you will also know my Father. From now on you do know him and have seen him."

⁸ "Lord," said Philip, "show us the Father, and that's enough for us."

⁹ Jesus said to him, "Have I been among you all this time and you do not know me, Philip? The one who has seen me has seen the Father. How can you say, 'Show us the Father'? ¹⁰ Don't you believe that I am in the Father and the Father is in me? The words I speak to you I do not speak on my own. The Father who lives in me does his works. ¹¹ Believe me that I am in the Father and the Father is in me. Otherwise, believe because of the works themselves.

¹² "Truly I tell you, the one who believes in me will also do the works that I do. And he will do even greater works than these, because I am going to the Father. ¹³ Whatever you ask in my name, I will do it so that the Father may be glorified in the Son. ¹⁴ If you ask me anything in my name, I will do it."

JESUS PROMISES ANOTHER COUNSELOR, THE SPIRIT OF TRUTH   JN 14:15-31A

¹⁵ "If you love me, you will keep my commands. ¹⁶ And I will ask the Father, and he will give you another Counselor to be with you forever. ¹⁷ He is the Spirit of truth. The world is unable to receive him because it doesn't see him or know him. But you do know him, because he remains with you and will be in you.

¹⁸ "I will not leave you as orphans; I am coming to you. ¹⁹ In a little while the world will no longer see me, but you will see me. Because I live, you will live too. ²⁰ On that day you will know that I am in my Father, you are in me, and I am in you. ²¹ The one who has my commands and keeps them is the one who loves me. And the one who loves me will be loved by my Father. I also will love him and will reveal myself to him."

²² Judas (not Iscariot) said to him, "Lord, how is it you're going to reveal yourself to us and not to the world?"

²³ Jesus answered, "If anyone loves me, he will keep my word. My Father will love him, and we will come to him and make our home with him. ²⁴ The one who doesn't love me will not keep my words. The word that you hear is not mine but is from the Father who sent me.

²⁵ "I have spoken these things to you while I remain with you. ²⁶ But the Counselor, the Holy Spirit, whom the Father will send in my name, will teach you all things and remind you of everything I have told you.

²⁷ "Peace I leave with you. My peace I give to you. I do not give to you as the world gives. Don't let your heart be troubled or fearful. ²⁸ You have heard me tell you, 'I am going away and I am coming to you.' If you loved me, you would rejoice that I am going to the Father, because the Father is greater than I. ²⁹ I have told you now before it happens so that when it does happen you may believe. ³⁰ I will not talk with you much longer, because the ruler of the world is coming. He has no power over me. ³¹ On the contrary, so that the world may know that I love the Father, I do as the Father commanded me."

Only Luke and John offer this short transitional statement. Matthew and Mark include a shift in location at the beginning of the next event.

³⁹ He went out and made his way as usual to the Mount of Olives, and the disciples followed him.   "Get up; let's leave this place."
⁴⁰ When he reached the place, he told them, "Pray that you may not fall into temptation."

JESUS TEACHES ABOUT THE VINE AND THE BRANCHES   JN 15:1-17

¹ "I am the true vine, and my Father is the gardener. ² Every branch in me that does not produce fruit he removes, and he prunes every branch that produces fruit so that it will produce more fruit. ³ You are already clean because of the word I have spoken to you. ⁴ Remain in me, and I in you. Just as a branch is unable to produce fruit by itself unless it remains on the vine, neither can you unless you remain in me. ⁵ I am the vine; you are the branches. The one who remains in me and I in him produces much fruit, because you can do nothing without me. ⁶ If anyone does not remain in me, he is thrown aside like a branch and he withers. They gather them, throw them into the fire, and they are burned. ⁷ If you remain in me and my words remain in you, ask whatever you want and it will be done for you. ⁸ My Father is glorified by this: that you produce much fruit and prove to be my disciples.

⁹ "As the Father has loved me, I have also loved you. Remain in my love. ¹⁰ If you keep my commands you will remain in my love, just as I have kept my Father's commands and remain in his love.

¹¹ "I have told you these things so that my joy may be in you and your joy may be complete.

¹² "This is my command: Love one another as I have loved you. ¹³ No one has greater love than this: to lay down his life for his friends. ¹⁴ You are my friends if you do what I command you. ¹⁵ I do not call you servants anymore, because a servant doesn't know what his master is doing. I have called you friends, because I have made known to you everything I have heard from my Father. ¹⁶ You did not choose me, but I chose you. I appointed you to go and produce fruit and that your fruit should remain, so that whatever you ask the Father in my name, he will give you.

¹⁷ "This is what I command you: Love one another."

JESUS WARNS AGAINST FUTURE PERSECUTIONS   JN 15:18–16:4

¹⁸ "If the world hates you, understand that it hated me before it hated you. ¹⁹ If you were of the world, the world would love you as its own. However, because you are not of the world, but I have chosen you out of it, the world hates you. ²⁰ Remember the word I spoke to you: 'A servant is not greater than his master.' If they persecuted me, they will also persecute you. If they kept my word, they will also keep yours. ²¹ But they will do all these things to you on account of my name, because they don't know the one who sent me. ²² If I had not come and spoken to them, they would not be guilty of sin. Now they have no excuse for their sin. ²³ The one who hates me also hates my Father. ²⁴ If I had not done the works among them that no one else has done, they would not have sin. Now they have seen and hated both me and my Father. ²⁵ But this happened so that the statement written in their law might be fulfilled: **They hated me for no reason.**

²⁶ "When the Counselor comes, the one I will send to you from the Father — the Spirit of truth who proceeds from the Father — he will testify about me. ²⁷ You also will testify, because you have been with me from the beginning.

[1] "I have told you these things to keep you from stumbling. [2] They will ban you from the synagogues. In fact, a time is coming when anyone who kills you will think he is offering service to God. [3] They will do these things because they haven't known the Father or me. [4] But I have told you these things so that when their time comes you will remember I told them to you. I didn't tell you these things from the beginning, because I was with you."

JESUS TEACHES ABOUT THE MINISTRY OF THE SPIRIT JN 16:5-15

[5] "But now I am going away to him who sent me, and not one of you asks me, 'Where are you going?' [6] Yet, because I have spoken these things to you, sorrow has filled your heart. [7] Nevertheless, I am telling you the truth. It is for your benefit that I go away, because if I don't go away the Counselor will not come to you. If I go, I will send him to you. [8] When he comes, he will convict the world about sin, righteousness, and judgment: [9] About sin, because they do not believe in me; [10] about righteousness, because I am going to the Father and you will no longer see me; [11] and about judgment, because the ruler of this world has been judged.

[12] "I still have many things to tell you, but you can't bear them now. [13] When the Spirit of truth comes, he will guide you into all the truth. For he will not speak on his own, but he will speak whatever he hears. He will also declare to you what is to come. [14] He will glorify me, because he will take from what is mine and declare it to you. [15] Everything the Father has is mine. This is why I told you that he takes from what is mine and will declare it to you."

JESUS TEACHES ABOUT PRAYING IN HIS NAME JN 16:16-33

[16] "A little while and you will no longer see me; again a little while and you will see me."

[17] Then some of his disciples said to one another, "What is this he's telling us: 'A little while and you will not see me; again a little while and you will see me' and, 'because I am going to the Father'?" [18] They said, "What is this he is saying, 'A little while'? We don't know what he's talking about."

[19] Jesus knew they wanted to ask him, and so he said to them, "Are you asking one another about what I said, 'A little while and you will not see me; again a little while and you will see me'? [20] Truly I tell you, you will weep and mourn, but the world will rejoice. You will become sorrowful, but your sorrow will turn to joy. [21] When a woman is in labor, she has pain because her time has come. But when she has given birth to a child, she no longer remembers the suffering because of the joy that a person has been born into the world. [22] So you also have sorrow now. But I will see you again. Your hearts will rejoice, and no one will take away your joy from you.

[23] "In that day you will not ask me anything. Truly I tell you, anything you ask the Father in my name, he will give you. [24] Until now you have asked for nothing in my name. Ask and you will receive, so that your joy may be complete.

[25] "I have spoken these things to you in figures of speech. A time is coming when I will no longer speak to you in figures, but I will tell you plainly about the Father. [26] On that day you will ask in my name, and I am not telling you that I will ask the Father on your behalf. [27] For the Father himself loves you, because you have loved me and have believed that I came from God. [28] I came from the Father and have come into the world. Again, I am leaving the world and going to the Father."

[29] His disciples said, "Look, now you're speaking plainly and not using any figurative language. [30] Now we know that you know everything and don't need anyone to question you. By this we believe that you came from God."

[31] Jesus responded to them, "Do you now believe? [32] Indeed, an hour is coming, and has come, when each of you will be scattered to his own home, and you will leave me alone. Yet I am not alone, because the Father is with me. [33] I have told you these things so that in me you may have peace. You will have suffering in this world. Be courageous! I have conquered the world."

JESUS PRAYS FOR HIMSELF, HIS DISCIPLES, AND ALL BELIEVERS   JN 17:1-26

[1] Jesus spoke these things, looked up to heaven, and said: "Father, the hour has come. Glorify your Son so that the Son may glorify you, [2] since you gave him authority over all flesh, so that he may give eternal life to everyone you have given him. [3] This is eternal life: that they may know you, the only true God, and the one you have sent — Jesus Christ. [4] I have glorified you on the earth by completing the work you gave me to do. [5] Now, Father, glorify me in your presence with that glory I had with you before the world existed.

[6] "I have revealed your name to the people you gave me from the world. They were yours, you gave them to me, and they have kept your word. [7] Now they know that everything you have given is from you, [8] because I have given them the words you gave me. They have received them and have known for certain that I came from you. They have believed that you sent me.

[9] "I pray for them. I am not praying for the world but for those you have given me, because they are yours. [10] Everything I have is yours, and everything you have is mine, and I am glorified in them. [11] I am no longer in the world, but they are in the world, and I am coming to you. Holy Father, protect them by your name that you have given me, so that they may be one as we are one. [12] While I was with them, I was protecting them by your name that you have given me. I guarded them and not one of them is lost, except the son of destruction, so that the Scripture may be fulfilled. [13] Now I am coming to you, and I speak these things in the world so that they may have my joy completed in them. [14] I have given them your word. The world hated them because they are not of the world, just as I am not of the world. [15] I am not praying that you take them out of the world but that you protect them from the evil one. [16] They are not of the world, just as I am not of the world. [17] Sanctify them by the truth; your word is truth. [18] As you sent me into the world, I also have sent them into the world. [19] I sanctify myself for them, so that they also may be sanctified by the truth.

[20] "I pray not only for these, but also for those who believe in me through their word. [21] May they all be one, as you, Father, are in me and I am in you. May they also be in us, so that the world may believe you sent me. [22] I have given them the glory you have given me, so that they may be one as we are one. [23] I am in them and you are in me, so that they may be made completely one, that the world may know you have sent me and have loved them as you have loved me.

[24] "Father, I want those you have given me to be with me where I am, so that they will see my glory, which you have given me because you loved me before the world's foundation. [25] Righteous Father, the world has not known you. However, I have known you, and they have known that you sent me. [26] I made your name known to them and will continue to make it known, so that the love you have loved me with may be in them and I may be in them."

JESUS AGONIZES IN THE GARDEN   MT 26:36-46   MK 14:32-42   LK 22:40-46

Jesus's agonizing prayer in the garden of Gethsemane is attested by the three Synoptic authors. Matthew and Luke are quite similar in their account of the event. Luke is shorter but includes a number of important details omitted by the other two. First, he mentions an angel who ministers to Jesus in his time of need. Luke refers to angels quite frequently in his narrative, making the inclusion of such a reference here a fitting detail for him to recall. Second, he heightens the intensity of Jesus's experience by mentioning that his sweat was as "great drops of blood." Describing Jesus's agony in physical terms would also have been a fitting description given the historical tradition that Luke was a physician. Together, these two unique details shift the focus from the weary disciples to the intensity of Jesus's emotional struggle.

36 Then Jesus came with them to a place called Gethsemane, and he told the disciples, "Sit here while I go over there and pray." **37** Taking along Peter and the two sons of Zebedee, he began to be sorrowful and troubled. **38** He said to them, "I am deeply grieved to the point of death. Remain here and stay awake with me." **39** Going a little farther, he fell facedown and prayed, "My Father, if it is possible, let this cup pass from me. Yet not as I will, but as you will." **40** Then he came to the disciples and found them sleeping. He asked Peter, "So, couldn't you stay awake with me one hour? **41** Stay awake and pray, so that you won't enter into temptation. The spirit is willing, but the flesh is weak." **42** Again, a second time, he went away and prayed, "My Father, if this cannot pass unless I drink it, your will be done." **43** And he came again and found them sleeping, because they could not keep their eyes open. **44** After leaving them, he went away again and prayed a third time, saying the same thing once more. **45** Then he came to the disciples and said to them, "Are you still sleeping and resting? See, the time is near. The Son of Man is betrayed into the hands of sinners. **46** Get up; let's go. See, my betrayer is near."

32 Then they came to a place named Gethsemane, and he told his disciples, "Sit here while I pray." **33** He took Peter, James, and John with him, and he began to be deeply distressed and troubled. **34** He said to them, "I am deeply grieved to the point of death. Remain here and stay awake." **35** He went a little farther, fell to the ground, and prayed that if it were possible, the hour might pass from him. **36** And he said, "*Abba*, Father! All things are possible for you. Take this cup away from me. Nevertheless, not what I will, but what you will." **37** Then he came and found them sleeping. He said to Peter, "Simon, are you sleeping? Couldn't you stay awake one hour? **38** Stay awake and pray so that you won't enter into temptation. The spirit is willing, but the flesh is weak." **39** Once again he went away and prayed, saying the same thing. **40** And again he came and found them sleeping, because they could not keep their eyes open. They did not know what to say to him. **41** Then he came a third time and said to them, "Are you still sleeping and resting? Enough! The time has come. See, the Son of Man is betrayed into the hands of sinners. **42** Get up; let's go. See, my betrayer is near."

40 When he reached the place, he told them, "Pray that you may not fall into temptation." **41** Then he withdrew from them about a stone's throw, knelt down, and began to pray, **42** "Father, if you are willing, take this cup away from me—nevertheless, not my will, but yours, be done." **43** Then an angel from heaven appeared to him, strengthening him. **44** Being in anguish, he prayed more fervently, and his sweat became like drops of blood falling to the ground. **45** When he got up from prayer and came to the disciples, he found them sleeping, exhausted from their grief. **46** "Why are you sleeping?" he asked them. "Get up and pray, so that you won't fall into temptation."

JUDAS BETRAYS JESUS, WHO GETS ARRESTED   MT 26:47-56   MK 14:43-52   LK 22:47-53   JN 18:1-12

All four Gospel writers record the arrest of Jesus at the hands of his betrayer, Judas. Each author, nevertheless, has his own emphases. Matthew is characteristically concerned with showing how the unfolding of the events fulfills Scripture. Mark has a similar interest in fulfillment but adds an interesting detail about a naked bystander—an insertion that many believe to be a cryptic reference to the author himself. Luke adds more vivid detail to the event, including Jesus's healing of a servant whose ear was severed. Not surprisingly, John offers the most detail about the characters. In addition, Judas's role is overshadowed by Jesus's surrender. Through this, John demonstrates how Jesus remains in complete control of the unfolding events. Collectively, the four accounts give a full-orbed picture.

47 While he was still speaking, Judas, one of the Twelve, suddenly arrived. A large mob with swords and clubs was with him

43 While he was still speaking, Judas, one of the Twelve, suddenly arrived. With him was a mob, with swords and clubs, from the

47 While he was still speaking, suddenly a mob came, and one of the Twelve named Judas was leading them. He came near Jesus to

1 After Jesus had said these things, he went out with his disciples across the Kidron Valley, where there was a garden, and he and his

---

from the chief priests and elders of the people. [48] His betrayer had given them a sign: "The one I kiss, he's the one; arrest him." [49] So immediately he went up to Jesus and said, "Greetings, Rabbi!" and kissed him.

[50] "Friend," Jesus asked him, "why have you come?"

Then they came up, took hold of Jesus, and arrested him. [51] At that moment one of those with Jesus reached out his hand and drew his sword. He struck the high priest's servant and cut off his ear.

[52] Then Jesus told him, "Put your sword back in its place because all who take up the sword will perish by the sword. [53] Or do you think that I cannot call on my Father, and he will provide me here and now with more than twelve legions of angels? [54] How, then, would the Scriptures be fulfilled that say it must happen this way?"

[55] At that time Jesus said to the crowds, "Have you come out with swords and clubs, as if I were a criminal, to capture me? Every day I used to sit, teaching in the temple, and you didn't arrest me. [56] But all this has happened so that the writings of the prophets would be fulfilled." Then all the disciples deserted him and ran away.

chief priests, the scribes, and the elders. [44] His betrayer had given them a signal. "The one I kiss," he said, "he's the one; arrest him and take him away under guard." [45] So when he came, immediately he went up to Jesus and said, "Rabbi!" and kissed him. [46] They took hold of him and arrested him. [47] One of those who stood by drew his sword, struck the high priest's servant, and cut off his ear.

[48] Jesus said to them, "Have you come out with swords and clubs, as if I were a criminal, to capture me? [49] Every day I was among you, teaching in the temple, and you didn't arrest me. But the Scriptures must be fulfilled."

[50] Then they all deserted him and ran away. [51] Now a certain young man, wearing nothing but a linen cloth, was following him. They caught hold of him, [52] but he left the linen cloth behind and ran away naked.

kiss him, [48] but Jesus said to him, "Judas, are you betraying the Son of Man with a kiss?"

[49] When those around him saw what was going to happen, they asked, "Lord, should we strike with the sword?" [50] Then one of them struck the high priest's servant and cut off his right ear.

[51] But Jesus responded, "No more of this!" And touching his ear, he healed him. [52] Then Jesus said to the chief priests, temple police, and the elders who had come for him, "Have you come out with swords and clubs as if I were a criminal? [53] Every day while I was with you in the temple, you never laid a hand on me. But this is your hour — and the dominion of darkness."

disciples went into it. [2] Judas, who betrayed him, also knew the place, because Jesus often met there with his disciples. [3] So Judas took a company of soldiers and some officials from the chief priests and the Pharisees and came there with lanterns, torches, and weapons.

[4] Then Jesus, knowing everything that was about to happen to him, went out and said to them, "Who is it that you're seeking?"

[5] "Jesus of Nazareth," they answered.

"I am he," Jesus told them.

Judas, who betrayed him, was also standing with them. [6] When Jesus told them, "I am he," they stepped back and fell to the ground.

[7] Then he asked them again, "Who is it that you're seeking?"

"Jesus of Nazareth," they said.

[8] "I told you I am he," Jesus replied. "So if you're looking for me, let these men go." [9] This was to fulfill the words he had said: "I have not lost one of those you have given me."

[10] Then Simon Peter, who had a sword, drew it, struck the high priest's servant, and cut off his right ear. (The servant's name was Malchus.)

[11] At that, Jesus said to Peter, "Put your sword away! Am I not to drink the cup the Father has given me?"

[12] Then the company of soldiers, the commander, and the Jewish officials arrested Jesus and tied him up.

JESUS, FOLLOWED BY PETER, IS TAKEN TO THE HIGH PRIEST MT 26:57-58 MK 14:53-54 LK 22:54 JN 18:13-16

Matthew, Mark, and Luke all recount that Jesus was taken first to the house of the high priest, Caiaphas, although Luke's account is considerably shorter. In all three accounts, Peter factors significantly as the narrative builds momentum toward the fulfillment of the prediction of his denial. John retains the core of

---

MATTHEW MARK LUKE JOHN

the Synoptics but includes a few notable details. First, he mentions Annas, the father-in-law of Caiaphas, and draws attention to an unwitting statement Annas made earlier in the narrative. Second, John offers a cryptic reference to "another disciple" who accompanied Peter (presumably, John himself). Both details lend credibility to the account and fit John's governing purpose to present reliable testimony of the pivotal events of Jesus's suffering in order to engender belief.

[57] Those who had arrested Jesus led him away to Caiaphas the high priest, where the scribes and the elders had convened. [58] Peter was following him at a distance right to the high priest's courtyard. He went in and was sitting with the servants to see the outcome.	[53] They led Jesus away to the high priest, and all the chief priests, the elders, and the scribes assembled. [54] Peter followed him at a distance, right into the high priest's courtyard. He was sitting with the servants, warming himself by the fire.	[54] They seized him, led him away, and brought him into the high priest's house. Meanwhile Peter was following at a distance.	[13] First they led him to Annas, since he was the father-in-law of Caiaphas, who was high priest that year. [14] Caiaphas was the one who had advised the Jews that it would be better for one man to die for the people. [15] Simon Peter was following Jesus, as was another disciple. That disciple was an acquaintance of the high priest; so he went with Jesus into the high priest's courtyard. [16] But Peter remained standing outside by the door. So the other disciple, the one known to the high priest, went out and spoke to the girl who was the doorkeeper and brought Peter in.

JESUS BEFORE THE SANHEDRIN MT 26:59-66   MK 14:55-64

Only Matthew and Mark record this covert meeting of the Sanhedrin in which they attempt to garner false testimony against Jesus. The two accounts are similar except that, in Mark, Jesus's reply to the question about his messianic identity is more direct. Matthew's more evasive statement, "You have said it," is no less affirmative, but it turns the inquisitor's words back on himself suggesting that Jesus did not completely agree with the connotation implied by the questioner. One might envision Jesus replying in both ways in a prolonged session marked by continued badgering by his opponents.

[59] The chief priests and the whole Sanhedrin were looking for false testimony against Jesus so that they could put him to death, [60] but they could not find any, even though many false witnesses came forward. Finally, two who came forward [61] stated, "This man said, 'I can destroy the temple of God and rebuild it in three days.'" [62] The high priest stood up and said to him, "Don't you have an answer to what these men are testifying against you?" [63] But Jesus kept silent. The high priest said to him, "I charge you under oath by the living God: Tell us if you are the Messiah, the Son of God." [64] "You have said it," Jesus told him. "But I tell you, in the future you will see **the Son of Man seated at the right hand** of Power and **coming on the clouds of heaven**." [65] Then the high priest tore his robes and said, "He has blasphemed! Why do we still need witnesses? See, now you've heard the blasphemy. [66] What is your decision?" They answered, "He deserves death!"	[55] The chief priests and the whole Sanhedrin were looking for testimony against Jesus to put him to death, but they could not find any. [56] For many were giving false testimony against him, and the testimonies did not agree. [57] Some stood up and gave false testimony against him, stating, [58] "We heard him say, 'I will destroy this temple made with human hands, and in three days I will build another not made by hands.'" [59] Yet their testimony did not agree even on this. [60] Then the high priest stood up before them all and questioned Jesus, "Don't you have an answer to what these men are testifying against you?" [61] But he kept silent and did not answer. Again the high priest questioned him, "Are you the Messiah, the Son of the Blessed One?" [62] "I am," said Jesus, "and you will see **the Son of Man seated at the right hand** of Power and **coming with the clouds of heaven**." [63] Then the high priest tore his robes and said, "Why do we still need witnesses? [64] You have heard the blasphemy. What is your decision?" They all condemned him as deserving death.

MATTHEW   MARK   LUKE   JOHN

The details surrounding Peter's first denial are consistent across all four Gospels. Peter was somewhere in the vicinity of the palace when a servant girl recognized him. Mark alone records the first crow of the rooster after Peter's initial denial. Looking back at Jesus's prediction of Peter's denial, however, it was Mark who noted that his three denials would be before the cock crowed "twice." The other Gospel writers, it seems, were less interested in the number of times the cock crowed than that Peter would deny Jesus three times before it crowed.

[69] Now Peter was sitting outside in the courtyard. A servant girl approached him and said, "You were with Jesus the Galilean too."

[70] But he denied it in front of everyone: "I don't know what you're talking about."

[66] While Peter was in the courtyard below, one of the high priest's maidservants came. [67] When she saw Peter warming himself, she looked at him and said, "You also were with Jesus, the man from Nazareth."

[68] But he denied it: "I don't know or understand what you're talking about." Then he went out to the entryway, and a rooster crowed.

[55] They lit a fire in the middle of the courtyard and sat down together, and Peter sat among them. [56] When a servant saw him sitting in the light, and looked closely at him, she said, "This man was with him too."

[57] But he denied it: "Woman, I don't know him."

[17] Then the servant girl who was the doorkeeper said to Peter, "You aren't one of this man's disciples too, are you?"

"I am not." he said. [18] Now the servants and the officials had made a charcoal fire, because it was cold. They were standing there warming themselves, and Peter was standing with them, warming himself.

ANNAS QUESTIONS JESUS

[19] The high priest questioned Jesus about his disciples and about his teaching.

[20] "I have spoken openly to the world," Jesus answered him. "I have always taught in the synagogue and in the temple, where all the Jews congregate, and I haven't spoken anything in secret. [21] Why do you question me? Question those who heard what I told them. Look, they know what I said."

[22] When he had said these things, one of the officials standing by slapped Jesus, saying, "Is this the way you answer the high priest?"

[23] "If I have spoken wrongly," Jesus answered him, "give evidence about the wrong; but if rightly, why do you hit me?" [24] Then Annas sent him bound to Caiaphas the high priest.

PETER'S SECOND AND THIRD DENIALS

One can piece together the setting of Peter's second and third denial by harmonizing the four accounts. Reading Luke, it appears that Peter's second denial was directed at a male, although Matthew and Mark claim that a servant girl initiated the query. However, it is clear from the setting that there were a number of individuals, both men and women, warming themselves by the fire that evening to whom Peter might have replied. John gives a few additional details such as the identity of the third inquisitor, who was a relative of the man whose ear Peter severed.

[71] When he had gone out to the gateway, another woman saw him and told those who were there, "This man was with Jesus the Nazarene!"

[72] And again he denied it with an oath: "I don't know the man!"

[69] When the maidservant saw him again, she began to tell those standing nearby, "This man is one of them."

[70] But again he denied it. After a little while those standing there said to Peter again, "You certainly

[58] After a little while, someone else saw him and said, "You're one of them too."

"Man, I am not!" Peter said.

[59] About an hour later, another kept insisting, "This man was

[25] Now Simon Peter was standing and warming himself. They said to him, "You aren't one of his disciples too, are you?"

He denied it and said, "I am not."

[26] One of the high priest's servants, a relative of the man whose

73 After a little while those standing there approached and said to Peter, "You really are one of them, since even your accent gives you away."

74 Then he started to curse and to swear with an oath, "I don't know the man!" Immediately a rooster crowed, 75 and Peter remembered the words Jesus had spoken, "Before the rooster crows, you will deny me three times." And he went outside and wept bitterly.

are one of them, since you're also a Galilean."

71 Then he started to curse and swear, "I don't know this man you're talking about!"

72 Immediately a rooster crowed a second time, and Peter remembered when Jesus had spoken the word to him, "Before the rooster crows twice, you will deny me three times." And he broke down and wept.

certainly with him, since he's also a Galilean."

60 But Peter said, "Man, I don't know what you're talking about!" Immediately, while he was still speaking, a rooster crowed. 61 Then the Lord turned and looked at Peter. So Peter remembered the word of the Lord, how he had said to him, "Before the rooster crows today, you will deny me three times." 62 And he went outside and wept bitterly.

ear Peter had cut off, said, "Didn't I see you with him in the garden?" 27 Peter denied it again. Immediately a rooster crowed.

GUARDS BEAT JESUS | MT 26:67-68 | MK 14:65 | LK 22:63-65

All three Synoptic authors consistently record the brutal treatment of Jesus by the temple guards following the covert meeting at Caiaphas's house.

67 Then they spat in his face and beat him; others slapped him 68 and said, "Prophesy to us, Messiah! Who was it that hit you?"

65 Then some began to spit on him, to blindfold him, and to beat him, saying, "Prophesy!" The temple servants also took him and slapped him.

63 The men who were holding Jesus started mocking and beating him. 64 After blindfolding him, they kept asking, "Prophesy! Who was it that hit you?" 65 And they were saying many other blasphemous things to him.

THE SANHEDRIN CONDEMNS JESUS | MT 27:1-2 | MK 15:1 | LK 22:66-71

The official meeting among the religious officials took place the next morning according to the Synoptic tradition. Matthew and Mark give little detail about this meeting, perhaps because it functioned only as a formality given the events of the night before. Since Luke alone records this official meeting, he includes the details of the hearing, many of which resemble the covert meeting of the night before. It would not be far-fetched to envision the same details taking place in a formal trial ensuring that the religious officials at least appeared to follow proper legal protocol.

1 When daybreak came, all the chief priests and the elders of the people plotted against Jesus to put him to death. 2 After tying him up, they led him away and handed him over to Pilate, the governor.

1 As soon as it was morning, having held a meeting with the elders, scribes, and the whole Sanhedrin, the chief priests tied Jesus up, led him away, and handed him over to Pilate.

66 When daylight came, the elders of the people, both the chief priests and the scribes, convened and brought him before their Sanhedrin. 67 They said, "If you are the Messiah, tell us."

But he said to them, "If I do tell you, you will not believe. 68 And if I ask you, you will not answer. 69 But from now on, the Son of Man will be seated at the right hand of the power of God."

70 They all asked, "Are you, then, the Son of God?"

And he said to them, "You say that I am."

71 "Why do we need any more testimony," they said, "since we've heard it ourselves from his mouth?"

---

³ Then Judas, his betrayer, seeing that Jesus had been condemned, was full of remorse and returned the thirty pieces of silver to the chief priests and elders. ⁴ "I have sinned by betraying innocent blood," he said.

"What's that to us?" they said. "See to it yourself!" ⁵ So he threw the silver into the temple and departed. Then he went and hanged himself.

⁶ The chief priests took the silver and said, "It's not permitted to put it into the temple treasury, since it is blood money." ⁷ They conferred together and bought the potter's field with it as a burial place for foreigners. ⁸ Therefore that field has been called "Blood Field" to this day. ⁹ Then what was spoken through the prophet Jeremiah was fulfilled: **They took the thirty pieces of silver, the price of him whose price was set by the Israelites, ¹⁰ and they gave them for the potter's field, as the Lord directed me.**

JESUS BEFORE PILATE

| | MT 27:11-14 | MK 15:2-5 | LK 23:1-7 | JN 18:28-38A |

All four Gospels grant significant space to the interchange between Jesus and Pilate, indicating its importance. Collectively, they offer a full picture of this event. Matthew and Mark have the briefest and most comparable versions, while Luke and John add details. For example, Luke records how Pilate sent Jesus to Herod, an aside that demonstrates Luke's interest in politics. John's account is by far the longest and shows the inherent irony in this unprincipled litigation brought against Jesus.

¹¹ Now Jesus stood before the governor. "Are you the King of the Jews?" the governor asked him.

Jesus answered, "You say so." ¹² While he was being accused by the chief priests and elders, he didn't answer.

¹³ Then Pilate said to him, "Don't you hear how much they are testifying against you?" ¹⁴ But he didn't answer him on even one charge, so that the governor was quite amazed.

² So Pilate asked him, "Are you the King of the Jews?"

He answered him, "You say so." ³ And the chief priests accused him of many things. ⁴ Pilate questioned him again, "Aren't you going to answer? Look how many things they are accusing you of!" ⁵ But Jesus still did not answer, and so Pilate was amazed.

¹ Then their whole assembly rose up and brought him before Pilate. ² They began to accuse him, saying, "We found this man misleading our nation, opposing payment of taxes to Caesar, and saying that he himself is the Messiah, a king." ³ So Pilate asked him, "Are you the king of the Jews?"

He answered him, "You say so." ⁴ Pilate then told the chief priests and the crowds, "I find no grounds for charging this man." ⁵ But they kept insisting, "He stirs up the people, teaching throughout all Judea, from Galilee where he started even to here." ⁶ When Pilate heard this, he asked if the man was a Galilean. ⁷ Finding that he was under Herod's jurisdiction, he sent him to Herod, who was also in Jerusalem during those days.

²⁸ Then they led Jesus from Caiaphas to the governor's headquarters. It was early morning. They did not enter the headquarters themselves; otherwise they would be defiled and unable to eat the Passover.

²⁹ So Pilate came out to them and said, "What charge do you bring against this man?"

³⁰ They answered him, "If this man weren't a criminal, we wouldn't have handed him over to you."

³¹ Pilate told them, "You take him and judge him according to your law."

"It's not legal for us to put anyone to death," the Jews declared. ³² They said this so that Jesus's words might be fulfilled indicating what kind of death he was going to die.

| ▮ MATTHEW | ▮ MARK | ▮ LUKE | ▮ JOHN |

^{33} Then Pilate went back into the headquarters, summoned Jesus, and said to him, "Are you the King of the Jews?"

^{34} Jesus answered, "Are you asking this on your own, or have others told you about me?"

^{35} "I'm not a Jew, am I?" Pilate replied. "Your own nation and the chief priests handed you over to me. What have you done?"

^{36} "My kingdom is not of this world," said Jesus. "If my kingdom were of this world, my servants would fight, so that I wouldn't be handed over to the Jews. But as it is, my kingdom is not from here."

^{37} "You are a king then?" Pilate asked.

"You say that I'm a king," Jesus replied. "I was born for this, and I have come into the world for this: to testify to the truth. Everyone who is of the truth listens to my voice."

^{38} "What is truth?" said Pilate.

JESUS BEFORE HEROD
LK 23:8-12

^{8} Herod was very glad to see Jesus; for a long time he had wanted to see him because he had heard about him and was hoping to see some miracle performed by him. ^{9} So he kept asking him questions, but Jesus did not answer him. ^{10} The chief priests and the scribes stood by, vehemently accusing him. ^{11} Then Herod, with his soldiers, treated him with contempt, mocked him, dressed him in bright clothing, and sent him back to Pilate. ^{12} That very day Herod and Pilate became friends. Previously, they had been enemies.

PILATE HANDS JESUS OVER TO BE CRUCIFIED
MT 27:15-26   MK 15:6-15   LK 23:13-25   JN 18:38B—19:16A

Together with the previous section ("Jesus before Pilate" on p. 126), Jesus's trial before Pilate is perhaps the lengthiest event within the Passion Narrative. All four Gospels, to varying degrees, seek to contrast the blamelessness of Jesus with the culpability of his accusers. Though the Jews are most accountable for Jesus's death, the role and intentions of Pilate remain a mystery. Nevertheless, from a human perspective both Rome and Israel are responsible. Yet more central to the four accounts, and especially John's, is the degree to which the events unfold as part of the larger divine redemptive plan.

^{15} At the festival the governor's custom was to release to the crowd a prisoner they wanted. ^{16} At that time they had a notorious prisoner called Barabbas. ^{17} So when they had gathered together, Pilate said to them, "Who is it you want me to release for you — Barabbas, or Jesus who is called Christ?" ^{18} For he knew it was because of envy that they had handed him over.

^{19} While he was sitting on the judge's bench, his wife sent word to him, "Have nothing to do with that righteous man, for today I've

^{6} At the festival Pilate used to release for the people a prisoner whom they requested. ^{7} There was one named Barabbas, who was in prison with rebels who had committed murder during the rebellion. ^{8} The crowd came up and began to ask Pilate to do for them as was his custom. ^{9} Pilate answered them, "Do you want me to release the King of the Jews for you?" ^{10} For he knew it was because of envy that the chief priests had handed him over. ^{11} But the chief priests stirred up the crowd so that he would release Barabbas

^{13} Pilate called together the chief priests, the leaders, and the people, ^{14} and said to them, "You have brought me this man as one who misleads the people. But in fact, after examining him in your presence, I have found no grounds to charge this man with those things you accuse him of. ^{15} Neither has Herod, because he sent him back to us. Clearly, he has done nothing to deserve death. ^{16} Therefore, I will have him whipped and then release him."

^{18} Then they all cried out together, "Take this man away!

After he had said this, he went out to the Jews again and told them, "I find no grounds for charging him. ^{39} You have a custom that I release one prisoner to you at the Passover. So, do you want me to release to you the King of the Jews?"

^{40} They shouted back, "Not this man, but Barabbas!" Now Barabbas was a revolutionary.

^{1} Then Pilate took Jesus and had him flogged. ^{2} The soldiers also twisted together a crown of thorns, put it on his head, and clothed him in a purple robe. ^{3} And

---

suffered terribly in a dream because of him."

20 The chief priests and the elders, however, persuaded the crowds to ask for Barabbas and to execute Jesus. **21** The governor asked them, "Which of the two do you want me to release for you?"

"Barabbas!" they answered.

22 Pilate asked them, "What should I do then with Jesus, who is called Christ?"

They all answered, "Crucify him!"

23 Then he said, "Why? What has he done wrong?"

But they kept shouting all the more, "Crucify him!"

24 When Pilate saw that he was getting nowhere, but that a riot was starting instead, he took some water, washed his hands in front of the crowd, and said, "I am innocent of this man's blood. See to it yourselves!"

25 All the people answered, "His blood be on us and on our children!" **26** Then he released Barabbas to them and, after having Jesus flogged, handed him over to be crucified.

to them instead. **12** Pilate asked them again, "Then what do you want me to do with the one you call the King of the Jews?"

13 Again they shouted, "Crucify him!"

14 Pilate said to them, "Why? What has he done wrong?"

But they shouted all the more, "Crucify him!"

15 Wanting to satisfy the crowd, Pilate released Barabbas to them; and after having Jesus flogged, he handed him over to be crucified.

Release Barabbas to us!" **19** (He had been thrown into prison for a rebellion that had taken place in the city, and for murder.)

20 Wanting to release Jesus, Pilate addressed them again, **21** but they kept shouting, "Crucify! Crucify him!"

22 A third time he said to them, "Why? What has this man done wrong? I have found in him no grounds for the death penalty. Therefore, I will have him whipped and then release him."

23 But they kept up the pressure, demanding with loud voices that he be crucified, and their voices won out. **24** So Pilate decided to grant their demand **25** and released the one they were asking for, who had been thrown into prison for rebellion and murder. But he handed Jesus over to their will.

they kept coming up to him and saying, "Hail, King of the Jews!" and were slapping his face.

4 Pilate went outside again and said to them, "Look, I'm bringing him out to you to let you know I find no grounds for charging him." **5** Then Jesus came out wearing the crown of thorns and the purple robe. Pilate said to them, "Here is the man!"

6 When the chief priests and the temple servants saw him, they shouted, "Crucify! Crucify!"

Pilate responded, "Take him and crucify him yourselves, since I find no grounds for charging him."

7 "We have a law," the Jews replied to him, "and according to that law he ought to die, because he made himself the Son of God."

8 When Pilate heard this statement, he was more afraid than ever. **9** He went back into the headquarters and asked Jesus, "Where are you from?" But Jesus did not give him an answer. **10** So Pilate said to him, "Do you refuse to speak to me? Don't you know that I have the authority to release you and the authority to crucify you?"

11 "You would have no authority over me at all," Jesus answered him, "if it hadn't been given you from above. This is why the one who handed me over to you has the greater sin."

12 From that moment Pilate kept trying to release him. But the Jews shouted, "If you release this man, you are not Caesar's friend. Anyone who makes himself a king opposes Caesar!"

13 When Pilate heard these words, he brought Jesus outside. He sat down on the judge's seat in a place called the Stone Pavement (but in Aramaic, *Gabbatha*). **14** It was the preparation day for the Passover, and it was about noon. Then he told the Jews, "Here is your king!"

15 They shouted, "Take him away! Take him away! Crucify him!"

Pilate said to them, "Should I crucify your king?"

"We have no king but Caesar!" the chief priests answered.

16 Then he handed him over to be crucified.

Matthew and Mark alone record the brutal treatment of Jesus following the indictment by Pilate. The graphic details are consistent across both.

27 Then the governor's soldiers took Jesus into the governor's residence and gathered the whole company around him. **28** They stripped him and dressed him in a scarlet robe. **29** They twisted together a crown of thorns, put it on his head, and placed a staff in his right hand. And they knelt down before him and mocked him: "Hail, King of the Jews!" **30** Then they spat on him, took the staff, and kept hitting him on the head. **31** After they had mocked him, they stripped him of the robe, put his own clothes on him,

16 The soldiers led him away into the palace (that is, the governor's residence) and called the whole company together. **17** They dressed him in a purple robe, twisted together a crown of thorns, and put it on him. **18** And they began to salute him, "Hail, King of the Jews!" **19** They were hitting him on the head with a stick and spitting on him. Getting down on their knees, they were paying him homage. **20** After they had mocked him, they stripped him of the purple robe and put his clothes on him.

The three Synoptic authors record Jesus's fateful journey to Golgotha and agree that a man named Simon of Cyrene was chosen to help carry the cross. Mark adds the names of Simon's sons, which may suggest that they were a part of the post-resurrection community of believers, but this is speculative. Luke adds Jesus's brief discourse to the women following him, showing the author's desire to set these events within an eschatological framework. Jesus's death will set in motion a series of epic events in the days to come.

and led him away to crucify him. **32** As they were going out, they found a Cyrenian man named Simon. They forced him to carry his cross.

They led him out to crucify him. **21** They forced a man coming in from the country, who was passing by, to carry Jesus's cross. He was Simon of Cyrene, the father of Alexander and Rufus.

26 As they led him away, they seized Simon, a Cyrenian, who was coming in from the country, and laid the cross on him to carry behind Jesus. **27** A large crowd of people followed him, including women who were mourning and lamenting him. **28** But turning to them, Jesus said, "Daughters of Jerusalem, do not weep for me, but weep for yourselves and your children. **29** Look, the days are coming when they will say, 'Blessed are the women without children, the wombs that never bore, and the breasts that never nursed!' **30** Then they will begin **to say to the mountains, 'Fall on us!' and to the hills, 'Cover us!'** **31** For if they do these things when the wood is green, what will happen when it is dry?"

32 Two others — criminals — were also led away to be executed with him.

The four Gospels are quite consistent with regard to the crucifixion of Jesus. In addition to the response of the onlookers, the Synoptic tradition highlights the response of the two thieves crucified with Jesus. Yet it is only Luke who draws attention to the thief who defends Jesus and to whom Jesus shows compassion. Perhaps for brevity, Matthew and Mark subsume both thieves into the broader group who hurl insults at Jesus. John includes yet another oblique reference to himself as the one whom Jesus chose to care for his mother. This presumably demonstrates Jesus's concern for the law to honor one's parents.

33 When they came to a place called *Golgotha* (which means Place of the Skull), **34** they gave him wine mixed with gall to

22 They brought Jesus to the place called *Golgotha* (which means Place of the Skull). **23** They tried to

33 When they arrived at the place called The Skull, they crucified him there, along with the criminals, one on the right and one on the left.

Then they took Jesus away. **17** Carrying the cross by himself, he went out to what is called Place of the Skull, which in Aramaic

drink. But when he tasted it, he refused to drink it. **35** After crucifying him, they divided his clothes by casting lots. **36** Then they sat down and were guarding him there. **37** Above his head they put up the charge against him in writing: THIS IS JESUS, THE KING OF THE JEWS.

38 Then two criminals were crucified with him, one on the right and one on the left. **39** Those who passed by were yelling insults at him, shaking their heads **40** and saying, "You who would destroy the temple and rebuild it in three days, save yourself! If you are the Son of God, come down from the cross!" **41** In the same way the chief priests, with the scribes and elders, mocked him and said, **42** "He saved others, but he cannot save himself! He is the King of Israel! Let him come down now from the cross, and we will believe in him. **43** He trusts in God; let God rescue him now—if he takes pleasure in him! For he said, 'I am the Son of God.'" **44** In the same way even the criminals who were crucified with him taunted him.

give him wine mixed with myrrh, but he did not take it.

24 Then they crucified him and divided his clothes, casting lots for them to decide what each would get. **25** Now it was nine in the morning when they crucified him. **26** The inscription of the charge written against him was: THE KING OF THE JEWS. **27** They crucified two criminals with him, one on his right and one on his left.

29 Those who passed by were yelling insults at him, shaking their heads, and saying, "Ha! The one who would destroy the temple and rebuild it in three days, **30** save yourself by coming down from the cross!" **31** In the same way, the chief priests with the scribes were mocking him among themselves and saying, "He saved others, but he cannot save himself! **32** Let the Messiah, the King of Israel, come down now from the cross, so that we may see and believe." Even those who were crucified with him taunted him.

34 Then Jesus said, "Father, forgive them, because they do not know what they are doing." And they divided his clothes and cast lots.

35 The people stood watching, and even the leaders were scoffing: "He saved others; let him save himself if this is God's Messiah, the Chosen One!" **36** The soldiers also mocked him. They came offering him sour wine **37** and said, "If you are the King of the Jews, save yourself!"

38 An inscription was above him: THIS IS THE KING OF THE JEWS.

39 Then one of the criminals hanging there began to yell insults at him: "Aren't you the Messiah? Save yourself and us!"

40 But the other answered, rebuking him: "Don't you even fear God, since you are undergoing the same punishment? **41** We are punished justly, because we're getting back what we deserve for the things we did, but this man has done nothing wrong." **42** Then he said, "Jesus, remember me when you come into your kingdom."

43 And he said to him, "Truly I tell you, today you will be with me in paradise."

is called *Golgotha*. **18** There they crucified him and two others with him, one on either side, with Jesus in the middle. **19** Pilate also had a sign made and put on the cross. It said: JESUS OF NAZARETH, THE KING OF THE JEWS. **20** Many of the Jews read this sign, because the place where Jesus was crucified was near the city, and it was written in Aramaic, Latin, and Greek. **21** So the chief priests of the Jews said to Pilate, "Don't write, 'The King of the Jews,' but that he said, 'I am the King of the Jews.'"

22 Pilate replied, "What I have written, I have written."

23 When the soldiers crucified Jesus, they took his clothes and divided them into four parts, a part for each soldier. They also took the tunic, which was seamless, woven in one piece from the top. **24** So they said to one another, "Let's not tear it, but cast lots for it, to see who gets it." This happened that the Scripture might be fulfilled that says: **They divided my clothes among themselves, and they cast lots for my clothing.** This is what the soldiers did.

25 Standing by the cross of Jesus were his mother, his mother's sister, Mary the wife of Clopas, and Mary Magdalene. **26** When Jesus saw his mother and the disciple he loved standing there, he said to his mother, "Woman, here is your son." **27** Then he said to the disciple, "Here is your mother." And from that hour the disciple took her into his home.

JESUS DIES ON THE CROSS   MT 27:45-56   MK 15:33-41   LK 23:44-49   JN 19:28-37

All four Gospels document the death of Jesus in remarkable detail. Each of the writers mention a variation of the last words of Jesus as he hung on the cross. Each author goes his own way, however, with regard to the unfolding events immediately following Jesus's death. Matthew, for example, recalls a series of supernatural events in which graves were opened and risen saints roamed the city. Such phenomena led to the centurion's confession. Mark doesn't include those details but retains the confession of the centurion in response to Jesus's death. Luke also highlights the centurion's response in contrast to the response of the crowds who "smote their breasts." John alone records the request of the Jews to hasten the deaths because of the approaching Sabbath. According the John, that the soldiers "pierced" Jesus's side, as opposed to breaking his legs, fulfilled the Scriptures and further demonstrates the credibility of his eyewitness testimony.

45 From noon until three in the afternoon darkness came over the whole land. 46 About three in the afternoon Jesus cried out with a loud voice, *"Elí, Elí, lemá sabachtháni?"* that is, "My God, my God, why have you abandoned me?"

47 When some of those standing there heard this, they said, "He's calling for Elijah."

48 Immediately one of them ran and got a sponge, filled it with sour wine, put it on a stick, and offered him a drink. 49 But the rest said, "Let's see if Elijah comes to save him."

50 But Jesus cried out again with a loud voice and gave up his spirit. 51 Suddenly, the curtain of the sanctuary was torn in two from top to bottom, the earth quaked, and the rocks were split. 52 The tombs were also opened and many bodies of the saints who had fallen asleep were raised. 53 And they came out of the tombs after his resurrection, entered the holy city, and appeared to many.

54 When the centurion and those with him, who were keeping watch over Jesus, saw the earthquake and the things that had happened, they were terrified and said, "Truly this man was the Son of God!"

55 Many women who had followed Jesus from Galilee and looked after him were there, watching from a distance. 56 Among them were Mary Magdalene, Mary the mother of James and Joseph, and the mother of Zebedee's sons.

33 When it was noon, darkness came over the whole land until three in the afternoon. 34 And at three Jesus cried out with a loud voice, *"Eloi, Eloi, lemá sabachtháni?"* which is translated, "My God, my God, why have you abandoned me?"

35 When some of those standing there heard this, they said, "See, he's calling for Elijah."

36 Someone ran and filled a sponge with sour wine, fixed it on a stick, offered him a drink, and said, "Let's see if Elijah comes to take him down."

37 Jesus let out a loud cry and breathed his last. 38 Then the curtain of the temple was torn in two from top to bottom. 39 When the centurion, who was standing opposite him, saw the way he breathed his last, he said, "Truly this man was the Son of God!"

40 There were also women watching from a distance. Among them were Mary Magdalene, Mary the mother of James the younger and of Joses, and Salome. 41 In Galilee these women followed him and took care of him. Many other women had come up with him to Jerusalem.

44 It was now about noon, and darkness came over the whole land until three, 45 because the sun's light failed. The curtain of the sanctuary was split down the middle. 46 And Jesus called out with a loud voice, "Father, **into your hands I entrust my spirit.**" Saying this, he breathed his last.

47 When the centurion saw what happened, he began to glorify God, saying, "This man really was righteous!" 48 All the crowds that had gathered for this spectacle, when they saw what had taken place, went home, striking their chests. 49 But all who knew him, including the women who had followed him from Galilee, stood at a distance, watching these things.

28 After this, when Jesus knew that everything was now finished that the Scripture might be fulfilled, he said, "I'm thirsty." 29 A jar full of sour wine was sitting there; so they fixed a sponge full of sour wine on a hyssop branch and held it up to his mouth.

30 When Jesus had received the sour wine, he said, "It is finished." Then bowing his head, he gave up his spirit.

31 Since it was the preparation day, the Jews did not want the bodies to remain on the cross on the Sabbath (for that Sabbath was a special day). They requested that Pilate have the men's legs broken and that their bodies be taken away. 32 So the soldiers came and broke the legs of the first man and of the other one who had been crucified with him. 33 When they came to Jesus, they did not break his legs since they saw that he was already dead. 34 But one of the soldiers pierced his side with a spear, and at once blood and water came out. 35 He who saw this has testified so that you also may believe. His testimony is true, and he knows he is telling the truth. 36 For these things happened so that the Scripture would be fulfilled: **Not one of his bones will be broken.** 37 Also, another Scripture says: **They will look at the one they pierced.**

All of the Gospels agree that Joseph of Arimathea took the lead in burying Jesus. Matthew and Mark mention the two Marys who appear frequently across the Passion Narrative. John alone mentions the participation of Nicodemus, a converted religious official and prominent character in the Fourth Gospel. Collectively, the four accounts validate the legitimacy of Jesus's physical death and introduce unlikely witnesses (i.e., women and religious officials) to the resurrection to come.

57 When it was evening, a rich man from Arimathea named Joseph came, who himself had also become a disciple of Jesus. **58** He approached Pilate and asked for Jesus's body. Then Pilate ordered that it be released. **59** So Joseph took the body, wrapped it in clean, fine linen, **60** and placed it in his new tomb, which he had cut into the rock. He left after rolling a great stone against the entrance of the tomb. **61** Mary Magdalene and the other Mary were seated there, facing the tomb.

42 When it was already evening, because it was the day of preparation (that is, the day before the Sabbath), **43** Joseph of Arimathea, a prominent member of the Sanhedrin who was himself looking forward to the kingdom of God, came and boldly went to Pilate and asked for Jesus's body. **44** Pilate was surprised that he was already dead. Summoning the centurion, he asked him whether he had already died. **45** When he found out from the centurion, he gave the corpse to Joseph. **46** After he bought some linen cloth, Joseph took him down and wrapped him in the linen. Then he laid him in a tomb cut out of the rock and rolled a stone against the entrance to the tomb. **47** Mary Magdalene and Mary the mother of Joses were watching where he was laid.

50 There was a good and righteous man named Joseph, a member of the Sanhedrin, **51** who had not agreed with their plan and action. He was from Arimathea, a Judean town, and was looking forward to the kingdom of God. **52** He approached Pilate and asked for Jesus's body. **53** Taking it down, he wrapped it in fine linen and placed it in a tomb cut into the rock, where no one had ever been placed. **54** It was the preparation day, and the Sabbath was about to begin. **55** The women who had come with him from Galilee followed along and observed the tomb and how his body was placed. **56** Then they returned and prepared spices and perfumes. And they rested on the Sabbath according to the commandment.

38 After this, Joseph of Arimathea, who was a disciple of Jesus — but secretly because of his fear of the Jews — asked Pilate that he might remove Jesus's body. Pilate gave him permission; so he came and took his body away. **39** Nicodemus (who had previously come to him at night) also came, bringing a mixture of about seventy-five pounds of myrrh and aloes. **40** They took Jesus's body and wrapped it in linen cloths with the fragrant spices, according to the burial custom of the Jews. **41** There was a garden in the place where he was crucified. A new tomb was in the garden; no one had yet been placed in it. **42** They placed Jesus there because of the Jewish day of preparation and since the tomb was nearby.

THE TOMB IS CLOSELY GUARDED   MT 27:62-66

62 The next day, which followed the preparation day, the chief priests and the Pharisees gathered before Pilate **63** and said, "Sir, we remember that while this deceiver was still alive he said, 'After three days I will rise again.' **64** So give orders that the tomb be made secure until the third day. Otherwise, his disciples may come, steal him, and tell the people, 'He has been raised from the dead,' and the last deception will be worse than the first."

65 "You have a guard of soldiers," Pilate told them. "Go and make it as secure as you know how." **66** They went and secured the tomb by setting a seal on the stone and placing the guard.

THE RESURRECTED JESUS COMPLETES HIS MINISTRY

Although several other women made the Sunday morning journey to the tomb, the four Gospels agree that Mary Magdalene was present to find the tomb empty. In addition, both Matthew and Mark recall at least one angel present at the tomb. Matthew recalls the angel sitting on the stone, while Mark mentions one inside the tomb. Perhaps Luke resolves the apparent discrepancy by recalling two men who "stood by them." Matthew includes the vivid detail of a "violent earthquake" and the subsequent descending of the "angel of the Lord." The Gospel writers clearly agree on the essential core of this event, which serves as the hallmark of the post-resurrection community of believers.

1 After the Sabbath, as the first day of the week was dawning, Mary Magdalene and the other Mary went to view the tomb. **2** There was a violent earthquake, because an angel of the Lord descended from heaven and approached the tomb. He rolled back the stone and was sitting on it. **3** His appearance was like lightning, and his clothing was as white as snow. **4** The guards were so shaken by fear of him that they became like dead men.

5 The angel told the women, "Don't be afraid, because I know you are looking for Jesus who was crucified. **6** He is not here. For he has risen, just as he said. Come and see the place where he lay. **7** Then go quickly and tell his disciples, 'He has risen from the dead and indeed he is going ahead of you to Galilee; you will see him there.' Listen, I have told you."

8 So, departing quickly from the tomb with fear and great joy, they ran to tell his disciples the news.

1 When the Sabbath was over, Mary Magdalene, Mary the mother of James, and Salome bought spices, so that they could go and anoint him. **2** Very early in the morning, on the first day of the week, they went to the tomb at sunrise. **3** They were saying to one another, "Who will roll away the stone from the entrance to the tomb for us?" **4** Looking up, they noticed that the stone — which was very large — had been rolled away.

5 When they entered the tomb, they saw a young man dressed in a white robe sitting on the right side; they were alarmed. **6** "Don't be alarmed," he told them. "You are looking for Jesus of Nazareth, who was crucified. He has risen! He is not here. See the place where they put him. **7** But go, tell his disciples and Peter, 'He is going ahead of you to Galilee; you will see him there just as he told you.'" **8** They went out and ran from the tomb, because trembling and astonishment overwhelmed them. And they said nothing to anyone, since they were afraid.

1 On the first day of the week, very early in the morning, they came to the tomb, bringing the spices they had prepared. **2** They found the stone rolled away from the tomb. **3** They went in but did not find the body of the Lord Jesus. **4** While they were perplexed about this, suddenly two men stood by them in dazzling clothes. **5** So the women were terrified and bowed down to the ground.

"Why are you looking for the living among the dead?" asked the men. **6** "He is not here, but he has risen! Remember how he spoke to you when he was still in Galilee, **7** saying, 'It is necessary that the Son of Man be betrayed into the hands of sinful men, be crucified, and rise on the third day'?" **8** And they remembered his words.

9 Returning from the tomb, they reported all these things to the Eleven and to all the rest. **10** Mary Magdalene, Joanna, Mary the mother of James, and the other women with them were telling the apostles these things. **11** But these words seemed like nonsense to them, and they did not believe the women.

1 On the first day of the week Mary Magdalene came to the tomb early, while it was still dark. She saw that the stone had been removed from the tomb. **2** So she went running to Simon Peter and to the other disciple, the one Jesus loved, and said to them, "They've taken the Lord out of the tomb, and we don't know where they've put him!"

Luke and John recall Peter and John's visit to the empty tomb. Luke limits his description to only Peter's encounter. Yet John, in cryptic fashion as has been his style throughout the Passion Narrative, includes an account of his own encounter with the empty tomb. Such a description only adds to the credibility of his testimony.

[12] Peter, however, got up and ran to the tomb. When he stooped to look in, he saw only the linen cloths. So he went away, amazed at what had happened.

[3] At that, Peter and the other disciple went out, heading for the tomb. [4] The two were running together, but the other disciple outran Peter and got to the tomb first. [5] Stooping down, he saw the linen cloths lying there, but he did not go in. [6] Then, following him, Simon Peter also came. He entered the tomb and saw the linen cloths lying there. [7] The wrapping that had been on his head was not lying with the linen cloths but was folded up in a separate place by itself. [8] The other disciple, who had reached the tomb first, then also went in, saw, and believed. [9] For they did not yet understand the Scripture that he must rise from the dead. [10] Then the disciples returned to the place where they were staying.

THE RISEN JESUS REVEALS HIMSELF TO THE WOMEN   MT 28:9-10   MK 16:9-11   JN 20:11-18

Mary Magdalene was apparently of such importance that she warranted her own resurrection appearance scene. A number of commentaries have satisfactorily addressed the timeline of Jesus's post-resurrection appearances. Matthew is very general in his description and implies that there were a number of women present. Mark and John, however, focus on Mary. Mark gives the reader some background on her checkered history. John offers the most vivid detail of the encounter. That Matthew recalls the women holding Jesus's feet in an act of worship does not conflict with Jesus's prohibition to "Don't cling to me" in John. After all, there were a number of post-resurrection instances where Jesus invited human touch. John is merely drawing attention to Jesus's future ascension, a theme Matthew does not address.

[9] Just then Jesus met them and said, "Greetings!" They came up, took hold of his feet, and worshiped him. [10] Then Jesus told them, "Do not be afraid. Go and tell my brothers to leave for Galilee, and they will see me there."

[9] Early on the first day of the week, after he had risen, he appeared first to Mary Magdalene, out of whom he had driven seven demons. [10] She went and reported to those who had been with him, as they were mourning and weeping. [11] Yet, when they heard that he was alive and had been seen by her, they did not believe it.

[11] But Mary stood outside the tomb, crying. As she was crying, she stooped to look into the tomb. [12] She saw two angels in white sitting where Jesus's body had been lying, one at the head and the other at the feet. [13] They said to her, "Woman, why are you crying?"

"Because they've taken away my Lord," she told them, "and I don't know where they've put him."

[14] Having said this, she turned around and saw Jesus standing there, but she did not know it was Jesus. [15] "Woman," Jesus said to her, "why are you crying? Who is it that you're seeking?"

Supposing he was the gardener, she replied, "Sir, if you've carried him away, tell me where you've put him, and I will take him away."

[16] Jesus said to her, "Mary."

Turning around, she said to him in Aramaic, *Rabboni!*—which means "Teacher."

[17] "Don't cling to me," Jesus told her, "since I have not yet ascended to the Father. But go to my brothers and tell them that I am ascending to my Father and your Father, to my God and your God."

[18] Mary Magdalene went and announced to the disciples, "I have seen the Lord!" And she told them what he had said to her.

¹¹ As they were on their way, some of the guards came into the city and reported to the chief priests everything that had happened. ¹² After the priests had assembled with the elders and agreed on a plan, they gave the soldiers a large sum of money ¹³ and told them, "Say this, 'His disciples came during the night and stole him while we were sleeping.' ¹⁴ If this reaches the governor's ears, we will deal with him and keep you out of trouble." ¹⁵ They took the money and did as they were instructed, and this story has been spread among Jewish people to this day.

JESUS APPEARS TO TWO TRAVELERS   MK 16:12-13   LK 24:13-35

In what many Bible translations refer to as the "Road to Emmaus," Luke presents an account of this well-known post-resurrection appearance by Jesus. Yet even with all his details, Luke leaves the reader wondering just what Jesus taught these two travelers as he unfolded the ways in which the Hebrew Scriptures pointed to him.

¹² After this, he appeared in a different form to two of them walking on their way into the country. ¹³ And they went and reported it to the rest, who did not believe them either.

¹³ Now that same day two of them were on their way to a village called Emmaus, which was about seven miles from Jerusalem. ¹⁴ Together they were discussing everything that had taken place. ¹⁵ And while they were discussing and arguing, Jesus himself came near and began to walk along with them. ¹⁶ But they were prevented from recognizing him. ¹⁷ Then he asked them, "What is this dispute that you're having with each other as you are walking?" And they stopped walking and looked discouraged.

¹⁸ The one named Cleopas answered him, "Are you the only visitor in Jerusalem who doesn't know the things that happened there in these days?"

¹⁹ "What things?" he asked them.

So they said to him, "The things concerning Jesus of Nazareth, who was a prophet powerful in action and speech before God and all the people, ²⁰ and how our chief priests and leaders handed him over to be sentenced to death, and they crucified him. ²¹ But we were hoping that he was the one who was about to redeem Israel. Besides all this, it's the third day since these things happened. ²² Moreover, some women from our group astounded us. They arrived early at the tomb, ²³ and when they didn't find his body, they came and reported that they had seen a vision of angels who said he was alive. ²⁴ Some of those who were with us went to the tomb and found it just as the women had said, but they didn't see him."

²⁵ He said to them, "How foolish you are, and how slow to believe all that the prophets have spoken! ²⁶ Wasn't it necessary for the Messiah to suffer these things and enter into his glory?" ²⁷ Then beginning with Moses and all the Prophets, he interpreted for them the things concerning himself in all the Scriptures.

²⁸ They came near the village where they were going, and he gave the impression that he was going farther. ²⁹ But they urged him, "Stay with us, because it's almost evening, and now the day is almost over." So he went in to stay with them.

³⁰ It was as he reclined at the table with them that he took the bread, blessed and broke it, and gave it to them. ³¹ Then their eyes were opened, and they recognized him, but he disappeared from their sight. ³² They said to each other, "Weren't our hearts burning within us while he was talking with us on the road and explaining the Scriptures to us?" ³³ That very hour they got up and returned to Jerusalem. They found the Eleven and those with them gathered together, ³⁴ who said, "The Lord has truly been raised and has appeared to Simon!" ³⁵ Then they

began to describe what had happened on the road and how he was made known to them in the breaking of the bread.

JESUS APPEARS TO THE DISCIPLES

MK 16:14   LK 24:36-43   JN 20:19-23

Mark, Luke, and John all offer a less than flattering portrait of Jesus's closest followers upon his first self-disclosure to them following his resurrection. Mark is characteristically shorter, and his portrait of the disciples is perhaps the most critical. Luke is comparable but includes more details of the setting. John is the most unique with his account of Jesus breathing upon the disciples who subsequently "receive the Holy Spirit." No other Gospel records this event, but most scholars believe it represents John's symbolic promise of the outpouring of the Holy Spirit at Pentecost.

[14] Later he appeared to the Eleven themselves as they were reclining at the table. He rebuked their unbelief and hardness of heart, because they did not believe those who saw him after he had risen.

[36] As they were saying these things, he himself stood in their midst. He said to them, "Peace to you!" [37] But they were startled and terrified and thought they were seeing a ghost. [38] "Why are you troubled?" he asked them. "And why do doubts arise in your hearts? [39] Look at my hands and my feet, that it is I myself! Touch me and see, because a ghost does not have flesh and bones as you can see I have." [40] Having said this, he showed them his hands and feet. [41] But while they still were amazed and in disbelief because of their joy, he asked them, "Do you have anything here to eat?" [42] So they gave him a piece of a broiled fish, [43] and he took it and ate in their presence.

[19] When it was evening of that first day of the week, the disciples were gathered together with the doors locked because they feared the Jews. Jesus came, stood among them, and said to them, "Peace be with you."
[20] Having said this, he showed them his hands and his side. So the disciples rejoiced when they saw the Lord.
[21] Jesus said to them again, "Peace to you. As the Father has sent me, I also send you."
[22] After saying this, he breathed on them and said, "Receive the Holy Spirit. [23] If you forgive the sins of any, they are forgiven them; if you retain the sins of any, they are retained."

JESUS APPEARS TO THOMAS

JN 20:24-29

[24] But Thomas (called "Twin"), one of the Twelve, was not with them when Jesus came. [25] So the other disciples were telling him, "We've seen the Lord!"
But he said to them, "If I don't see the mark of the nails in his hands, put my finger into the mark of the nails, and put my hand into his side, I will never believe."
[26] A week later his disciples were indoors again, and Thomas was with them. Even though the doors were locked, Jesus came and stood among them and said, "Peace be with you."
[27] Then he said to Thomas, "Put your finger here and look at my hands. Reach out your hand and put it into my side. Don't be faithless, but believe."
[28] Thomas responded to him, "My Lord and my God!"
[29] Jesus said, "Because you have seen me, you have believed. Blessed are those who have not seen and yet believe."

[1] After this, Jesus revealed himself again to his disciples by the Sea of Tiberias. He revealed himself in this way:

[2] Simon Peter, Thomas (called "Twin"), Nathanael from Cana of Galilee, Zebedee's sons, and two others of his disciples were together.

[3] "I'm going fishing," Simon Peter said to them.

"We're coming with you," they told him. They went out and got into the boat, but that night they caught nothing.

[4] When daybreak came, Jesus stood on the shore, but the disciples did not know it was Jesus. [5] "Friends," Jesus called to them, "you don't have any fish, do you?"

"No," they answered.

[6] "Cast the net on the right side of the boat," he told them, "and you'll find some." So they did, and they were unable to haul it in because of the large number of fish. [7] The disciple, the one Jesus loved, said to Peter, "It is the Lord!"

When Simon Peter heard that it was the Lord, he tied his outer clothing around him (for he had taken it off) and plunged into the sea. [8] Since they were not far from land (about a hundred yards away), the other disciples came in the boat, dragging the net full of fish.

[9] When they got out on land, they saw a charcoal fire there, with fish lying on it, and bread. [10] "Bring some of the fish you've just caught," Jesus told them. [11] So Simon Peter climbed up and hauled the net ashore, full of large fish — 153 of them. Even though there were so many, the net was not torn.

[12] "Come and have breakfast," Jesus told them. None of the disciples dared ask him, "Who are you?" because they knew it was the Lord. [13] Jesus came, took the bread, and gave it to them. He did the same with the fish. [14] This was now the third time Jesus appeared to the disciples after he was raised from the dead.

[15] When they had eaten breakfast, Jesus asked Simon Peter, "Simon, son of John, do you love me more than these?"

"Yes, Lord," he said to him, "you know that I love you."

"Feed my lambs," he told him. [16] A second time he asked him, "Simon, son of John, do you love me?"

"Yes, Lord," he said to him, "you know that I love you."

"Shepherd my sheep," he told him.

[17] He asked him the third time, "Simon, son of John, do you love me?"

Peter was grieved that he asked him the third time, "Do you love me?" He said, "Lord, you know everything; you know that I love you."

"Feed my sheep," Jesus said. [18] "Truly I tell you, when you were younger, you would tie your belt and walk wherever you wanted. But when you grow old, you will stretch out your hands and someone else will tie you and carry you where you don't want to go." [19] He said this to indicate by what kind of death Peter would glorify God. After saying this, he told him, "Follow me."

20
So Peter turned around and saw the disciple Jesus loved following them, the one who had leaned back against Jesus at the supper and asked, "Lord, who is the one that's going to betray you?" [21] When Peter saw him, he said to Jesus, "Lord, what about him?"

[22] "If I want him to remain until I come," Jesus answered, "what is that to you? As for you, follow me."

[23] So this rumor spread to the brothers and sisters that this disciple would not die. Yet Jesus did not tell him that he would not die, but, "If I want him to remain until I come, what is that to you?"

JESUS GIVES THE GREAT COMMISSION

MT 28:16-20   MK 16:15-18

The differences in the Great Commission, as reported by Matthew and Mark, have engendered much debate. While the two accounts are certainly not incompatible, the consensus among many scholars is that Mark's ending was likely added later (by someone other than Mark) as an attempt to give a more "appropriate" ending comparable to the other Gospels. As with other variations, large or small, the modern reader must consider that such a tradition was embraced by many throughout church history, most of whom believed the saying originated with Jesus.

[16] The eleven disciples traveled to Galilee, to the mountain where Jesus had directed them. [17] When they saw him, they worshiped, but some doubted. [18] Jesus came near and said to them, "All authority has been given to me in heaven and on earth. [19] Go, therefore, and make disciples of all nations, baptizing them in the name of the Father and of the Son and of the Holy Spirit, [20] teaching them to observe everything I have commanded you. And remember, I am with you always, to the end of the age."

[15] Then he said to them, "Go into all the world and preach the gospel to all creation. [16] Whoever believes and is baptized will be saved, but whoever does not believe will be condemned. [17] And these signs will accompany those who believe: In my name they will drive out demons; they will speak in new tongues; [18] they will pick up snakes; if they should drink anything deadly, it will not harm them; they will lay hands on the sick, and they will get well."

JESUS APPEARS TO THE DISCIPLES IN JERUSALEM

LK 24:44-49

[44] He told them, "These are my words that I spoke to you while I was still with you—that everything written about me in the Law of Moses, the Prophets, and the Psalms must be fulfilled." [45] Then he opened their minds to understand the Scriptures. [46] He also said to them, "This is what is written: The Messiah would suffer and rise from the dead the third day, [47] and repentance for forgiveness of sins would be proclaimed in his name to all the nations, beginning at Jerusalem. [48] You are witnesses of these things. [49] And look, I am sending you what my Father promised. As for you, stay in the city until you are empowered from on high."

Mark and Luke alone record the grand ascension of Jesus with comparable details. The slight variation between the two accounts can be explained in light of the fact that Luke's Gospel is only the first part of his story. The book of Acts tells the second half. With this in mind, it is not surprising that Luke omits Mark's reference to the disciples "preaching everywhere," given that the expansion of the gospel through the apostolic ministry is linked, in Acts, to the giving of the Spirit at Pentecost.

[19] So the Lord Jesus, after speaking to them, was taken up into heaven and sat down at the right hand of God. [20] And they went out and preached everywhere, while the Lord worked with them and confirmed the word by the accompanying signs.

[50] Then he led them out to the vicinity of Bethany, and lifting up his hands he blessed them. [51] And while he was blessing them, he left them and was carried up into heaven. [52] After worshiping him, they returned to Jerusalem with great joy. [53] And they were continually in the temple praising God.

JOHN'S FIRST TESTIMONY   JN 20:30-31

[30] Jesus performed many other signs in the presence of his disciples that are not written in this book. [31] But these are written so that you may believe that Jesus is the Messiah, the Son of God, and that by believing you may have life in his name.

JOHN'S SECOND TESTIMONY   JN 21:24-25

[24] This is the disciple who testifies to these things and who wrote them down. We know that his testimony is true.

[25] And there are also many other things that Jesus did, which, if every one of them were written down, I suppose not even the world itself could contain the books that would be written.

NOTES

NOTES

NOTES

NOTES

NOTES